THE SEVEN CURSES OF LONDON

THE SEVEN CURSES OF LONDON

James Greenwood

Introduction by Jeffrey Richards

BASIL BLACKWELL · OXFORD

Introduction © Jeffrey Richards 1981

First published 1869 by Stanley Rivers and Co.

Reprinted with a new introduction 1981

Basil Blackwell Publisher Limited
108 Cowley Road, Oxford OX4 1JF, England

British Library Cataloguing in Publication Data

Greenwood, James
  The seven curses of London.
  1. London – Social conditions – 19th century
  I. Title
  942.1'081   HN 398.L/

  ISBN 0–631–12778–X

Typesetting by Freeman Graphic, Tonbridge
Printed and bound in Great Britain at the Camelot Press Limited,
Southampton

Introduction

by Jeffrey Richards

The Industrial Revolution wrought such a dramatic transformation in this kingdom that commentators as diverse as Marx and Disraeli began to perceive the emergence of two nations – the rich and the poor. The conditions of life in what Henry Mayhew called 'the undiscovered country of the poor' were revealed by a succession of enquiries, both official and unofficial, into such questions as public health, housing and child labour. But alongside these enquiries there grew up from the 1850s onwards a literary genre that became known as 'social exploration'. It sought to dramatize and flesh out the basic facts with incident and anecdote, and thus make them accessible to a wider public. Perhaps the most celebrated of the mid-Victorian exponents of the genre was Henry Mayhew, whose *Morning Post* articles and four-volume survey of London life and labour (1861–62), with their combination of statistics, interviews and anecdotes, set the pattern for others to follow and helped to bring into sharp focus 'the condition of England' question which was to haunt the Victorian mind. [1]

At once the most famous and the most representative of the post-Mayhew generation of social explorers was James Greenwood (1832–1929). He was one of eleven children of a Kensington carriage upholsterer. Both James and his eldest brother Frederick were bitten by the literary bug while working as compositors in a printing works, and entered that raffish, prolific, penurious world of Victorian journalism which had already produced both Mayhew and Dickens. This was a world in which articles, essays, stories and novels cascaded indiscriminately from the pens of a tribe of clannish, improvident, imaginative Bohemians. James was to fit easily

[1] P. J. Keating (ed.), *Into Unknown England 1866–1913: Selections from the Social Explorers* (London, 1976).

into this milieu, his hardback output eventually running, according to the British Museum Catalogue, to some thirty-nine items, including novels, children's books, volumes of short stories and collections of journalism. [2]

In 1865 Frederick Greenwood, who had established a reputation as essayist and reviewer, was appointed the first editor of *The Pall Mall Gazette*, which was to become one of the most celebrated journals in Victorian London. James went to work for his brother and it was at Frederick's suggestion that he spent a night in disguise in the casual ward of a workhouse. The result was a series of articles entitled 'A Night in a Workhouse', which, in its vividly written revelation of an aspect of life unknown to the gentleman readers of the *Gazette*, caused a sensation when it appeared in 1866. It was reprinted in *The Times*, issued as a pamphlet, and made the reputation of Greenwood, whose *nom de plume* the 'Amateur Casual' became famous overnight. Salvation Army leader General Booth later wrote: 'From the storm of indignation over that one night in a casual ward may be traced the beginnings of the reform of our poor law.' [3]

James was now launched on his career as a social explorer, and took pride in his investigative journalism, describing himself as 'one whose delight it is to do his humble endeavour towards exposing and extirpating social abuses'. [4] He left *The Pall Mall Gazette* for *The Daily Telegraph*, for which he was to write regularly, often under the pseudonymn 'One of the Crowd', for the rest of the century. He gained further notoriety in 1874 with his *Telegraph* story of a fight between a man and a dog in the Potteries, an article which launched a correspondence in *The Times* and prompted questions in Parliament. [5]

There is no doubt that he was a brilliant journalist and publicist, and put his talents to work in several causes. One was the pay and conditions of railwaymen. In the early 1870s a campaign built up about the excessively long working hours and relatively poor pay of railwaymen, which were giving rise, among other effects, to a

---

[2] The early history of the Greenwood family is told in J. W. Robertson Scott, *The Story of the Pall Mall Gazette* (Oxford, 1950).

[3] ibid, pp. 166–9. The articles are reprinted in Keating, *Into Unknown England*, pp. 33–54.

[4] J. Greenwood, *The Wilds of London* (London, 1876), Preface.

[5] The article is reprinted in Keating, *Into Unknown England*, pp. 54–64.

dramatic increase in accidents. The Derby MP, Michael Bass, took up the railwaymen's cause and engaged Greenwood to publicize it. Greenwood travelled thousands of miles on British railways finding out about working conditions and in a series of articles published in the *Telegraph* in December 1871 wrote movingly and authoritatively about the exploitation of railway workers. Once again his revelations caused a sensation. In the same month the first railwaymen's union, the Amalgamated Society of Railway Servants, was formed. The historian of the rail unions, P. S. Bagwell, has concluded that the union might never have seen the light of day but for the help of influential public figures, and that 'Greenwood's articles were of great value in helping to create an informed public opinion favourable to the foundation of a railwaymen's trade union'. [6]

Another cause which deeply interested him was children. He had a large family of his own, and he wrote children's books, of a peculiarly bloodthirsty kind. [7] Although they are totally forgotten now, one of them, *King Lion*, was an important and acknowledged influence on Kipling and one of the sources of inspiration for *The Jungle Book*. [8] In 1895 Greenwood promoted the idea of sending poor children to the country for summer holidays and cooperated with the Ragged School Union in arranging this. He also persuaded the editor of the *Telegraph* to launch an appeal to provide Christmas hampers for crippled children, a subscription which raised £80,000. [9] It is no coincidence that 'neglected children' comes first in his seven curses and his exposure in that section of the scandal of 'baby-farming' gave valuable publicity to an evil which reformers were seeking to eliminate by legislation. Equally important was his continuing interest in the problems of working-class youths. Waldo McGillicuddy Eagar, the historian of the Boys' Clubs movement, writes: 'a tribute must be paid to James Greenwood who more than any other man made the no-longer-child-not-yet-man a matter of concern to the British public'. [10]

Greenwood's best novel, *The True History of a Little Ragamuffin* (1866), is a meticulously detailed, extremely readable semi-

---

[6] P. S. Bagwell, *The Railwaymen* (London, 1963), pp. 46–51.

[7] E. Quayle, *The Collector's Book of Boys' Stories* (London, 1973), pp. 83–4.

[8] R. Lancelyn Green, *Tellers of Tales* (London, 1965), p. 226.

[9] J. Hall Richardson, *From the City to Fleet Street* (London, 1927), pp. 253–4.

[10] W. M. Eagar, *Making Men: The History of Boys' Clubs and Related Movements in Great Britain* (London, 1953), p. 44.

documentary account of the career of a typical street arab, re-creating the settings and causes from personal observation and avoiding the mawkish sentimentality and sanctimonious moral-izing that marked so much 'street arab' literature. His subsequent fiction, however, never reached the standard set in *Ragamuffin*, remaining, according to P. J. Keating 'a mixture of the domestic sentimentality of Dickens and the more brutal and bizarre element of "the Newgate novel"'. [11] J. Hall Richardson, a colleague on *The Telegraph*, talks of Greenwood 'flickering out in police court papers' at the turn of the century. [12] His penultimate publication is indeed a collection of police-court stories, published in 1902. In fact, he survived until he was 96, but he had long outlived his age.

The importance of *The Seven Curses* is twofold. Within his own *oeuvre*, it is Greenwoood's sole attempt at a grand summing-up of the problems of the metropolis. Its particular qualities are the journalistic ones that were his forte. It is reportage rather than scientific assessment, impressionistic rather than statistical, emotional rather than analytical. He loves searching out the inter-esting, the colourful and the curious, thieves' slang and beggars' dodges, human interest stories and lively anecdotes. But just as interesting for the historian are his explanations of and solutions for the curses, rarely original and almost always reiterations of long-canvassed views. In virtually all of them he is strongly repres-entative of the social thinking of middle-class commentators of the 1860s and provides us with a compendium of their attitudes.

The background against which Greenwood wrote was one of economic and social crisis. The mid-sixties had seen bank failure and financial collapse accompanied by harsh winters, bread riots and a cholera epidemic. The focus of attention was clearly centred on the swelling numbers of the poor. But what was the cause of the poverty in London? Present-day scholarship has readily identified the cause as economic: low wages, seasonality of employment, the decline and collapse of key industries in East London (silk weaving and ship building), the small-unit structure of industrial pro-duction, which could only be run on low costs and therefore necessitated 'sweated labour'. The situation was exacerbated by a housing crisis, due to the demolition of the central slum areas to

---

[11] P. J. Keating, *The Working Classes in Victorian Fiction* (London, 1971), p. 39.
[12] Richardson, *From the City to Fleet Street*, p. 97.

facilitate road and railway construction and commercial development. Replacement housing for the displaced masses was not forthcoming and they simply moved into the adjacent slum areas, creating massive overcrowding and its attendant problems.

Contemporaries, however, identified the cause of poverty as demoralization, in line with the dominant middle-class Victorian view that poverty was an expression of personal and above all moral failure. This idea lies behind everything that Greenwood wrote. His very title *The Seven Curses of London* calls to mind the moral concept of 'The Seven Deadly Sins'. It is Greenwood's seventh curse, the waste of charity, that lies at the heart of this world-view. In common with many concerned figures, he wanted to distinguish between the deserving and the undeserving poor, for it was widely believed that the poor were being engulfed in a flood of charity. There had been a considerable increase in private charity in the 1850s and 1860s as the middle classes moved out of the centre of London and took up residence in the expanding suburbs, thus creating a real geographical gulf between the classes. Charity was seen as a way of salving consciences, imposing social control and bridging this gulf. The extent of private charity had in fact been partly necessitated by the complete breakdown of the Poor Law system in the poorer areas of London. The system operated on the assumption that there would be a mix of poor and rich in each area, but this had ceased to be the case with the separation of the classes into their own distinctive districts. The result, with each Poor Law Union responsible for the relief of its own poor, was that the poorer districts, with a necessarily greater number of people in need of relief, paid the highest rates, and the richest districts the lowest. In times of crisis, the system broke under the strain.

Private charity came to be seen as a problem when, in response to the crisis of the mid-sixties, a flood of privately raised money poured into the East End of London in the form of relief. Some observers believed that this flow of charity 'pauperized' the honest poor, discouraging thrift and self-help and promoting idleness; also that it succoured the undeserving and dishonest poor, the rogues and the skrimshankers.

This outcry about demoralization led to the formulation by various concerned groups of three objectives, all of which Greenwood endorsed and canvassed: first, to coordinate and regulate private charity; second, to prevent it overlapping with Poor Relief and to distinguish strictly between Poor Relief and charity; and third, to reform the Poor Law assessment. The third objective was in part accomplished by the 1867 Metropolitan Poor Act which transferred a considerable proportion of the expense of local Poor Law administration to a common Poor Fund, to which each Union was to contribute according to its rateable value. The first and second objectives were achieved by the setting up in 1869 of the Society for Organizing Charitable Relief and Repressing Mendicity, better known as the Charity Organization Society. It set out to coordinate and strictly control charitable activity and to work closely with the Poor Law Board to ensure that there was no mixing of charity and poor relief. In addition, it aimed to repress beggars and beggary. Simultaneously the Poor Law Board sought to lay down a policy which ensured that the Poor Law was seen as a penalty for moral and economic failure, in effect a return to the principles behind the 1834 New Poor Law. They wanted no additional charity given to those in receipt of poor relief. They wanted outdoor relief, to which the seasonally unemployed were prone to resort, to be phased out, and the workhouse reserved for the destitute, who were by definition feckless.

The distinction made by both the COS and the Poor Law Board was quite clear. Private charity was to be used sparingly for the relief on a temporary basis of the deserving poor, who had through no fault of their own fallen on hard times. The Poor Law was to deal with the undeserving poor, and consequently the workhouse, that institution most loathed and feared by the working classes of nineteenth-century Britain, was to continue to be as grim, cheerless and uninviting as possible.

The critics of the 1860s and 1870s saw economic explanations for poverty as mere excuses for worthlessness and so, throughout the 1870s, the COS led an attack on indiscriminate charitable institutions such as free dispensaries, soup kitchens and outdoor relief, which were thought to molly-coddle the poor and promote idleness. They sought also to repress beggars and vagrants, those the Elizabethans had called 'the able-bodied poor', by tightening up workhouse conditions and setting up an especially tough regime at Poplar, to which unregenerate beggars might be sent.

Beggars and vagrants were the archetypal 'undeserving poor' and were a particular *bête noire* of Greenwood, who made them his third curse, exposing their tricks and dodges. The standard Poor

Law policy throughout the nineteenth century was to make help for them so disagreeable that they would not apply for it. So separate vagrant wards were provided at workhouses, with compulsory baths, no heating, inadequate equipment, a ban on pipes and cards, and an enforced work task, usually corn grinding or stone breaking. It was a constant fear of the Poor Law administrators that life in the workhouse ward might be so attractive that vagrants would not look for work. This fear intensified in the wake of the crisis of the 1860s when an estimated population of 30,000 vagrants swelled to 80,000. The reaction of the authorities was to make the regulations progressively harsher and the work burden heavier to break these tramps and moral failures of their stubborn fecklessness and workshy recalcitrance. [13]

Greenwood's general approach is that of a liberal and a humanitarian. Yet at the same time he is moralistic and, in keeping with the prevailing view of the age, interprets the problems of the metropolis as at bottom moral problems. He does not see the poor as innately immoral but 'demoralized', and the causes of this demoralization constitute his seven curses. But it is fascinating to see from time to time an ambivalence surfacing, a contradiction between the received doctrines of social commentators and a compassion awakened by personal observation. No commentator knew the inside of the workhouse better than the 'Amateur Casual'. It was this firsthand acquaintance which led to Greenwood expressing the view that the poor could not be lumped together, that some became poor through 'sheer misfortune and hard necessity' and that anyone could become poor with bad luck. His own experience, then, caused him to take a different line about the workhouse from the COS. Where they sought to make workhouse conditions harsher and to stop outdoor relief, even if this resulted in the breakup of families, Greenwood wanted to keep families together, to reform the 'labour test' which gave the workhouse masters a licence for tyranny, to vary the work provided and to make individual personal assessments of paupers in order to help them get

[13] The best account of the problems of the metropolis in this period is G. Stedman Jones, *Outcast London* (Oxford, 1971). But see also D. Owen, *English Philanthropy 1600–1960* (London, 1965); S. and B. Webb, *English Poor Law History*, 3 vols. (London, 1927–29); N. Longmate, *The Workhouse* (London, 1974); M. E. Rose, *The Relief of Poverty 1834–1914* (London, 1972); J. H. Treble, *Urban Poverty in Britain 1830–1914* (London, 1979).

work. However, again in common with a prevalent contemporary view, Greenwood believed that 'the cheapest, most lasting and in every way the best remedy' for pauperism was emigration – though naturally only the worthy and deserving poor should be exported, in order to maintain decent standards in the colonies.

Greenwood's first curse is 'neglected children', a problem which had preoccupied commentators since the beginning of the century. Greenwood estimated that there were 350,000 'pauper children' in parochial care. They, however, were by definition not neglected. It was the 100,000 street arabs he estimated to be roaming London who were the neglected ones. The 'pauper children', according to Greenwood, comprised the illegitimate and the abandoned, the children of the sick and the poor, the inmates of workhouse and prison. He defended them against arguments that they should be harshly treated to prevent their growing attracted to pauperism instead of honest work. But he was more concerned about the street arabs. Where did they come from? Modern research has attributed the armies of neglected children to the high birth and death rates which made a large child-surplus inevitable; the break-up of families by hardship, death, homelessness, removal; the scale of internal migration within cities and external migration into cities; the shortage of work to absorb the child population. Green-wood, on the other hand, settled on the exploitation of young children by sweat-shop proprietors as the main cause. These pro-prietors, he believed, employed children for their cheapness, and when they reached a certain age, turned them out in order to employ younger, still cheaper children. This certainly went on but cannot be seen as the principal cause. Greenwood in fact erred in assuming that all the abandoned, illegitimate and poverty-stricken children were in the workhouse, for this was clearly not the case. Many of those he would categorize as 'pauper children' lived on the streets and roamed with the street arabs. So poverty lay at the root of this problem. [14]

It is interesting to see Greenwood propounding an essentially economic explanation for neglected children, even if it is the wrong one. But when it comes to solutions, moral aspects are again upper-most. Greenwood did not believe that philanthropy was the answer to the problem; it only tackled the results. Although there were

[14] I. Pinchbeck and M. Hewitt, *Children in English Society*, vol. 2 (London, 1973).

many orphanages, asylums and refuges, particularly in the second half of the century, Greenwood called for an extension of education and the demolition of the slums to eradicate the causes of the problem. By education he meant instilling proper values and standards of behaviour – moral rather than scholarly education. It was this idea that lay behind the Ragged Schools, set up by evangelical bodies to teach self-help, morality and discipline. By 1861, these numbered 176 and boasted an average daily attendance of 25,000. But the need for an extension of formal education was already so widely accepted that in 1870 Parliament enacted Forster's Education Act, which took a decisive step forward towards the free compulsory education for all that was finally attained in 1891.

Greenwood's next solution was the abolition of the slums, where overcrowding bred immorality and provided permanent examples of bad conduct. But it seems never to have occurred to him to specify replacement homes. He wrote perplexedly about the poor clinging to their slum dwellings even while they were being demolished. He apparently views it as natural perversity, rather than the simple fact that they had nowhere else to go. The demolition of the central London rookeries, without thought for the human consequences, was the result of such blinkered vision. In the last resort, however, Greenwood did not believe that the problem could be eliminated totally. Street arabs, like the poor, would always be with us.

Two specific problems exercised him in this field. One, a perennial hobby-horse, was the baleful influence of penny dreadfuls and the criminal plays of the penny gaffs on impressionable young minds. The idea that they degraded and demoralized young people was advanced with the same fervour with which succeeding generations would indict their latterday equivalents – films, television, horror comics, 'space invaders' machines. But Greenwood did concede that working-class boys were not naturally more susceptible to these lures than their social superiors; it was simply that they lacked moral guidance. [15]

The other problem was that of baby-farming and bogus adoption, which was giving rise to major public concern just as he wrote. It was really only in the second half of the nineteenth century that

[15] P. Sheridan, *The Penny Theatres of Victorian London* (London, 1981); P. Dunae, 'Penny dreadfuls: late nineteenth century boys' literature and crime', *Victorian Studies* 22 (1979), pp. 133–50.

cruelty to children became a matter of public concern. Baby-farming, by which unscrupulous people took unwanted babies off their parents' hands for a consideration, highlighted the problem and had by the 1860s become a public scandal. Greenwood's vivid description of the Oxleeks' establishment in *The Seven Curses* gave it publicity, and the trial and execution of baby-farmer Margaret Waters in 1870 for the murder of a child in her care was the culmination of a decade of mounting concern. In 1870 the Infant Life Protection Society was formed to press for parliamentary action against baby-farmers. The Society sought to introduce a bill for the licensing and regulating of baby-farmers, something Greenwood had called for in his book. In 1872 the Infant Life Protection Act was passed. But the evil continued and another outcry, after the trial and execution of baby-farmer Mrs Dyer in 1896 for strangling and throwing in the Thames babies in her care, led to a tightening of the Act the following year.

There was a thin line between juvenile vagrants and juvenile criminals, and the question of crime leads Greenwood to his second curse – professional thieves. Crime had been a preoccupation of commentators since the century began, and many were the doom-laden prophecies about the imminent collapse of society under the growing weight of urban crime. Engels wrote in 1844: 'There is more crime in Britain than in any other country in the world.' But attitudes began to change in the second half of the century, and crime came to be viewed no longer as apocalyptic but as a defined social problem, which could be tackled along with cholera and illiteracy. It is an attitude which may be seen reflected in Greenwood's constructive and sympathetic approach. [16]

The debate about law and order then elicited much the same responses as it does now. There were hard-liners and soft-liners; Greenwood definitely came in the latter category. He maintained that criminals were people and retained their human characteristics, a far from widely-held view. He expressed sympathy, declaring that 'the thief always was and always will be the hardest worked and most miserable of all labourers'. [17] He called for greater help and understanding for criminals, particularly for recently released pris-

---

[16] J. J. Tobias, *Crime and Industrial Society in the Nineteenth Century* (London, 1972).
[17] Greenwood, *The Wilds of London*, p. 254.

oners. He argued for an extension and liberalization of the 'ticket of leave' (parole) system. He opposed the application of more stringent penalties. But his sympathy for working-class criminals was matched by his hatred of 'respectable' criminals. He was morally affronted by the double standard prevalent in the judgement of crime, pointing to the large number of professional and middle-class criminals who were getting away with swindles and embezzlements. Dishonest shopkeepers, he thought, were far worse criminals than those people who stole food to live, for by their use of false weights and their adulteration of food and drink they were cheating the poor. Adulteration was another of his hobby-horses, and again it was a current one. It had been a matter of public concern and discussion since the 1850s, but the Adulteration of Foods Act of 1860 had done little to check it. The result of agitation, faithfully reflected by Greenwood in his journalism, was that new Acts were passed in 1872 and 1875, leading to the appointment of public analysts, whose activities did much to check the practice of adulteration.

As might have been expected, he was greatly concerned about juvenile crime. He argued that juveniles did not choose to be criminals, but were brought up in criminal environments and inherited dishonesty like a disease. He further blamed the penny dreadfuls and penny gaffs for glamorizing crime, and saw the solution as the removal of juvenile criminals from their slum environment and the provision of work or education for them. This same rationale lay behind the foundation in the 1850s of reformatories and industrial schools, to which the decline in juvenile crime has been in part attributed.

Statistics are notoriously difficult to interpret but after taking into account invisible items such as the differences between actual and recorded crime, shifts in public attitudes, legal and administrative changes, alterations in policing and regional differences, they do seem to indicate a decline in the crime rate after the mid-century. In the case of violent crime, pickpocketing and juvenile crime, this is a significant decline. [18]

The reasons for the decline in the crime rate are not hard to find. Not only was there a general improvement in social and economic

---

[18] V. A. C. Gattrell and T. B. Hadden, 'Criminal statistics and their interpretation', in E. A. Wrigley (ed.), *Nineteenth Century Society* (Cambridge, 1972), pp. 336–96.

conditions and of the standard of living of the lower classes over the century as a whole, but there were also improvements in policing and in prison discipline, advances in communications and street lighting, the cleaning out of the 'citadels of crime' – the rookeries of central London, changes in the law, and the lightening of penalties, which made juries readier to convict.

Social scientists and historians have identified the causes of crime as poverty, lack of education, bad housing, drink, rapid population growth, social instability and rootlessness. It seems that there were also cyclical patterns in crime, in tandem with economic conditions; in times of depression offences against property increased and drunken assaults declined, and in times of prosperity the reverse happened. But Greenwood drew attention not to poverty, nor population growth, nor social and economic conditions. His causes were again moral factors: drink, overcrowding, lack of education and instruction, all of which contributed to demoralization. However, statistics both national and local do confirm that convicted offenders came mainly from the working class, that the key age for crime was 16–25, that the largest proportion of indictable crimes was larceny, and that offenders showed a high degree of illiteracy, thus confirming the pattern of criminality discerned by Greenwood at the time.

Greenwood is notably reticent about matters sexual. When discussing street children, for instance, he never once alludes to their 'extraordinary licentiousness' and 'unnatural precocity' as noted by Henry Mayhew. [19] When discussing prostitution, his fourth curse, he manifests a mixture of prudery and crusading zeal. He apologizes profusely for raising so unpleasant a subject, but defends its inclusion as a matter of public interest.

He was concerned to discuss the structure and extent of prostitution in London. For this he relied on ten-year-old police statistics which put the number of London prostitutes at 8,600. But police estimates were notoriously conservative, and press estimates, which leant to the other extreme, went up to 120,000. A number frequently quoted in mid-century was 50,000. But the actual number must remain uncertain. [20]

[19] H. Mayhew, *London Labour and the London Poor* (London, 1861–62), vol. 1 p. 477.
[20] F. Finnegan, *Poverty and Prostitution* (Cambridge, 1979); E. M. Sigsworth and T. J. Wyke, 'A study of Victorian prostitution and venereal disease', M. Vicinus

He seems little concerned with the causes of prostitution, though they were much discussed and thought to include poverty, over-crowding, shortage of employment, seduction, parental neglect and drink, a range that modern research has endorsed. Instead he settles for the moralistic view that prostitution is often due to natural feminine weakness and overgenerosity of spirit, a view advanced by Dr William Acton in his celebrated book *Prostitution*, which Greenwood recommends to his male readers ('The volume . . . is of necessity not one that might be introduced into the drawing room, but it is one that all thinking men would do well to procure and peruse'). From his own observation he adds to this the role of music hall as den of vice. His view is essentially what would today be called male chauvinist, as evidenced by the approval with which he quotes a writer who distinguishes between mere seduction ('which will never be visited with extreme severity among men of the world') and seduction and desertion, which involved the abandonment of obligation and was therefore reprehensible.

None of Greenwood's ideas in this field were new, and for much of the fourth curse, of which he apparently had little firsthand investigative experience, he relied on the researches and opinions of Acton, adding his own editorial comment where appropriate. Greenwood's attitude was a mixture of compassion and revulsion. But as with the poor and the beggars, he wanted to distinguish between the deserving and the undeserving: between those women who had fallen through weakness rather than evil, and those who were steeped in sin and irredeemable, 'like the horde of human tigresses who swarm in the pestilent dens by the riverside at Ratcliff and Shadwell'.

For solutions, he echoed Acton in his call for the legal supervision and regulation of prostitution, rejecting the argument that this would give legal sanction to a vice. He called for heavy financial penalties on male seducers, not as a punishment but as a deterrent and to help finance the support of bastard children. He also called for the assisted emigration of reformed prostitutes and the increased provision of asylums for them.

Acton was passionately concerned to protect men, particularly men in the armed forces, from fallen women, and so supported the

(ed.), *Suffer and Be Still: Women in the Victorian Age* (London, 1980), pp. 77–99; E. Trudgill, 'Prostitution and paterfamilias', in H. J. Dyos and M. Wolff, *The Victorian City* (London, 1973), vol. 2 pp. 693–705.

Contagious Diseases Acts of 1864, 1866 and 1869, which were intended to reduce the incidence of venereal disease in the forces. He also wanted their scope extended nation-wide. The Acts ordered the registration and supervision of prostitutes in certain named centres and, if diseased, their detention in hospital. But the Acts provoked a strong reaction and in 1869 two societies were formed to campaign for their repeal. The Acts were suspended in 1883 and repealed in 1886. The grounds for opposition were class bias against the working class, sex bias in that men were not punished along with women, the moral argument that the state was condoning a vice, the liberal argument against the unprecedented extension of police powers and the medical argument that women only were detained and that men could continue to spread the disease. The only one of these arguments that worried Greenwood was the extension of police powers. He was concerned about their abuse: 'it is highly necessary that the said power . . . should be scrupulously watched by those who are set in authority over [the police]'. [21]

Turning to leisure, Greenwood attacked the two preeminent working-class leisure pursuits – drinking and gambling. In the mainstream of opinion again, Greenwood described drunkenness (fifth on his list) as 'the crowning curse' which 'has wrought more mischief than all the other social evils put together'. It plays a part in all other sins, infects all other classes of society. So the repression of drunkenness was clearly an essential element in the remoralization of the poor.

The public house was an institution central to working-class life. Besides drink, it provided heat, light, food, newspapers, lodgings, a meeting place for societies and political groups, an organization centre for gambling, savings, excursions, an escape from drabness, squalor and monotony. It was this centrality that the temperance movement in all its manifestations sought to undermine. The movement began life in 1828 and remained a vital force in British society throughout the century. It became politically militant in 1853 with the formation of the United Kingdom Alliance, which actively sought prohibition by Act of Parliament. Supported by influential and articulate groups in society, such as feminists,

---

[21] P. McHugh, *Prostitution and Victorian Social Reform* (London, 1980); J. Walkowitz, *Prostitution and Victorian Society* (Cambridge, 1980).

Nonconformists and newly enfranchised leaders of the 'labour aristocracy', it made temperance a major political issue. But it never obtained its parliamentary objective. For quite apart from the opposition of the powerful 'Drink Interest', the temperance movement committed two major errors. In concentrating on drunkenness as a moral failing, it paid too little attention to environmental factors, and in too often splitting into different groups, it dissipated the strength of its attack. However, it did succeed in focusing society's attention on the problem, and it provided an important meeting ground for the classes, bridging the social gulf by the creation of a community of interest and an agitational framework whose pattern could be utilized for other causes. Its positive results included the promotion of a better diet for the working classes and the advancement of the role of the home and an enhanced status for women. Greenwood criticized some aspects of the temperance campaign – its failure to use statistics, the deploying of broad generalizations about drinking and pubs which he knew not to be true, the use of children to sermonize about abstinence – but on the whole he supported the movement and its aims.

Despite all the activity of temperance groups, however, per capita consumption of alcohol continued to rise until the 1870s, and when it began to fall thereafter, it did so for reasons not directly linked with the temperance movement. Two of the major influences fostering drunkenness came under attack: bad housing and the lack of alternative leisure pursuits. Slum clearance and the promotion of the middle-class concept of 'home life' attacked the pub from one direction, and the rise of alternative leisure pursuits attacked it from the other. Sport, music, the music hall and popular theatre, the provision of municipal parks, libraries and art galleries, coupled with the rise of the electric tram providing cheap and accessible transport, all threatened the hitherto unchallenged leisure eminence of the pub. The logical and inevitable outcome of these developments was that after the Great War, drunkenness ceased to be the major social problem that had so haunted the Victorian imagination. [22]

Greenwood's sixth curse was working-class gambling, which up to 1914 meant betting on horses. A recent study has suggested that

[22] B. Harrison, *Drink and the Victorians* (London, 1971); A. E. Dingle, 'Drink and working-class living standards in Britain 1870–1914', *Economic History Review* 25 (1972), pp. 608–22.

the 1880s saw the beginning of mass gambling because that decade saw a rise in the level of disposable income among the working classes and the utilization of the electric telegraph and the popular press to facilitate the speedy and comprehensive publication of starting prices and race results. [23] But gambling had always been an integral part of working-class leisure, and as early as the 1850s its scale was causing concern to the authorities. There had been such a large increase in the number of 'betting houses', bookmaking operations based on public houses – an estimated 100–150 in London – that Parliament legislated to ban them in 1853. The focus of betting shifted from the public house to the street, and in the late 1860s had become once again so widespread as to provoke a police crackdown. The opposition to it was essentially class biased. Rich men's gaming clubs and gambling arrangements were exempted from legal penalty, on the grounds, as Lord Brougham declared in 1844, that 'gambling . . . was far more injurious to morals among the inferior classes than among the superior classes'. It was once again the 'demoralization argument', advanced frequently in Parliament during debates on working-class gambling, the idea that the 'get rich quick' ethic which inspired gambling was injurious to the work ethic. [24]

Greenwood saw it as an increasingly proliferating evil, evidenced by the quadrupling in number of the sporting papers in the previous twenty years, the organization of lotteries in pubs and the increase in race course betting. He was particularly concerned about the corruption of the young by tipsters, who were given to luring the unwary into the habit-forming pastime of the wager. He attributed the 'horse betting mania' to increased leisure time and 'each man's faith in the ignorance of his neighbour and his high respect for his own sagacity and his "good luck"'. But like so many contemporary commentators on leisure, he failed to appreciate its potency as a more congenial form of self-help than saving, an unfailing source of escapist excitement and mental stimulation, a crucial topic of conversation and a provider of social status to the successful gambler. It was this combination of attractions which prevented its ever being suppressed.

[23] R. McKibbin, 'Working-class gambling in Britain 1880–1939', *Past and Present* 82 (1979), pp. 147–78.
[24] W. Vamplew, *The Turf: a Social and Economic History of Horse Racing* (London, 1976), pp. 199–231.

There was of course an eighth curse, greater than all the others, contributing to all the others – and that was poverty. Before that curse could be tackled – and on a scale which inevitably implied unprecedented government intervention – there had to be a revolution in thought and attitude far greater than anything that Greenwood or his contemporaries could have foreseen. The outlook and interpretation of society's ills enshrined in *The Seven Curses of London* was to be overtaken by another and more serious economic crisis in the 1880s, when society was shocked by three successive days of looting and rioting in the West End (February 1887), which made palpable the fear of revolution. The ideas of the COS became discredited, particularly after the publication of the findings of Charles Booth, who made the first systematic scientific study of poverty and discovered that 35 per cent of the population of the East End lived in poverty. In the wake of this and similar surveys, which outlined the concepts of the poverty cycle and the poverty line and demonstrated that poverty was generally not the result of moral failure but of low earnings, irregular employment, large families, sickness and old age, new schools of thought developed which argued for government action to rectify this situation just as it had sought to solve the problems of health and education. Fabian Socialism, the 'New Liberalism' and Social Imperialism, the shaping ideologies of the last decades of the century, all embraced standpoints which were to lead in the long run to the Welfare State. [25]

---

[25] I am indebted to my colleagues Dr S. Constantine, Dr E. J. Evans and Dr J. K. Walton for reading and commenting on earlier drafts of this introduction.

Contents

I. NEGLECTED CHILDREN.

Chapter I.

STARTLING FACTS.

Chapter II.

RESPECTING THE PARENTAGE OF SOME OF OUR GUTTER POPULATION.

Chapter III.

BABY-FARMING.

Chapter IV.

WORKING BOYS.

Chapter V.

THE PROBLEM OF DELIVERANCE.

II. PROFESSIONAL THIEVES.

Chapter VI.

THEIR NUMBER AND DIFFICULTIES.

Chapter VII.

HOMES AND HAUNTS OF THE BRITISH THIEF.

Chapter VIII.

JUVENILE THIEVES.

Chapter IX.

THE THIEF NON-PROFESSIONAL.

Chapter X.

CRIMINAL SUPPRESSION AND PUNISHMENT.

III. PROFESSIONAL BEGGARS.

Chapter XII.

THE BEGGAR OF OLDEN TIME.

Chapter XIII.

THE WORK OF PUNISHMENT AND RECLAMATION.

Chapter XIV.

BEGGING "DODGES."

Chapter XV.

GENTEEL ADVERTISING BEGGARS.

IV. FALLEN WOMEN.

Chapter XVI.

THIS CURSE.

Chapter XVII.

THE PLAIN FACTS AND FIGURES OF PROSTITUTION.

Chapter XVIII.

THE PRESENT CONDITION OF THE QUESTION.

Chapter XIX.

SUGGESTIONS.

V. THE CURSE OF DRUNKENNESS.

Chapter XX.

ITS POWER.

I.

NEGLECTED CHILDREN.

CHAPTER I.

Startling Facts.

The Pauper Population.—Pauper Children.—Opinions concerning their proper Treatment.—A Hundred Thousand Children loose in London Streets.—Neglected Babies.—Juvenile "Market Prowlers."

It is a startling fact that, in England and Wales alone, at the present time, the number of children under the age of sixteen, dependent more or less on the parochial authorities for maintenance, amounts to three hundred and fifty thousand.

It is scarcely less startling to learn that annually more than a hundred thousand criminals emerge at the doors of the various prisons, that, for short time or long time, have been their homes, and with no more substantial advice than "to take care that they don't make their appearance there again," are turned adrift once more to face the world, unkind as when they last stole from it. This does not include our immense army of juvenile vagrants. How the information has been arrived at is more than I can tell; but it is an accepted fact that, daily, winter and summer, within the limits of our vast and wealthy city of London, there wander, destitute of proper guardianship, food, clothing, or employment, a *hundred thousand* boys and girls in fair training for the treadmill and the oakum shed, and finally for Portland and the convict's mark.

It is these last-mentioned hundred thousand, rather than the three hundred and fifty thousand previously mentioned, that are properly classed under the heading of this first chapter. Practically, the three hundred and fifty thousand little paupers that cumber the poor-rates are without the category of neglected ones. In all probability, at least one-half of that vast number never were victims of neglect, in the true sense of the term. Mr. Bumble derives his foster children from sources innumerable. There are those that are born in the "house," and who, on some pretext, are abandoned by their unnatural mother. There are the "strays," discovered by the police on their beats, and consigned, for the present, to the workhouse, and never owned. There is the off-

3

spring of the decamping weaver, or shoemaker, who goes on tramp "to better himself;" but, never succeeding, does not regard it as worth while to tramp home again to report his ill-luck. These, and such as these, may truly ascribe their pauperism to neglect on somebody's part; but by far the greater number are what they are through sheer misfortune. When death snatches father away from the table scarcely big enough to accommodate the little flock that cluster about it—snatches him away in the lusty prime of life, and without warning, or, worse still, flings him on a bed of sickness, the remedies for which devour the few pounds thriftily laid aside for such an emergency, and, after all, are of no avail, what other asylum but the workhouse offers itself to mother and children? How many cases of this kind the parish books could reveal, one can only guess; quite enough, we may be sure, to render unpalatable that excessive amount of caution observed by those in power against "holding out a premium" to pauperism. It is somewhat amazing to hear great authorities talk sometimes. Just lately, Mr. Bartley, reading at the Society of Arts a paper entitled, "The training and education of pauper children," took occasion to remark:—

"These children cannot be looked upon exactly in the same way as paupers proper, inasmuch as their unfortunate position is entirely due to circumstances over which they could have no control. They are either the offspring of felons, cripples, and idiots, or orphans, bastards, and deserted children, and claim the protection of the law, frequently from their tenderest years, from having been deprived of the care of their natural guardians without fault or crime of their own. Such being their condition, they must either steal or starve in the streets, or the State must take charge of them. It may further be affirmed that, in a strictly commercial point of view, it is more economical to devote a certain amount in education and systematic training than by allowing them to grow up in the example of their parents and workhouse companions, to render their permanent support, either in a prison or a workhouse, a burden on the industrious classes. The State, in fact, acknowledges this, and accordingly a provision is theoretically supplied for all pauper children, not only for their bodily wants, but, to a certain extent, for their mental improvement. At the same time, it is also necessary that the extreme should not be run into, viz., that of treating them so liberally as to hold out a premium to pauperism. In no case should their comfort be better than, nor in fact as good as, an industrious labourer has within his reach."

Mr. Bartley is a gentleman whose knowledge of the subject he treats of exceeds that of most men; moreover, he is a man who, in his acts and nature, shows himself actuated by a kind heart, governed by a sound head; but, with all deference, it is difficult to agree altogether with the foregoing remarks of his: and they are the better worth noticing, because precisely the same sentiment breathes through almost every modern, new, and improved system of parochial reform. Why should these unfortunate creatures, "their unfortunate position being entirely due to circumstances over which they had no control," be made less comfortable in their condition than the industrious labourer,—who, by the way, may be an agricultural labourer, with his starvation wages of nine shillings a week and his damp and miserable hovel of two rooms to board and lodge his numerous family? What sort of justice is it to keep constantly before their unoffending eyes the humiliating fact that they have no standing even on the bottom round of the social ladder, and that their proper place is to crouch meekly and un-complainingly at the foot of it? Even supposing that they, the pauper children, are "either the offspring of felons, cripples, and idiots, or orphans, bastards, and deserted children," which is assuming to the verge of improbability, still, since it is acknow-ledged that the state in which we discover them "is due to no fault or crime of their own," why should we hesitate to make them commonly comfortable? To fail so to do when it is in our power, and when, according to their innocence and helplessness, it is their due, is decidedly at variance with the commonly-understood principles of Christian charity. It will be needless, however, here to pursue the subject of pauper management, since another section of this book has been given to its consideration. Anyhow, our three hundred and fifty thousand pauper children can have no claim to be reckoned among the "neglected." They are, or should be, a class whose hard necessity has been brought under the notice of the authorities, and by them considered and provided for.

There are other neglected children besides those already enu-merated, and who are not included in the tenth part of a million who live in the streets, for the simple reason that they are too young to know the use of their legs. They are "coming on," how-ever. There is no present fear of the noble annual crop of a hundred thousand diminishing. They are so plentifully propagated that a savage preaching "civilization" might regard it as a mercy that the localities of their infant nurture are such as suit the ravening appe-tites of cholera and typhus. Otherwise they would breed like rabbits in an undisturbed warren, and presently swarm so abun-dantly that the highways would be over-run, making it necessary

to pass an Act of Parliament, improving on the latest enacted for
dogs, against the roaming at large of unmuzzled children of the
gutter. Observe the vast number of "city Arabs," to be encountered in a walk, from Cheapside to the Angel at Islington, say. You
cannot mistake them. There are other children who are constantly
encountered in the street, male and female, who, though perhaps
neither so ragged and dirty as the genuine juvenile vagrants, are
even more sickly and hungry looking; but it is as easy to distinguish between the two types—between the *home-owning* and the
homeless, as between the sleek pet dog, and the cur of the street,
whose ideas of a "kennel" are limited to that represented by the
wayside gutter, from which by good-luck edibles may be extrac-
ted. Not only does the youthful ragamuffin cry aloud for remedy
in every street and public way of the city, he thrusts his ugly
presence on us continuously, and appeals to us in bodily shape. In
this respect, the curse of neglected children differs widely from
any of the others, beggars alone excepted, perhaps. And even as
regards beggars, to see them is not always to believe in them as
human creatures helpless in the sad condition in which they are
discovered, and worthy of the best help we can afford to bestow
on them. It is next to impossible by outward signs merely to discriminate between the impostor and the really unfortunate and
destitute. The pallid cheek and the sunken eye, may be a work of
art and not of nature, and in the cunning arrangement of rags, so
as to make the most of them, the cheat must always have an
advantage over the genuine article. Weighing the evidence *pro* and
con., the object of it creeping even at his snail's pace may be out
of sight before we arrive at what appears to us a righteous verdict,
and our scrupulous charity reserved for another occasion. But no
such perplexing doubts and hesitation need trouble us in selecting
the boy gutter bred and born from the one who lays claim to a
home, even though it may be no more than a feeble pretence, consisting of a family nightly gathering in some dirty sty that serves as
a bedroom, and a morning meeting at a board spread with a substitute for a breakfast. In the latter there is an expression of
countenance utterly wanting in the former; an undescribable shy-
ness, and an instinctive observance of decency, that has been rain-
washed and sun-burnt out of the gipsy of the London highway
since the time of his crawling out of the gooseberry sieve, with a
wisp of hay in it that served him as a cradle.

And here I can fancy I hear the incredulous reader exclaim,
"But that is mere imagery of course; ragamuffin babies never are
cradled in gooseberry sieves, with a wisp of hay to lie on." Let me

assure you, dear madam, it is not imagery, but positive fact. The strangest receptacles do duty as baby cradles at times. In another part of our book, it will be shown that a raisin-box may be so adapted, or even an egg-box; the latter with a bit of straw in it as a cradle for an invalid baby with a broken thigh! But as regards the gooseberry sieve, it is a fact that came under the writer's immediate observation. Accompanied by a friend, he was on a visit of exploration into the little-known regions of Baldwin's Gardens, in Leather Lane, and entering a cellar there, the family who occupied it were discovered in a state of dreadful commotion. The mother, a tall, bony, ragged shrew, had a baby tucked under one arm, while she was using the other by the aid of a pair of dilapidated nozzleless bellows in inflicting a tremendous beating on a howling young gentleman of about eleven years old. "Tut! tut! what is the matter, Mrs. Donelly? Rest your arm a moment, now, and tell us all about it." "Matther! shure it's matther enough to dhrive a poor widdy beyant her sinses!" And then her rage turning to sorrow, she in pathetic terms described how that she left that bad boy Johnny only for a few moments in charge of the "darlint comfortable ashleap in her bashket," and that he had neglected his duty, and that the baste of a donkey had smelt her out, and "ate her clane out o' bed."

I have had so much experience in this way, that one day I may write a book on the Haunts and Homes of the British Baby. It was not long after the incident of the gooseberry sieve, that I discovered in one small room in which a family of six resided, three little children, varying in age from three to eight, perhaps, stark naked. It was noon of a summer's day, and there they were nude as forest monkeys, and so hideously dirty that every rib-bone in their poor wasted little bodies showed plain, and in colour like mahogany. Soon as I put my head in at the door they scattered, scared as rabbits, to the "bed," an arrangement of evil-smelling flock and old potato-sacks, and I was informed by the mother that they had not a rag to wear, and had been in their present condition for *more than three months.*

Let us return, however, to the hordes of small Arabs found wandering about the streets of the city. To the mind of the initiated, instantly recurs the question, "whence do they all come? They are not imported like those other pests of society, "German band boys or organ grinders;" they must have been babies once upon a time; where did they grow up? In very dreary and retired regions, my dear sir, though for that matter if it should happen that you are perambulating fashionable Regent-street or aristocratic Belgravia, when you put to yourself the perplexing question, you may be nigher to a visible solution of the mystery than you would care to know. Where does the shoeless ragged, dauntless, and often desperate boy of the gutter breed? Why, not unfrequently as close almost to the mansions of the rich and highly respectable as the sparrows in their chimney stacks. Nothing is more common than to discover a hideous stew of courts and alleys reeking in poverty and wretchedness almost in the shadow of the palatial abodes of the great and wealthy. Such instances might be quoted by the dozen.

It is seldom that these fledglings of the hawk tribe quit their nests or rather their nesting places until they are capable, although on a most limited scale, of doing business on their own account. Occasionally a specimen may be seen in the vicinity of Covent Garden or Farringdon Market, seated on a carriage extemporized out of an old rusty teatray and drawn along by his elder relatives, by means of a string. It may not be safely assumed, however, that the latter are actuated by no other than affectionate and disinterested motives in thus treating their infant charge to a ride. It is much more probable that being left at home in the alley by their mother, who is engaged elsewhere at washing or "charing," with strict injunctions not to leave baby for so long as a minute, and being goaded to desperation by the thoughts of the plentiful feed of cast-out plums and oranges to be picked up in "Common Garden" at this "dead ripe" season of the year, they have hit on this ingenious expedient by which the maternal mandate may be obeyed to the letter, and their craving for market refuse be at the same time gratified.

By-the-bye, it may here be mentioned as a contribution towards solving the riddle, "How do these hundred thousand street prowlers contrive to exist?" that they draw a considerable amount of their sustenance from the markets. And really it would seem that by some miraculous dispensation of Providence, garbage was for their sake robbed of its poisonous properties, and endowed with virtues such as wholesome food possesses. Did the reader ever see the young market hunters at such a "feed" say in the month of August or September? It is a spectacle to be witnessed only by early risers who can get as far as Covent Garden by the time that the wholesale dealing in the open falls slack—which will be about eight o'clock; and it is not to be believed unless it is seen. They will gather about a muck heap and gobble up plums, a sweltering mass of decay, and oranges and apples that have quite lost their original shape and colour, with the avidity of ducks or pigs. I speak according to my knowledge, for I have seen them at it. I have seen one of these gaunt wolfish little children with his tattered cap full of plums of a sort one of which I would not have permitted a child of mine to eat for all the money in the Mint, and this at a season when the sanitary authorities in their desperate alarm at the spead of cholera had turned bill stickers, and were begging and imploring the people to abstain from this, that, and the other, and especially to beware of fruit unless perfectly sound and ripe. Judging from the earnestness with which this last provision was urged, there must have been cholera enough to have slain a dozen strong men in that little ragamuffin's cap, and yet he munched on till that frowsy receptacle was emptied, finally licking his fingers with a relish. It was not for me to forcibly dispossess the boy of a prize that made him the envy of his plumless companions, but I spoke to the market beadle about it, asking him if it would not be possible, knowing the propensities of these poor little wretches, so to dispose of the poisonous offal that they could not get at it; but he replied that it was nothing to do with him what they ate so long as they kept their hands from picking and steal-ing; furthermore he politely intimated that "unless I had nothing better to do" there was no call for me to trouble myself about the "little warmint," whom nothing would hurt. He confided to me his private belief that they were "made inside something after the orsestretch, and that farriers' nails wouldn't come amiss to 'em if they could only get 'em down." However, and although the evidence was rather in the sagacious market beadle's favour, I was unconverted from my original opinion, and here take the liberty of urging on any official of Covent Garden or Farringdon Market who may happen to read these pages the policy of adopting my suggestion as to the safe bestowal of fruit offal during the sickly season. That great danger is incurred by allowing it to be con-sumed as it now is, there cannot be a question. Perhaps it is too much to assume that the poor little beings whom hunger prompts to feed off garbage do so with impunity. It is not improbable that, in many cases, they slink home to die in their holes as poisoned rats do. That they are never missed from the market is no proof of the contrary. Their identification is next to impossible, for they are like each other as apples in a sieve, or peas in one pod. More-over, to tell their number is out of the question. It is as incompre-hensible as is their nature. They swarm as bees do, and arduous indeed would be the task of the individual who undertook to reckon up the small fry of a single alley of the hundreds that abound in Squalor's regions. They are of as small account in the public estimation as stray street curs, and, like them, it is only where they evince a propensity for barking and biting that their existence is recognised. Should death tomorrow morning make a clean sweep of the unsightly little scavengers who grovel for a meal amongst the market offal heaps, next day would see the said heaps just as industriously surrounded.

CHAPTER II.

Respecting the Parentage of some of our Gutter Population.

Instructive and interesting though it may be to inquire into the haunts and habits of these wretched waifs and "rank outsiders" of humanity, of how much importance and of useful purpose is it to dig yet a little deeper and discover who are the parents—the mothers especially—of these babes of the gutter.

Clearly they had no business there at all. A human creature, and more than all, a *helpless* human creature, endowed with the noblest shape of God's creation, and with a soul to save or lose, is as much out of place grovelling in filth and contamination as would be a wild cat crouching on the hearth-rug of a nursery. How come they there, then? Although not bred absolutely in the kennel, many merge into life so very near the edge of it, that it is no wonder if even their infantine kickings and sprawlings are enough to topple them over. Some there are, not vast in number, perhaps, but of a character to influence the whole, who are dropped into the gutter from such a height that they may never crawl out of it—they are so sorely crippled. Others, again, find their way to the gutter by means of a process identical with that which serves the conveyance to sinks and hidden sewers of the city's ordinary refuse and off-scourings. Of this last-mentioned sort, however, it will be necessary to treat at length presently.

I think that it may be taken as granted that gross and deliberate immorality is not mainly responsible for our gutter population. Neither can the poverty of the nation be justly called on to answer for it. On the contrary, unless I am greatly mistaken, the main tributary to the foul stream has its fountain-head in the keen-witted, ready-penny commercial enterprise of the small-capital, business-minded portion of our vast community.

11

In no respect are we so unlike our forefathers as in our struggles after "mastership" in business, however petty. This may be a sign of commercial progress amongst us, but it is doubtful if it tends very much to the healthful constitution of our humanity. "Work hard and win a fortune," has become a dry and mouldy maxim, distasteful to modern traders, and has yielded to one that is much smarter, viz., "There is more got by scheming than by hard work."

By scheming the labour of others, that is; little children—anyone. It is in the infant labour market especially that this new and dashing spirit of commercial enterprise exercises itself chiefly. There are many kinds of labour that require no application of muscular strength; all that is requisite is dexterity and lightness of touch, and these with most children are natural gifts. They are better fitted for the work they are set to than adults would be, while the latter would require as wages shillings where the little ones are content with pence. This, perhaps, would be tolerable if their earnings increased with their years; but such an arrangement does not come within the scheme of the sweaters and slop-factors, Jew and Christian, who grind the bones of little children to make them not only bread, but luxurious living and country houses, and carriages to ride in. When their "hands" cease to be children, these enterprising tradesmen no longer require their services, and they are discharged to make room for a new batch of small toilers, eager to engage themselves on terms that the others have learned to despise, while those last-mentioned unfortunates are cast adrift to win their bread—somehow.

Anyone curious to know the sort of working young female alluded to may be gratified a hundred times over any day of the week, if he will take the trouble to post himself, between the hours of twelve and two, at the foot of London or Blackfriars bridge. There he will see the young girl of the slop-shop and the city "warehouse" hurrying homeward on the chance of finding a meagre makeshift—"something hot"—that may serve as a dinner.

It is a sight well worth the seeking of any philanthropic person interested in the present condition and possible future of the infant labour market. How much or how little of truth there may be in the lament one occasionally hears, that our endurance is failing us, and that we seldom reach the ripe old age attained by our ancestors, we will not here discuss; at least there can be no doubt of this—that we grow old much earlier than did our great grandfathers; and though our "three-score years and ten" may be shortened by fifteen or twenty years, the downhill portion of our existence is at least as protracted as that of the hale men of old who could leap a gate at sixty. This must be so, otherwise the ancient law, defining an infant as "a person under the age of fourteen," could never have received the sanction of legislators. Make note of these "infants" of the law as they come in knots of two and three, and sometimes in an unbroken "gang," just as they left the factory, putting their best feet foremost in a match against time; for all that is allowed them is one hour, and within that limited period they have to walk perhaps a couple of miles to and fro, resting only during that brief space in which it is their happy privilege to exercise their organs of mastication.

Good times indeed were those olden ones, if for no other reason than that they knew not such infants as these! Of the same stuff in the main, one and all, but by no means of the same pattern. Haggard, weary-eyed infants, who never could have been babies; little slips of things, whose heads are scarcely above the belt of the burly policeman lounging out his hours of duty on the bridge, but who have a brow on which, in lines indelible, are scored a dreary account of the world's hard dealings with them. Painfully puckered mouths have these, and an air of such sad, sage experience, that one might fancy, not that these were young people who would one day grow to be old women but rather that, by some inversion of the natural order of things, they had once been old and were growing young again—that they had seen seventy, at least, but had doubled on the brow of the hill of age, instead of crossing it, and retraced their steps, until they arrived back again at thirteen; the old, old heads planted on the young shoulders revealing the secret.

This, the most melancholy type of the grown-up neglected infant, is, however, by no means the most painful of those that come trooping past in such a mighty hurry. Some are dogged and sullen-looking, and appear as though steeped to numbness in the comfortless doctrine, "What can't be cured must be endured;" as if they had acquired a certain sort of surly relish for the sours of existence, and partook of them as a matter of course, without even a wry face. These are not of the sort that excite our compassion the most; neither are the ailing and sickly-looking little girls, whose tender constitutions have broken down under pressure of the poison inhaled in the crowded workroom, and long hours, and countless trudgings, early and late, in the rain and mire, with no better covering for their shoulders than a flimsy mantle a shower would wet through and through, and a wretched pair of old boots that squelch on the pavement as they walk. Pitiful as are these forlorn ones to behold, there is, at least, a grim satisfaction in knowing that with them it cannot last. The creature who causes us most alarm is a girl of a very different type.

This is the flashy, flaunting "infant," barely fourteen, and with scarce four feet of stature, but self-possessed and bold-eyed enough to be a "daughter of the regiment"— of a militia regiment even. She consorts with birds of her own feather. Very little experience enables one to tell at a glance almost how these girls are employed, and it is quite evident that the terrible infant in question and her companions are engaged in the manufacture of artificial flowers. Their teeth are discoloured, and there is a chafed and chilblainish appearance about their nostrils, as though suffering under a malady that were best consoled with a pocket-hand-kerchief. The symptoms in question, however, are caused by the poison used in their work—arsenite of copper, probably, that deadly mineral being of a "lovely green," and much in favour amongst artificial florists and their customers. Here they come, unabashed by the throng, as though the highway were their home, and all mankind their brothers; she, the heroine with a bold story to tell, and plenty of laughter and free gesticulation as sauce with it. She is of the sort, and, God help them! they may be counted by hundreds in London alone, in whom keen wit would appear to be developed simultaneously with ability to walk and talk. Properly trained, these are the girls that grow to be clever, capable women— women of spirit and courage and shrewd discernment. The worst of it is that the seed implanted will germinate. Hunger cannot starve it to death, or penurious frosts destroy it. Untrained, it grows apace, overturning and strangling all opposition and asserting its paramount importance.

This is the girl who is the bane and curse of the workroom crowded with juvenile stitchers or pasters, or workers in flowers or beads. Her constant assumption of lightheartedness draws them towards her, her lively stories are a relief from the monotonous drudgery they are engaged on. Old and bold in petty wickedness, and with audacious pretensions to acquaintance with vice of a graver sort, she entertains them with stories of "sprees" and "larks" she and her friends have indulged in. She has been to "plays" and to "dancing rooms," and to the best of her ability and means she demonstrates the latest fashion in her own attire, and wears her draggletail flinders of lace and ribbon in such an easy and old-fashioned manner, poor little wretch, as to impress one with the conviction that she must have been used to this sort of thing since the time of her shortcoating; which must have been many, many years ago. She has money to spend; not much, but sufficient for the purchase of luxuries, the consumption of which inflict cruel pangs on the hungry-eyed beholders. She is a person whose intimacy is worth cultivating, and they do cultivate it, with what result need not be here described.

At fifteen the London factory-bred girl in her vulgar way has the worldly knowledge of the ordinary female of eighteen or twenty. She has her "young man," and accompanies him of evenings to "sing-songs" and raffles, and on high days and holidays to Hampton by the shilling van, or to Greenwich by the sixpenny boat. At sixteen she wearies of the frivolities of sweethearting, and the young man being agreeable the pair embark in housekeeping, and "settle down."

Perhaps they marry, and be it distinctly understood, whatever has been said to the contrary, the estate of matrimony amongst her class is not lightly esteemed. On the contrary, it is a contract in which so much pride is taken that the certificate attesting its due performance is not uncommonly displayed on the wall of the living-room as a choice print or picture might be; with this singular and unaccountable distinction that when a *clock* is reckoned with the other household furniture, the marriage certificate is almost invariably hung under it. It was Mr. Catlin of the Cow Cross Mission who first drew my attention to this strange observance, and in our many explorations into the horrible courts and alleys in the vicinity of his mission-house he frequently pointed out instances of this strange custom; but even he, who is as learned in the habits and customs of all manner of outcasts of civilisation as any man living, was unable to explain its origin. When questioned on the subject the common answer was, "They say that it's lucky."

It is the expense attending the process that makes matrimony the exception and not the rule amongst these people. At least this is their invariable excuse. And here, as bearing directly on the question of "neglected infants," I may make mention of a practice that certain well-intentioned people are adopting with a view to diminishing the prevalent sin of the unmarried sexes herding in their haunts of poverty, and living together as man and wife.

The said practice appears sound enough on the surface. It consists simply in marrying these erring couples gratis. The missionary or scripture reader of the district who, as a rule, is curiously intimate with the family affairs of his flock, calls privately on those young people whose clock, if they have one, ticks to a barren wall, and makes the tempting offer—banns put up, service performed, beadle and pew opener satisfied, and all free! As will not uncommonly happen, if driven into a corner for an excuse, the want of a jacket or a gown "to make a 'spectable 'pearance in" is pleaded; the negociator makes a note of it, and in all probability the dif-

ficulty is provided against, and in due course the marriage is con-
summated.

This is all very well as far as it goes, but to my way of thinking
the scheme is open to many grave objections. In the first place the
instinct that incites people to herd like cattle in a lair is scarcely
the same as induces them to blend their fortunes and live "for
better, for worse" till the end of their life. It requires no great
depth of affection on the man's part to lead him to take up with
a woman who, in consideration of board and lodging and masculine protection will create some semblance of a home for him. In
his selection of such a woman he is not governed by those grave
considerations that undoubtedly present themselves to his mind
when he meditates wedding himself irrevocably to a mate. Her
history, previous to his taking up with her, may be known to him,
and though perhaps not all that he could wish, she is as good to
him as she promised to be, and they get along pretty well and
don't quarrel very much.

Now, although not one word can be urged in favour of this
iniquitous and shocking arrangement, is it quite certain that a
great good is achieved by inducing such a couple to tie themselves
together in the sacred bonds of matrimony? It is not a marriage of
choice as all marriages should be. If the pair had been bent on
church marriage and earnestly desired it, it is absurd to suppose
that the few necessary shillings, the price of its performance,
would have deterred them. If they held the sacred ceremony of so
small account as to regard it as well dispensed with as adopted, it
is no very great triumph of the cause of religion and morality that
the balance is decided by a gown or a jacket, in addition to the
good will of the missionary (who, by-the-bye, is generally the dis-
tributor of the alms of the charitable) being thrown into the scale.

To be sure the man is not compelled to yield to the persuasions
of those who would make of him a creditable member of society;
he is not compelled to it, but he can hardly be regarded as a free
agent. If the pair have children already, the women will be only
too anxious to second the solicitation of her friend, and so secure
to herself legal protection in addition to that that is already
secured to her through her mate's acquired regard for her. Then it
is so difficult to combat the simple question, "Why not?" when all
is so generously arranged—even to the providing a real gold ring to
be worn in place of the common brass make-believe—and nothing
remains but to step round to the parish church, where the minister
is waiting, and where in a quarter of an hour, the great, and good,
and lasting work may be accomplished. The well-meaning mission-

ary asks, "Why not?" The woman, urged by moral or mercenary motives, echoes the momentous query, and both stand with arms presented, in a manner of speaking, to hear the wavering one's objection. The wavering one is not generally of the far-seeing sort. In his heart he does not care as much as a shilling which way it is. He does not in the least trouble himself from the religious and moral point of view. When his adviser says, "Just consider how much easier your conscience will be if you do this act of justice to the woman whom you have selected as your helpmate," he wags his head as though admitting it, but having no conscience about the matter he is not very deeply impressed. Nine times out of ten the summing-up of his deliberation is, "I don't care; it won't cost *me* nothing; let 'em have their way."

But what, probably, is the upshot of the good missionary's endeavours and triumph? In a very little time the gilt with which the honest adviser glossed the chain that was to bind the man irrevocably to marriage and morality wears off. The sweat of his brow will not keep it bright; it rusts it. He feels, in his own vulgar though expressive language, that he has been "bustled" into a bad bargain. "It is like this 'ere," a matrimonial victim of the class once confided to me; "I don't say as she isn't as good as ever, but I'm blowed if she's all that better as I was kidded to believe she would be."

"But if she is as good as ever, she is good enough."

"Yes, but you haven't quite got the bearing of what I mean, sir, and I haint got it in me to put it in the words like you would. Good enough before isn't good enough now, cos it haint hoptional, don't you see? No, you don't. Well, look here. S'pose I borrer a barrer. Well, it's good enough and a conwenient size for laying out my stock on it. It goes pooty easy, and I pays eighteen pence a week for it and I'm satisfied. Well, I goes on all right and without grumbling, till some chap he ses to me, 'What call have you got to borrer a barrer when you can have one of your own; you alwis *want* a barrer, don't you know, why not make this one your own?' 'Cos I can't spare the money,' I ses. 'Oh,' he ses, 'I'll find the money and the barrer's yourn, if so be as you'll promise and vow to take up with no other barrer, but stick to this one so long as you both shall live.' Well, as aforesaid, it's a tidy, useful barrer, and I agrees. But soon as it's *mine*, don't you know, I ain't quite so careless about it. I overhauls it, in a manner of speaking, and I'm more keerful in trying the balance of it in hand when the load's on it. Well, maybe I find out what I never before troubled myself to look for. There's a screw out here and a bolt wanted there. Here it's weak, and there it's ugly. I dwells on it in my mind constant. I've never got that there barrer out of my head, and p'raps I make too much of the weak pints of it. I gets to mistrust it. 'It's all middling right, just now, old woman—old barrer, I mean,' I ses to myself, 'but you'll be a playing me a trick one day, I'm afraid.' Well, I go on being afraid, which I shouldn't be if I was only a borrower."

"But you should not forget that the barrow, to adopt your own ungallant figure of speech, is not accountable for these dreads and suspicions of yours; it will last you as long and as well as though you had continued a borrower; you will admit that, at least!"

"I don't know. *Last,* yes! That's the beggaring part of it. Ah, well! p'raps it's all right, but I'm blest if I can stand being haunted like I am now."

Nothing that I could say would add force to the argument of my costermonger friend, as set forth in his parable of the "barrer." Applying it to the question under discussion, I do not mean to attribute to the deceptiveness of the barrow or to its premature breaking down, the spilling into the gutter of all the unhappy children there discovered. My main reason for admitting the evidence in question was to endeavour to show that as a pet means of improving the morality of our courts and alleys, and consequently of diminishing the gutter population, the modern idea of arresting fornication and concubinage, by dragging the pair there and then to church, and making them man and wife, is open to serious objections. The state of matrimony is not good for such folk. It was never intended for them. It may be as necessary to healthful life as eating is, but no one would think of taking a man starved, and in the last extremity for lack of wholesome aliment, and setting before him a great dish of solid food. It may be good for him by-and-by, but he must be brought along by degrees, and fitted for it. Undoubtedly a great source of our abandoned gutter children may be found in the shocking herding together of the sexes in the vile "slums" and back places of London, and it is to be sincerely hoped that some wise man will presently devise a speedy preventive.

In a recent report made to the Commissioners of Sewers for London, Dr. Letheby says: "I have been at much pains during the last three months to ascertain the precise conditions of the dwellings, the habits, and the diseases of the poor. In this way 2,208 rooms have been most circumstantially inspected, and the general result is that nearly all of them are filthy or overcrowded or imperfectly drained, or badly ventilated, or out of repair. In 1,989 of these rooms, all in fact that are at present inhabited, there are 5,791 inmates, belonging to 1,576 families; and to say nothing of the too frequent occurrence of what may be regarded as a necessitous overcrowding, where the husband, the wife, and young family of four or five children are cramped into a miserably small and ill-conditioned room, there are numerous instances where adults of both sexes, belonging to different families, are lodged in the same room, regardless of all the common decencies of life, and where from three to five adults, men and women, besides a train or two of children, are accustomed to herd together like brute beasts or savages; and where every human instinct of propriety and decency is smothered. Like my predecessor, I have seen grown persons of both sexes sleeping in common with their parents, brothers and sisters, and cousins, and even the casual acquaintance of a day's tramp, occupying the same bed of filthy rags or straw; a woman suffering in travail, in the midst of males and females of different families that tenant the same room, where birth and death go hand in hand; where the child but newly born, the patient cast down with fever, and the corpse waiting for interment, have no separation from each other, or from the rest of the inmates. Of the many cases to which I have alluded, there are some which have commanded my attention by reason of their unusual depravity— cases in which from three to four adults of both sexes, with many children, were lodging in the same room, and often sleeping in the same bed. I have note of three or four localities, where forty-eight men, seventy-three women, and fifty-nine children are living in thirty-four rooms. In one room there are two men, three women, and five children, and in another one man, four women, and two children; and when, about a fortnight since, I visited the back room on the ground floor of No. 5, I found it occupied by one man, two women, and two children; and in it was the dead body of a poor girl who had died in childbirth a few days before. The body was stretched out on the bare floor, without shroud or coffin. There it lay in the midst of the living, and we may well ask how it can be otherwise than that the human heart should be dead to all the gentler feelings of our nature, when such sights as these are of common occurrence.

"So close and unwholesome is the atmosphere of some of these rooms, that I have endeavoured to ascertain, by chemical means, whether it does not contain some peculiar product of decomposition that gives to it its foul odour and its rare powers of engendering disease. I find it is not only deficient in the due proportion of oxygen, but it contains three times the usual amount of carbonic acid, besides a quantity of aqueous vapour charged with alkaline matter that stinks abominably. This is doubtless the product of putrefaction, and of the various foetid and stagnant exhalations that pollute the air of the place. In many of my former reports, and in those of my predecessor, your attention has been drawn to this pestilential source of disease, and to the consequence of heaping human beings into such contracted localities; and I again revert to it because of its great importance, not merely that it perpetuates fever and the allied disorders, but because there stalks side by side with this pestilence a yet deadlier presence, blighting the moral existence of a rising population, rendering their hearts hopeless, their acts ruffianly and incestuous, and scattering, while society averts her eye, the retributive seeds of increase for crime, turbulence and pauperism."

CHAPTER III

Baby-farming.

"Baby-Farmers" and Advertising "Child Adopters."—"F. X." of Stepney.—
The Author's Interview with Farmer Oxleck.—The Case of Baby Frederick
Wood.

Although it is not possible, in a book of moderate dimensions, such as this, to treat the question of neglected children with that extended care and completeness it undoubtedly deserves, any attempt at its consideration would be glaringly deficient did it not include some reference to the modern and murderous institution known as "baby farming."

We may rely on it that we are lamentably ignorant both of the gigantic extent and the pernicious working of this mischief. It is only when some loud-crying abuse of the precious system makes itself heard in our criminal courts, and is echoed in the newspapers, or when some adventurous magazine writer in valiant pursuit of his avocation, directs his inquisitive nose in the direction indicated, that the public at large hear anything either of the farmer or the farmed.

A year or so ago a most atrocious child murder attracted towards this ugly subject the bull's-eye beams of the press, and for some time it was held up and exhibited in all its nauseating nakedness. It may be safely asserted that during the protracted trial of the child murderess, Mrs. Winser, there was not one horrified father or mother in England who did not in terms of severest indignation express his or her opinion of how abominable it was that such scandalous traffic in baby flesh and blood should, through the law's inefficiency, be rendered possible. But it was only while we, following the revolting revelations, were subject to a succession of shocks and kept in pain, that we were thus virtuous. It was only while our tender feelings were suffering excruciation from the harrowing story of baby torture that we shook in wrath against the torturer. Considering what our sufferings were (and from the manner of our crying out they must have been truly awful) we recovered with a speed little short of miraculous. Barely was the trial of the murderess concluded and the court cleared, than our fierce indignation subsided from its bubbling and boiling, and quickly settled down to calm and ordinary temperature. Nay it is hardly too much to say that our over-wrought sympathies as regards baby neglect and murder fell so cold and flat that little short of a second edition of Herod's massacre might be required to raise them again.

This is the unhappy fate that attends nearly all our great social grievances. They are overlooked or shyly glanced at and kicked aside for years and years, when suddenly a stray spark ignites their smouldering heaps, and the eager town cooks a splendid supper of horrors at the gaudy conflagration; but having supped full, there ensues a speedy distaste for flame and smoke, and in his heart every one is chiefly anxious that the fire may burn itself out, or that some kind hand will smother it. "We have had enough of it." That is the phrase. The only interest we ever had in it, which was nothing better than a selfish and theatrical interest, is exhausted. We enjoyed the bonfire amazingly, but we have no idea of tucking back our coat-sleeves and handling a shovel or a pick to explore the unsavoury depth and origin of the flareup, and dig and dam to guard against a repetition of it. It is sufficient for us that we have endured without flinching the sensational horrors dragged to light; let those who dragged them forth bury them again; or kill them; or be killed by them. We have had enough of them.

Great social grievances are not to be taken by storm. They merely bow their vile heads while the wrathful blast passes, and regain their original position immediately afterwards. So it was with this business of baby-farming, and the tremendous outcry raised at the time when the wretch Winser was brought to trial. There are certain newspapers in whose advertisement columns the baby-farmer advertises for "live stock" constantly, and at the time it was observed with great triumph by certain people that since the vile hag's detection the advertisements in question had grown singularly few and mild. But the hope that the baby-farmer had retired, regarding his occupation as gone, was altogether delusive. He was merely lying quiet for a spell, quite at his ease, making no doubt that business would stir again presently. Somebody else was doing his advertising, that was all. If he had had any reasonable grounds for supposing that the results of the appalling facts brought to light would be that the Legislature would bestir itself and take prompt and efficacious steps towards abolishing him, it would have been different. But he had too much confidence in the sluggardly law to suppose anything of the kind. He knew that the details of the doings of himself and his fellows would presently sicken those who for a time had evinced a relish for them, and that in a short time they would bid investigators and newspapers say no more—they had had enough of it! When his sagacity was verified, he found his way leisurely back to the advertising columns again.

I have spoken of the baby-farmers as masculine, but that was merely for convenience of metaphor. No doubt that the male sex have a considerable interest in the trade, but the negociators, and ostensibly the proprietors, are women. As I write, one of the said newspapers lies before me. It is a daily paper, and its circulation, an extensive one, is essentially amongst the working classes, *especially amongst working girls and women.*

The words italicised are worth particular attention as regards this particular part of my subject. Here is a daily newspaper that is mainly an advertising broadsheet. It is an old-established news-paper, and its advertisement columns may be said fairly to reflect the condition of the female labour market over vast tracts of the London district. Column after column tells of the wants of ser-vants and masters. "Cap-hands," "feather-hands," "artificial flower-hands," "chenille-hands," hands for the manufacture of "chignons" and "hair-nets" and "bead work," and all manner of "plaiting" and "quilling" and "gauffering" in ribbon and net and muslin, contributing towards the thousand and one articles that stock the "fancy" trade. There are more newspapers than one that aspire as mediums between employers and employed, but this, before all others, is *the* newspaper, daily conned by thousands of girls and women in search of work of the kind above mentioned, and it is in this newspaper that the baby-farmer fishes wholesale for customers.

I write "wholesale," and surely it is nothing else. To the un-initiated in this peculiar branch of the world's wickedness it would seem that, as an article of negociation, a baby would figure rarer than anything, and in their innocence they might be fairly guided to this conclusion on the evidence of their personal experience of the unflinching love of parents, though never so poor, for their children; yet in a single number of this newspaper, published every day of the week and all the year round, be it borne in mind, appear no less than *eleven* separate advertisements, emanating from individuals solicitous for the care, weekly, monthly, yearly— anyhow, of other people's children, and that on terms odorous of starvation at the least in every meagre figure.

It is evident at a glance that the advertisers seek for customers and expect none other than from among the sorely pinched and poverty-stricken class that specially patronise the newspaper in question. The complexion, tone, and terms of their villanously cheap suggestions for child adoption are most cunningly shaped to meet the possible requirements of some unfortunate work-girl, who, earning while at liberty never more than seven or eight shillings a week, finds herself hampered with an infant for whom no father is forthcoming. There can scarcely be imagined a more terrible encumbrance than a young baby is to a working girl or woman so circumstanced. Very often she has a home before her disaster announced itself—her first home, that is, with her parents —and in her shame and disgrace she abandons it, determined on hiding away where she is unknown, "keeping herself to herself." She has no other means of earning a livelihood excepting that she has been used to. She is a "cap-hand," or an "artificial flower-hand," and such work is always entirely performed at the warehouse immediately under the employer's eye. What is she to do? She cannot possibly carry her baby with her to the shop and keep it with her the livelong day. Were she inclined so to do, and could somehow contrive to accomplish the double duty of nurse and flower-weaver, it would not be allowed. If she stays at home in the wretched little room she rents with her infant she and it must go hungry. It is a terrible dilemma for a young woman "all but" good, and honestly willing to accept the grievous penalty she must pay if it may be accomplished by the labour of her hands. Small and puny, however, the poor unwelcome little stranger may be, it is a perfect ogre of rapacity on its unhappy mother's exertions. Now and then an instance of the self-sacrificing devotion exhibited by those unhappy mothers for their fatherless children creeps into print. There was held in the parish of St. Luke's, last summer, an inquest on the body of a neglected infant, aged seven months. The woman to whose care she was confided had got drunk, and left the poor little thing exposed to the cold, so that it died. The mother paid the drunken nurse four-and-sixpence a week for the child's keep, and it was proved in evidence that she (the mother) had been earning at her trade of paper-bag making never more than six-and-threepence per week during the previous five months. That was four-and-sixpence for baby and *one-and-ninepence* for herself.

I don't think, however, that the regular baby-farmer is a person habitually given to drink. The successful and lucrative prosecution of her business forbids the indulgence. Decidedly not one of the eleven advertisements before mentioned read like the concoctions of persons whose heads were muddled with beer or gin. Here is the first one:—

NURSE CHILD WANTED, OR TO ADOPT.—The Advertiser, a Widow with a little family of her own, and a moderate allowance from her late husband's friends, would be glad to accept the charge of a young child. Age no object. If sickly would receive a parent's care. Terms, Fifteen Shillings a month; or would adopt entirely if under two months for the small sum of Twelve pounds.

Women are shrewder than men at understanding these matters, and the advertisement is addressed to women; but I doubt if a man would be far wrong in setting down the "widow lady with a little family of her own," as one of those monsters in woman's clothing who go about seeking for babies to devour. Her "moderate allowance," so artlessly introduced, is intended to convey to the unhappy mother but half resolved to part with her encumbrance, that possibly the widow's late husband's friends settle her butcher's and baker's bills, and that under such circumstances the widow would actually be that fifteen shillings a month in pocket, for the small trouble of entering the little stranger with her own interesting little flock. And what a well-bred, cheerful, and kindly-behaved little flock it must be, to have no objection to add to its number a young child aged one month or twelve, sick or well! Fancy such an estimable person as the widow lady appraising her parental care at so low a figure as three-and-ninepence a week—sevenpence farthing a day, including Sundays! But, after all, that is not so cheap as the taking the whole and sole charge of a child, sick or well, mind you, to nourish and clothe, and educate it from the age of two months till twelve years, say! To be sure, the widow lady stipulates that the child she is ready to "adopt" must be under two months, and we all know how precarious is infantine existence, and at what a wonderfully low rate the cheap undertakers bury babies in these days.

Another of the precious batch of eleven speaks plainer, and comes to the point without any preliminary walking round it:—

ADOPTION.—A person wishing a lasting and comfortable home for a young child of either sex will find this a good opportunity. Advertisers having no children of their own are about to proceed to America. Premium, Fifteen pounds. Respectable references given and required. Address F.X—.

All that is incomplete in the above is the initials; but one need not ask for the "O" that should come between the "F" and "X." After perusing the pithy advertisement, I interpreted its meaning simply this:—Any person possessed of a child he is anxious to be rid of, here is a good chance for him. Perhaps "F. X." is going to

America; perhaps he's not. That is *his* business. The party having a child to dispose of, need not trouble itself on that score. For "respectable references" read "mutual confidence." I'll take the child, and ask no questions of the party, and the party shall fork over the fifteen pounds, and ask no questions of me. That will make matters comfortable for both parties, 'specially if the meeting is at a coffee-house, or at some public building, for if I don't know the party's address, of course he can have no fear that I shall turn round on him, and return the child on his hands. The whole affair might be managed while an omnibus is waiting to take up a passenger. A simple matter of handing over a bulky parcel and a little one—the child and the money—and all over, without so much as "good night," if so be the party is a careful party, and wouldn't like even his voice heard.

It may be objected that the seduced factory girl is scarcely likely to become the victim of "F. X.," inasmuch as she never had fifteen pounds to call her own in the whole course of her life, and is less likely than ever to grow so rich now. And that is quite true, but as well as a seduced, there must be a seducer. Not a man of position and means, probably; more likely the fast young son of parents in the butchering, or cheesemongering, or grocery interest —a dashing young blade, whose ideas of "seeing life" is seeking that unwholesome phase of it presented at those unmitigated dens of vice, the "music halls," at one of which places, probably, the acquaintance terminating so miserably, was commenced. Or, may be, instead of the "young master," it is the shopman who is the male delinquent; and, in either case, anything is preferable to a "row," and an exposure. Possibly the embarrassed young mother, by stress of necessity, and imperfect faith in the voluntary goodness of her lover, is driven to make the best of the defensive weapons that chance has thus placed in her hands, and her urging for "some little assistance" becomes troublesome. This being the case, and the devil stepping in with "F.X.'s" advertisement in his hand, the difficulty is immediately reduced to one of raising fifteen pounds. No more hourly anxiety lest "something should turn up" to explode the secret under the very nose of parents or master, no more restrictions from amusements loved so well because of a dread lest that pale-faced baby-carrying young woman should intrude her reproachful presence, and her tears, into their midst. Only one endeavour—a big one, it is true, but still, only one—and the ugly ghost is laid at once and for ever! Perhaps the young fellow has friends of whom he can borrow the money. May be he has a watch, and articles of clothing and jewellery, that will pawn for the amount. If he has neither, still he is not entirely without resources. Music-halls and dancing-rooms cannot be patronised on bare journeyman's wages, and probably already the till has bled slightly—let it bleed more copiously! And the theft is perpetrated, and "F.X." releases the guilty pair of the little creature that looks in its helplessness and innocence so little like a bugbear. And it isn't at all unlikely that, after all, papa regards himself as a fellow deserving of condemnation, perhaps, but entitled to some pity, and, still more, of approval for his self-sacrificing. Another fellow, finding himself in such a fix, would have snapped his fingers in Polly's face, and told her to do her worst, and be hanged to her; but, confound it all, he was not such a brute as *that*. Having got the poor girl into trouble, he had done all he could to get her out of it—clean out of it, mind you. Not only had he done all that he could towards this generous end, but considerably more than he ought; he had risked exposure as a thief, and the penalty of the treadmill, and all for her sake! And so thick-skinned is the young fellow's morality, that possibly he is really not aware of the double-dyed villain he has become; that to strip his case of the specious wrappings in which he would envelop it, he is nothing better than a mean scoundrel who has stooped to till-robbery in order to qualify himself as an accessory to child murder, or worse—the casting of his own offspring, like a mangy dog, on the streets, to die in a gutter, or to live and grow up to be a terror to his kind—a ruffian, and a breeder of ruffians. Nor need it be supposed that this last is a mere fancy sketch. There can be no doubt that if the history of every one of the ten thousand of the young human pariahs that haunt London streets could be inquired into, it would be found that no insignificant percentage of the whole were children abandoned and left to their fate by mock "adopters," such as "F. X."

It is these "adopters" of children who should be specially looked after, since, assuming that heartless roguery is the basis of their business dealing, it becomes at once manifest that their main source of profit must lie in their ability to get rid of their hard bargains as soon as possible. From fifteen to five-and-twenty pounds would appear to be the sums usually asked, and having once got possession of the child, every day that the mockery of a *bona fide* bargain is maintained, the value of the blood-money that came with it diminishes. The term "blood-money," however, should be accepted in a qualified sense. It is quite common for these people to mention as one of the conditions of treaty that a sickly child would not be objected to, and provided it were very sickly, it might in ordinary cases have a fair chance of dying a natural death; but the course commonly pursued by the professional childmonger is not to murder it either by sudden and violent means, or by the less merciful though no less sure process of cold, neglect, and starvation. Not only does death made public (and in these wide-awake times it is not easy to hide a body, though a little one, where it may not speedily be found) attract an amount of attention that were best avoided, but it also entails the expenses of burial. A much easier way of getting rid of a child,— especially if it be of that convenient age when it is able to walk but not to talk, is to convey it to a strange quarter of the town and there abandon it.

And there is something else in connection with this painful phase of the question of neglected children that should not be lost sight of. It must not be supposed that every child abandoned in the streets is discovered by the police and finds its way first to the station-house, and finally to the workhouse. Very many of them, especially if they are pretty-looking and engaging children, are voluntarily adopted by strangers. It might not be unreasonably imagined that this can only be the case when the cruel abandonment takes place in a neighbourhood chiefly inhabited by well-to-do people. And well would it be for the community at large if this supposition were the correct one; then there would be a chance that the poor neglected little waif would be well cared for and preserved against the barbarous injustice of being compelled to fight for his food even before he had shed his milk-teeth. But wonderful as it may seem, it is not in well-to-do quarters that the utterly abandoned child finds protection, but in quarters that are decidedly the worst to do, and that, unfortunately, in every possible respect than any within the city's limits. The tender consideration of poverty for its kind is a phase of humanity that might be studied both with instruction and profit by those who, through their gold-rimmed spectacles regard deprivation from meat and clothes and the other good things of this world as involving a corresponding deficiency of virtue and generosity. They have grown so accustomed to associate cherubs with chubbiness, and chubbiness with high respectability and rich gravies, that they would, if such a thing were possible, scarcely be seen conversing with an angel of bony and vulgar type. Nevertheless, it is an undoubted fact, that for one child taken from the streets in the highly respectable West-end, and privately housed and taken care of, there might be shown fifty who have found open door and lasting entertainment in the most poverty-stricken haunts of London.

In haunts of vice too, in hideous localities inhabited solely by loose women and thieves. Bad as these people are, they will not deny a hungry child. It is curious the extent to which this lingering of nature's better part remains with these "bad women." Love for little children in these poor creatures seems unconquerable. It would appear as though conscious of the extreme depth of degradation to which they have fallen, and of the small amount of sympathy that remains between them and the decent world, they were anxious to hold on yet a little longer, although by so slender a thread as unreasoning childhood affords. As everyone can attest, whose duty it has been to explore even the most notorious sinks of vice and criminality, it is quite common to meet with pretty little children, mere infants of three or four years old, who are the pets and toys of the inhabitants, especially of the women. The frequent answer to the inquiry, "Who does the child belong to?" is, "Oh, he's anybody's child," which sometimes means that it is the offspring of one of the fraternity who has died or is now in prison, but more often that he is a "stray" who is fed and harboured there simply because nobody owns him.

But as may be easily understood, the reign of "pets" of this sort is of limited duration. By the time the curly-headed little boy of four years old grows to be six, he must indeed be an inapt scholar if his two years' attendance at such a school has not turned his artless simplicity into mischievous cunning, and his 'pretty ways" into those that are both audacious and tiresome. Then clubbing takes the place of caressing, and the child is gradually left to shift for himself, and we meet him shortly afterwards an active and intelligent nuisance, snatching his hard-earned crust out of the mire as a crossing sweeper, fusee, or penny-paper selling boy, or else more evilly inclined, he joins other companions and takes up the trade of a whining beggar. Even at that tender age his eyes are opened to the ruinous fact that as much may be got by stealing as by working, and he "tails on," a promising young beginner, to the army of twenty thousand professional thieves that exact black mail in London.

Supposing it to be true, and for my part I sincerely believe it, that the ranks of neglected children who eventually become thieves, are recruited in great part from the castaways of the mock child adopter, then is solved the puzzle how it is that among a class the origin of almost every member of which can be traced back to the vilest neighbourhood of brutishness and ignorance, so many individuals of more than the average intellect are discovered. Any man who has visited a reformatory for boys must have observed this. Let him go into the juvenile ward or the school-room of a workhouse, either in town or country, and he will find four-fifths of the lads assembled wearing the same heavy stolid look, indicative of the same desperate resignation to the process of learning than which for them could hardly be devised a punishment more severe. But amongst a very large proportion of the boys who have been rescued not merely from the gutter but out of the very jaws of the criminal law, and bestowed in our reformatories, how different is their aspect! Quick-witted, ready of comprehension, bold-eyed, shrewdly-observant, one cannot but feel that it is a thousand pities that such boys should be driven to this harbour of refuge—that so much good manhood material should come so nigh to being wrecked. But how is it that with no more promising nurses than squalor and ignorance the boys of the reformatory should show so much superior to the boys whom a national institution, such as a workhouse is, has adopted, and had all to do with since their infancy? The theory that many of the boys who by rapid steps in crime find their way to a reformatory, are bastard children, for whose safe-keeping the baby farmer was once briefly responsible, goes far towards solving the riddle. The child-adopting fraternity is an extensive one, and finds clients in all grades of society, and there can be little doubt that in instances innumerable, while Alley Jack is paying the penalty of his evil behaviour by turning for his bread on the treadmill, his brothers, made legitimate by the timely reformation and marriage of Alley Jack's father, are figuring in their proper sphere, and leisurely and profitably developing the intellect they inherit from their brilliant papa. Alley Jack, too, has his share of the family talent—all the brain, all the sensitiveness, all the "blood" of the respectable stock a reckless sprig of which is responsible for Jack's being. It is only in the nature of things to suppose that Jack's blood is tainted with the wildness of wicked papa; and here we have in Alley Jack a type of that bold intellectual villain whose clique of fifty or so, as Lord Shaftesbury recently declared, is more to be dreaded than as many hundred of the dull and plodding sort of thief, the story of whose exploits figure daily in the newspapers.

We have, however, a little wandered away from the subject in hand, which is not concerning neglected children who have become thieves, but neglected children, simply, whose future is not as yet ascertained. Speaking of the professional child farmer, it has been already remarked that his sole object, as regards these innocents that are adopted for a sum paid down, is to get rid of them as secretly and quickly as possible. And assuming the preservation of health and life in the little mortal to be of the first importance, there can be no question that he has a better chance of both, even though his treacherous "adopter" deserts him on a doorstep, than if he were so kindly cruel as to tolerate his existence at the "farm." It is those unfortunate infants who are not "adopted," but merely housed and fed at so much per week or month, who are the greater sufferers. True, it is to the interest of the practitioners who adopt this branch of baby-farming to keep life in their little charges, since with their death terminates the more or less profitable contract entered into between themselves and the child's parent or guardian; but no less true is it that it is to the "farmers'" interest and profit to keep down their expenditure in the nursery at as low an ebb as is consistent with the bare existence of its luckless inhabitants. The child is welcome to live on starvation diet just as long as it may. It is very welcome indeed to do so, since the longer it holds out, the larger the number of shillings the ogres that have it in charge will be enabled to grind out of its poor little bones. These are not the "farmers" who append to their advertisements the notification that "children of ill-health are not objected to." They are by far too good judges for that. What they rejoice in is a fine, robust, healthy-lunged child, with whom some such noble sum as a shilling a day is paid. Such an article is as good as a gift of twenty pounds to them. See the amount of privation such a child can stand before it succumbs! The tenacity of life in children of perfectly sound constitution is proverbial. A ha'p'orth of bread, and a ha'p'orth of milk daily will suffice to keep the machinery of life from coming to a sudden standstill. By such a barely sufficient link will the poor little helpless victim be held to life, while what passes as natural causes attack and gradually consume it, and drag it down to its grave. This, in the baby-farmer's estimation, is a first-rate article—the pride of the market, and without doubt the most profitable. The safest too. Children will pine. Taken from their mother, it is only to be expected that they should. Therefore, when the poor mother, who is working of nights as well as days, that "nurse's money" may be punctually paid, visits her little one, and finds it thin and pale and wasting, she is not amazed, although her conscience smites her cruelly, and her heart is fit to break. She is only too thankful to hear "nurse" declare that she is doing all she can for the little darling. It is her only consolation, and she goes away hugging it while "nurse" and her old man make merry over gin bought with that hard, hard-earned extra sixpence that the poor mother has left to buy baby some little comfort.

I trust and hope that what is here set down will not be regarded

as mere tinsel and wordy extravagance designed to produce a
"sensation" in the mind of the reader. There is no telling into
whose hands a book may fall. Maybe, it is not altogether impossible eyes may scan this page that have been recently red with
weeping over the terrible secret that will keep but a little longer,
and for the inevitable launching of which provision must be made.
To such a reader, with all kindliness, I would whisper words of
counsel. Think now "twice," but many times before you adopt
the "readiest" means of shirking the awful responsibility you have
incurred. Rely on it, you will derive no lasting satisfaction out of
this "readiest" way, by which, of course, is meant the way to
which the villanous child-farmer reveals an open door. Be righteous-
ly courageous, and take any step rather, as you would I am sure if
you were permitted to raise a corner and peep behind the curtain
that conceals the hidden mysteries of adopted-child murder.

As a volunteer explorer into the depths of social mysteries, once
upon a time I made it my business to invade the den of a child-
farmer. The result of the experiment was printed in a daily newspaper or magazine at the time, so I will here make but brief allusion to it. I bought the current number of the newspaper more
than once here mentioned, and discovering, as usual, a considerable string of child-adopting and nursing advertisements, I replied
to the majority of them, professing to have a child "on my hands,"
and signing myself "M. D." My intention being to trap the villains,
I need not say that in every case my reply to their preliminary
communications was couched in such carefully-considered terms
as might throw the most suspicious off their guard. But I found
that I had under-estimated the cunning of the enemy. Although
the innocent-seeming bait was made as attractive and savoury as
possible, at least half of the farmers to whom my epistles were
addressed vouchsafed no reply. There was something about it not
to their liking, evidently.

Three or four of the hungry pike bit, however, one being a lady
signing herself "Y. Z." In her newspaper advertisement, if I rightly
remember, persons whom it concerned were to address, "Y. Z.,"
Post Office, —— Street, Stepney. "Y. Z." replying to mine so
addressed, said that, as before stated, she was willing to adopt a
little girl of weakly constitution at the terms I suggested, her
object being chiefly to secure a companion for her own little
darling, who had lately, through death, been deprived of his own
dear little sister. "Y. Z." further suggested that I should appoint a
place where we could "meet and arrange."

This, however, was not what I wanted. It was quite evident

from the tone of the lady's note that she was not at all desirous that the meeting should take place at her abode. Again I was to address, "Post Office." To bring matters to a conclusion, I wrote, declaring that nothing could be done unless I could meet "Y. Z." at her own abode. No answer was returned to this my last, and it was evidently the intention of "Y. Z." to let the matter drop.

I was otherwise resolved, however. I had some sort of clue, and was resolved to follow it up. By what subtle arts and contrivance I managed to trace "Y. Z." from "Post Office" to her abode need not here be recited. Armed with her real name and the number of the street in which she resided, I arrived at the house, and at the door of it just as the postman was rapping to deliver a letter to the very party I had come uninvited to visit. I may say that the house was of the small four or five-roomed order, and no more or less untidy or squalid than is commonly to be found in the back streets of Stepney or Bethnal Green.

"Oxleek" was the original of "Y. Z.," and of the slatternly, ragged-haired girl who opened the door I asked if that lady was at home. The young woman said that she was out—that she had "gone to the Li-ver." The young woman spoke with a rapid utterance, and was evidently in a mighty hurry to get back to some business the postman's knock had summoned her from.

"I beg your pardon, miss, gone to the —"

"Li-ver; where you pays in for young uns' berryins and that," she responded; "she ain't at home, but he is. I'll call him."

And so she did. And presently a husky voice from the next floor called out, "Hullo! what is it?"

"Here's a gentleman wants yer, and here's a letter as the postman jest left."

"Ask him if he's the doctor; I've got the young un, I can't come down," the husky voice was again heard to exclaim.

To be sure I was not a doctor, not a qualified practitioner that is to say, but as far as the Oxleek family knew me I was "M.D.;" and pacifying my grumbling conscience with this small piece of jesuitism, I blandly nodded my head to the young woman when she recited to me Mr. Oxleek's query.

"Then you'd better go up, and p'raps you wouldn't mind taking this letter up with you," said she.

I went up; it was late in the evening and candlelight, in the room on the next floor that is, but not on the stairs; but had it been altogether dark, I might have discovered Mr. Oxleek by the stench of his tobacco. I walked in at the half-open door.

There was Mr. Oxleek by the fire, the very perfection of an

indolent, ease-loving, pipe-smoking, beer-soaking wretch as ever sat for his portrait. He was a man verging on fifty, I should think, with a pair of broad shoulders fit to carry a side of beef, and as greasy about the cuffs and collar of his tattered jacket as though at some early period of his existence he had carried sides of beef. But that must have been many years ago, for the grease had all worn black with age, and the shoulders of the jacket were all fretted through by constant friction against the back of the easy-chair he sat in. He wore slippers—at least, he wore *one* slipper; the other one, all slouched down at heel, had slipped off his lazy foot a few inches too far for easy recovery, and there it lay. A villanously dirty face had Mr. Oxleek, and a beard of at least a month's growth. It was plain to be seen that one of Mr. Oxleek's most favourite positions of sitting was with his head resting against that part of the wall that was by the side of the mantelshelf, for there, large as a dinner plate, was the black greasy patch his dirty hair had made. He had been smoking, for there, still smouldering, was his filthy little pipe on the shelf, and by the side of it a yellow jug all streaked and stained with ancient smears of beer.

He was not quite unoccupied, however; he was nursing a baby! He, the pipe-sucking, beer-swigging, unshaven, dirty, lazy ruffian, was nursing a poor little creature less than a year old, as I should judge, with its small, pinched face reposing against his ragged waistcoat, in the pocket of which his tobacco was probably kept. The baby wore its bedgown, as though it had once been put to bed, and roused to be nursed. It was a very old and woefully begrimed bedgown, bearing marks of Mr. Oxleek's dirty paws, and of his tobacco dust, and of physic clumsily administered and spilt. It would appear too much like "piling up the agony" did I attempt to describe that baby's face. It was the countenance of an infant that had cried itself to sleep, and to whom pain was so familiar, that it invaded its dreams, causing its mites of features to twitch and quiver so that it would have been a mercy to wake it.

"Evening, sir; take a cheer!" remarked Mr. Oxleek, quite hospitably; "this is the young un, sir."

It was very odd. Clearly there was a great mistake somewhere, and yet as far as they had gone, the proceedings were not much at variance with the original text. I was "M.D.," and a doctor was expected. "This was the young un," Mr. Oxleek declared, and a young one, a bereaved young one who had lost his darling playmate, was a prominent feature in his wife's letter to me.

"Oh, is that the young one?" I remarked.

"Yes; a heap of trouble; going after the last, I'm afeard."

"The same symptoms, eh?"

"Just the same. Reg'ler handful she is, and no mistake."

This then was *not* the "young un" Mrs. Oxleek had written about. This was a girl, it seemed.

"Pray, how long is it since a medical man saw the child?" I inquired, I am afraid in a tone that roused suspicion in Mr. Oxleek's mind.

"Oh, you know, when he came last week—you're come instead of him? You *have* come instead of him, haven't you?"

"No, indeed," I replied. "I've come to talk about that advertisement of yours."

Mr. Oxleek for a moment looked blank, but only for a moment. He saw the trap just as he was about to set his foot in it, and withdrew in time.

"Not here," he remarked, impudently.

"But I must beg your pardon, it is here. You forget. I wrote to you as M.D."

By this time Mr. Oxleek had seized and lit his short pipe, and was puffing away at it with great vigour.

"You're come to the wrong shop, I tell you," he replied, from behind the impenetrable cloud; "we don't know no 'M.D.' nor M.P., nor M. anythink; it's a mistake."

"Perhaps if I show you your wife's writing, you will be convinced?"

"No, I shan't; it's all a mistake, I tell you."

I sat down on a chair.

"Will your wife be long before she returns?" I inquired.

"Can't say—oh, here she comes; *now* p'raps you'll believe that you're come to the wrong shop. My dear, what do we know about M.D.'s, or advertising, eh?"

"Nothing."

Mrs. Oxleek was a short, fat woman, with a sunny smile on her florid face, and a general air of content about her. She had brought in with her a pot of beer and a quantity of pork sausages for supper.

"Nothing," she repeated instantly, taking the cue, "who says that we do?"

"This gentleman's been a tacklin' me a good 'un, I can tell you! —says that he's got your writing to show for summat or other."

"Where is my writing?" asked Mrs. Oxleek, defiantly.

"This is it, if I am not mistaken, ma'am." And I displayed it.

"Ah! that's where it is, you see," said she, with a triumphant chuckle, "you *are* mistaken. You are only wasting your time, my good sir. My name isn't 'Y. Z.,' and never was. Allow me to light you down-stairs, my good sir."

And I did allow her. What else could I do? At the same time, and although my investigations led to nothing at all, I came away convinced, as doubtless the reader is, that there was no "Mistake," and that Mr. and Mrs. Oxleek were of the tribe of ogres who fatten on little children.

Singularly enough, as I revise these pages for the press, there appears in the newspapers a grimly apt illustration of the above statement. So exactly do the details of the case in question bear out the arguments used in support of my views of baby-farming, that I will take the liberty of setting the matter before the reader just as it was set before the coroner.

"An investigation of a singular character was held by Mr. Richards on Thursday night, at the Lord Campbell Tavern, Bow, respecting the death of Frederick Wood, aged two years and three months.

"Miss A. W——, of Hoxton, said deceased was a sickly child, and ten months ago witness took it to Mrs. Savill, of 24, Swayton Road, Bow. She paid her four-and-sixpence a week to take care of the child. She never saw more than two other babies at Mrs. Savill's house. She thought her child was thoroughly attended to. The deceased met with an accident and its thigh was broken, but the doctor said that the witness need not put herself out in the slightest degree, for the child was getting on very well. Witness could not get away from business more than once a week to see the child. She had not seen the child for five weeks.

"Mrs. Caroline Savill said she was the wife of a porter in the city. The deceased had been with her ten months. She put him to bed at nine o'clock on Saturday night, and at half-past eight on Sunday morning she said to her daughter, 'He looks strange,' and then she put a looking-glass to his mouth and found that he was dead.

"By the Coroner: She could account for the broken thigh. Last October when she was taking deceased up to bed, she slipped down and fell upon the child. She was quite certain that she was sober. It was a pair of old boots that caused her to slip. She had eleven children to keep at Bow.

"A Juryman: You keep, in fact, a baby-farm?

"Witness: That I must leave to your generosity, gentlemen. In continuation, witness stated that out of the eleven children *five had died.* There had been no inquest on either of them. The deceased's bed was an egg-box with some straw in it. The egg-box was a short one, and was sixteen inches wide. The child could not turn in it. She never tied deceased's legs together. She never discovered that the child's thigh was broken till the morning following the night when she fell on it. He cried and she put him to bed. She fell upon the edge of the stairs and her weight was on him. She sent for a doctor next day.

"Doctor Atkins said he was called to see the dead body of the deceased last Sunday. The child had a malformed chest. Death had arisen from effusion of serum on the brain from natural causes, and not from neglect. Witness had attended the deceased for the broken thigh. He believed that the bones had not united when death took place.

"The jury, after a long consultation, returned a verdict of 'death from natural causes;' and they wished to append a censure, but the coroner refused to record it."

That is the whole of the pretty story of which the reader must be left to form his own opinion. Should that opinion insist on a censure as one of its appendages, the reader must of course be held personally responsible for it. It is all over now. The poor little victim whom a Miss of his name placed with the Bow "child-farmer," "by leave of your generosity, gentlemen," is dead and buried. It would have been a mercy when his unsteady nurse fell on and crushed him on the edge of the stairs, if she had crushed his miserable life out, instead of only breaking a thigh. Since last October, with one small leg literally in the grave, he must have had a dismal time of it, poor little chap, and glad, indeed, must his spirit have been when its clay tenement was lifted out of his coffin cradle—the egg-box with the bit of straw in it—and consigned to the peaceful little wooden house that the cemetery claimed. It is all over with Frederick John Wood; and his mamma, or whoever she was who was at liberty only once a week to come and see him, is released from the crushing burden his maintenance imposed on her, and Mrs. Savill by this time has doubtless filled up the egg-box the little boy's demise rendered vacant. Why should she not, when she left the coroner's court without a stain on her character? It is all over. The curtain that was raised just a little has been dropped again, and the audience has dispersed, and nobody will think again of the tragedy the darkened stage is ready to produce again at the shortest notice, until the coroner's constable rings the bell and the curtain once more ascends.

And so we shall go on, unless the law steps in to our aid. Why does it not do so? It is stringent and vigilant enough as regards inferior animals. It has a stern eye for pigs, and will not permit them to be kept except on certain inflexible conditions. It holds dogs in leash, and permits them to live only as contributors to Her Majesty's Inland Revenue. It holds its whip over lodging-house keepers, and under frightful pains and penalties they may not swindle a lodger of one out of his several hundred regulation feet of air; but it takes no heed of the cries of its persecuted babes and sucklings. Anyone may start as a professed adopter of children. Anyone however ignorant, and brutal, and given to slipping down stairs, may start as a baby-farmer, with liberty to do as she pleases with the helpless creatures placed in her charge. What she pleases first of all to do, as a matter of course, is to pare down the cost of her charge's keep, so that she may make a living of the parings. As has been seen, she need not even find them beds to lie on; if she be extra economical, an egg-box with a handful of straw will do as well.

And is there no remedy for this? Would it not be possible, at least, to issue licences to baby-keepers as they are at present issued to cow-keepers? It may appear a brutal way of putting the matter, but it becomes less so when one considers how much at present the brutes have the best of it.

CHAPTER IV

Working Boys.

The London Errand Boy.—His Drudgery and Privations.—His Temptations.—
The London Boy after Dark.—The Amusements provided for him.

The law takes account of but two phases of human existence,—the child irresponsible, and the adult responsible, and overlooks as beneath its dignity the important and well-marked steps that lead from the former state to the latter.

Despite the illegality of the proceeding, it is the intention of the writer hereof to do otherwise, aware as he is, and as every thinking person may be, of how critical and all-important a period in the career of the male human creature, is "boyhood." Amongst people of means and education, the grave responsibility of seeing their rising progeny safely through the perilous "middle passage" is fully recognized; but it is sadly different with the labouring classes, and the very poor.

It is a lamentable fact that at that period of his existence when he needs closest watching, when he stands in need of healthful guidance, of counsel against temptation, a boy, the son of labouring parents, is left to himself, almost free to follow the dictates of his inclinations, be they good or bad. Nothing than this can be more injudicious, and as regards the boy's moral culture and worldly welfare, more unjust. Not, as I would have it distinctly understood, that the boy of vulgar breeding is by nature more pregnable to temptation than his same age brother of genteel extraction; not because, fairly tested with the latter, he would be the first to succumb to a temptation, but because, poor fellow, outward circumstances press and hamper him so unfairly.

It has recently come to my knowledge that at the present time there is striving hard to attract public attention and patronage an institution styled the "Errand Boys' Home." It would be difficult, indeed, to overrate the importance of such an establishment, properly conducted. Amongst neglected children of a larger growth, those of the familiar "errand boy" type figure first and

39

foremost. It would be instructive to learn how many boys of the kind indicated are annually drafted into our great criminal army, and still more so to trace back the swift downhill strides to the original little faltering step that shuffled from the right path to the wrong.

Anyone who has any acquaintance with the habits and customs of the labouring classes, must be aware that the "family" system is for the younger branches, as they grow up, to elbow those just above them in age out into the world; not only to make more room at the dinner-table, but to assist in its substantial adornment. The poorer the family, the earlier the boys are turned out, "to cut their own grass," as the saying is. Take a case—one in ten thousand —to be met with to-morrow or any day in the city of London. Tom is a little lad—one of seven or eight—his father is a labourer, earning, say, a guinea a week; and from the age of seven Tom has been sent to a penny-a-week school; partly for the sake of what learning he may chance to pick up, but chiefly to keep him "out of the streets," and to effect a simultaneous saving of his morals and of his shoe-leather. As before stated, Tom's is essentially a working family. It is Tom's father's pride to relate how that he was "turned out" at eight, and had to trudge through the snow to work at six o'clock of winter mornings; and, that though on account of coughs and chilblains and other frivolous and childish ailments, he thought it very hard at the time, he rejoices that he was so put to it, since he has no doubt that it tended to harden him and make him the man he is.

Accordingly, when Tom has reached the ripe age of ten, it is accounted high time that he "got a place," as did his father before him; and, as there are a hundred ways in London in which a sharp little boy of ten can be made useful, very little difficulty is experienced in Tom's launching. He becomes an "errand boy," a newspaper or a printing boy, in all probability. The reader curious as to the employment of juvenile labour, may any morning at six or seven o'clock in the morning witness the hurried trudging to work of as many Toms as the pavement of our great highways will conveniently accommodate, each with his small bundle of food in a little bag, to last him the day through. Something else he may see, too, that would be highly comic were it not for its pitiful side. As need not be repeated here, a boy's estimate of earthy bliss might be conveniently contained in a dinner-plate of goodly dimensions. When he first goes out to work, his pride and glory is the parcel of food his mother makes up for the day's consumption. There he has it—breakfast, dinner, tea! Possibly he might get as much, or very nearly, in the ordinary course of events at home, but in a piece-meal and ignoble way. He never in his life possessed such a wealth of food, all his own, to do as he pleases with. Eight—ten slices of bread and butter, and may be—especially if it happen to be Monday—a slice of meat and a lump of cold pudding, relics of that dinner of dinners, Sunday's dinner!

His, all his, with nobody to say nay; but still only wealth in prospective! It is now barely seven o'clock, and, by fair eating, he will not arrive at that delicious piece of cold pork with the crackling on it until twelve! It is a keen, bracing morning; he has already walked a mile or more; and it wants yet fully an hour and a half to the factory breakfast time. It is just as broad as it is long; suppose he draws on his breakfast allowance just to the extent of one slice? Only one, and that in stern integrity: the topmost slice without fee or favour! But, ah! the cruel fragrance of that juicy cut of spare-rib! It has impregnated the whole contents of the bundle; The crust of that abstracted slice is as savoury, almost, as the crisp-baked rind of the original. Six bites—"too brief for friendship, not for fame"—have consumed it, and left him, alas! hungrier than ever. Shall he? What—taste of the sacred slice? No. It isn't likely. The pork is for his dinner. But the pudding—that is a supplemental sort of article; a mere extravagance when added to so much perfection as the luscious meat embodies. And out he hauls it; the ponderous abstraction afflicting the hitherto compact parcel with such a shambling looseness, that it is necessary to pause in one of the recesses of the bridge to readjust and tighten it. But, ah! rash boy! Since thou wert not proof against the temptation lurking in that slice of bread-and-butter, but faintly odorous of that maddening flavour, how canst thou hope to save thyself now that thou hast tasted of the pudding to which the pork was wedded in the baker's oven? It were as safe to trust thee at hungry noon with a luscious apple-dumpling, and bid thee eat of the dough and leave the fruit. It is all over. Reason, discretion, the admonitions of a troubled conscience, were all gulped down with that last corner, crusty bit, so full of gravy. The bridge's next recess is the scene of another halt, and of an utterly reckless spoliation of the dwindled bundle. And now the pork is consumed, to the veriest atom, and nought remains but four reproachful bread slices, that skulk in a corner, and almost demand the untimely fate visited on their companions. Shall they crave in vain? No. A pretty bundle, *this,* to take to the factory for his mates to see. A good excuse will serve his purpose better. He will engulf the four slices as he did the rest, and fold up his bag neatly, and hide it in his pocket, and, when dinner-time comes, he will profess that there is something nice at home, and he is going there to partake of it; while, really, he will take a dismal stroll, lamenting his early weakness, and making desperate vows for the future.

It is not, however, with Tom as the lucky owner of a filled food-bag that we have here to deal, but with Tom who at least five days out of the six is packed off to work with just as much bread and butter as his poor mother can spare off the family loaf. Now "going out to work" is a vastly different matter from going from home to school, and innocently playing between whiles. In the first place, the real hard work he has to perform (and few people would readily believe the enormous amount of muscular exertion these little fellows are capable of enduring), develops his appetite for eating to a prodigious extent. He finds the food he brings from home as his daily ration but half sufficient. What are a couple of slices of bread, with perhaps a morsel of cheese, considered as a dinner for a hearty boy who has perhaps trudged from post to pillar a dozen miles or so since his breakfast, carrying loads more or less heavy? He hungers for more, and more is constantly in his sight if he only had the means, a penny or twopence even, to buy it. He makes the acquaintance of other boys; he is drawn towards them in hungry, envious curiosity, seeing them in the enjoyment of what he so yearns after, and they speedily inform him how easy it is to "make" not only a penny or twopence, but a sixpence or a shilling, if he has a mind. And they are quite right, these young counsellors of evil. The facilities for petty pilfering afforded to the shopkeeper's errand-boy are such as favour momentary evil impulses. He need not engage in subtle plans for the purloining of a shilling or a shilling's worth. The opportunity is at his fingers' ends constantly. Usually he has the range of the business premises. Few people mistrust a little boy, and he is left to mind the shop where the money-till is, and he has free access to the store-room or warehouse in which all manner of portable small goods are heaped in profusion. It is an awful temptation. It is not sufficient to urge that it should not be, and that in the case of a lad of well-regulated mind it would not be. It would perhaps be more to the purpose to substitute "well-regulated meals" for "well-regulated minds." Nine times out of ten the confessions of a discovered juvenile pilferer go to prove that he sinned for his belly's sake. He has no conscience above his waistband, poor little wretch; nor can much better be expected, when we consider that all his life, his experience and observation has taught him that the first grand aim of human in-genuity and industry is to place a hot baked dinner on the table of

Sundays. To be sure, in the case of his hard-working father he may never have known him resort to any other than honest industry; he never found out that his parent was any other than an honest man; and so long as his father or his employer does not find him out to be any other than an honest boy, matters may run smoothly.

It is least of all my intention to make out that every errand-boy is a petty thief; all that I maintain is that he is a human creature just budding into existence as it were in the broad furrowed field of life, and that his susceptibilities are tender, and should be protected from evil influence with even extraordinary care; and that instead of which he is but too often left to grow up as maybe. In their ignorance and hard driving necessity, his parents having given him a spell of penny schooling, and maintained him until he has become a marketable article, persuade themselves that they have done for him the best they can, and nothing remains but for him to obey his master in all things, and he will grow to be as bright a man as his father before him.

It is only necessary to point to the large number of such children, for they are no better, who annually swell our criminal lists, to prove that somewhere a screw is sadly loose, and that the sooner it is set right the better it will be for the nation. The Home for Errand Boys is the best scheme that has as yet been put forth towards meeting the difficulty. Its professed object, I believe, is to afford shelter and wholesome food and healthful and harmless recreation for boys who are virtually without a home, and who have "only a lodging." That is to say, a place to which they may retire to sleep come bed-time, and for which they pay what appears as a paltry sum when regarded as so many pence per night, but which tells up to a considerable sum by the end of a week.

The most important feature, however, of such a scheme as the Home for Errand Boys embraces, does not appear in the vaunted advantage of reduced cost. Its main attraction is the promise it holds out to provide its lodgers with suitable amusement after work hours and before bed-time. If this were done on an extensive scale, there is no telling how much real substantial good might be accomplished. It is after work hours that boys fall into mischief. There is no reason why these homes should not have existence in various parts of London. One such establishment indeed is of little practical use. If it were possible to establish such places (a careful avoidance of everything savouring of the "asylum" and the "reformatory" would of course be necessary) in half a dozen different spots in the immediate neighbourhood of the city, they would doubtless meet with extensive patronage. They might indeed be made to serve many valuable ends that do not appear at a first glance. If these "homes" were established east, west, north, and south, they might be all under one management, and much good be effected by recommending deserving members for employment. There might even be a provident fund, formed by contributions of a penny or so a week, out of which lads unavoidably out of employ could be supported until a job of work was found for them.

Allusion has, in a previous page, been made to that dangerous time for working boys—the time between leaving work and retiring to bed. It would be bad enough were the boy left to his own devices for squandering his idle time and his hard-earned pence. This task, however, is taken out of his hands. He has only to stroll up this street and down the next, and he will find pitfalls already dug for him; neatly and skilfully dug, and so prettily overspread with cosy carpeting, that they do not in the least appear like pitfalls. It may at first sight seem that "neglected children" are least of all likely to make it worth the while of these diggers of pits, but it should be borne in mind that the term in question is here applied in its most comprehensive sense, that there are children of all ages, and that there are many more ways than one of neglecting children. It is evident that young boys who are out at work from six till six say, and after that spend the evening pretty much how they please, are "neglected" in the most emphatic meaning of the term. Parents are not apt to think so. It is little that they have to concede him in return for his contributions to the common stock, and probably they regard this laxity of supervision as the working boy's due—as something he has earned, and which is his by right. The boy himself is nothing backward in claiming a privilege he sees accorded to so many other boys, and it is the least troublesome thing in the world for the parents to grant the favour. All that they stipulate for is that the boy shall be home and a-bed in such good time as shall enable him to be up and at work without the loss in the morning of so much as an hour; which is a loss of just as many pence as may happen.

It may not be here out of place to make more definite allusion to the "pitfalls" above-mentioned. Pitfall broadest and deepest is the theatrical exhibition, known as the "penny gaff." Some considerable time since I wrote on this subject in the columns of the "Morning Star;" and as precisely the old order of things prevails, and the arguments then used against them apply with equal force now, I will, with the reader's permission, save myself further trouble than that which transcription involves.

Every low district of London has its theatre, or at least an humble substitute for one, called in vulgar parlance a "gaff." A gaff is a place in which, according to the strict interpretation of the term, stage plays may not be represented. The actors of a drama may not correspond in colloquy, only in pantomime, but the pieces brought out at the "gaff" are seldom of an intricate character, and the not over-fastidious auditory are well content with an exhibition of dumb show and gesture, that even the dullest comprehension may understand. The prices of admission to these modest temples of the tragic muse, are judiciously regulated to the means of the neighbourhood, and range from a penny to threepence. There is no "half-price for children," and for the simple reason that such an arrangement would reduce the takings exactly fifty per cent. They are *all* children who support the gaff. Costermonger boys and girls, from eight or nine to fourteen years old, and errand boys and girls employed at factories. As before mentioned, every district has its own "gaff." There is one near Peter Street, Westminster; a second in the New Cut, at Lambeth; a third in Whitecross Street; a fourth, fifth, and sixth between Whitechapel Church and Ratcliff Highway. It may, without fear of contradiction, be asserted, that within a circuit of five miles of St. Paul's, at least twenty of these dangerous dens of amusement might be enumerated.

At best of times they are dangerous. The best of times being when current topics of a highly sensational character are lacking, and the enterprising manager is compelled to fall back on some comparatively harmless stock piece. But the "gaff" proprietor has an eye to business, and is a man unlikely to allow what he regards as his chances to slip by him. He at once perceives a chance in the modern mania that pervades the juvenile population for a class of literature commonly known as "highly sensational." He has no literature to vend, but he does not despair on that account. He is aware that not one in five of the youth who honour his establishment with their patronage can read. If he, the worthy gaff proprietor, had any doubts on the subject, he might settle them any day by listening at his door while an admiring crowd of "regular customers" flocking thereto speculated on the pleasures of the night as foretold in glowing colours on the immense placards that adorn the exterior of his little theatre. They can understand the pictures well enough, but the descriptive legends beneath them are mysteries to which few possess the key. If these few are maliciously reticent, the despair of the benighted ones is painful to witness, as with puckered mouths and knitted brows they essay to decipher the strange straight and crooked characters, and earnestly consult with each other as to when and where they had seen the like. Failing in this, the gaff proprietor may have heard them exclaim in tones of but half-assured consolation, "Ah, well! it doesn't matter what the *reading* is; the piece won't be spoke, it'll be *acted,* so we are sure to know all about it when we come to-night."

Under such circumstances, it is easy enough to understand the agonized anxiety of low-lived ignorant Master Tomkins in these stirring times of Black Highwaymen, and Spring Heel Jacks, and Boy Detectives. In the shop window of the newsvendor round the corner, he sees displayed all in a row, a long line of "penny numbers," the mere illustrations pertaining to which makes his heart palpitate, and his hair stir beneath his ragged cap. There he sees bold highwaymen busy at every branch of their delightful avocation, stopping a lonely traveller and pressing a pistol barrel to his affrighted head, and bidding him deliver his money or his life; or impeding the way of the mail coach, the captain, hat in hand, courteously robbing the inside passengers (prominent amongst whom is a magnificent female with a low bodice, who evidently is not insensible to the captain's fascinating manner), while members of his gang are seen in murderous conflict with the coachman and the guard, whose doom is but too surely foreshadowed. Again, here is a spirited woodcut of a booted and spurred highwayman in headlong flight from pursuing Bow Street officers who are close at his heels, and in no way daunted or hurt by the contents of the brace of pistols the fugitive has manifestly just discharged point blank at their heads.

But fairly in the way of the bold rider is a toll-gate, and in a state of wild excitement the toll-gate keeper is seen grasping the long bar that crosses the road. The tormenting question at once arises in the mind of Master Tomkins—is he pushing it or pulling it? Is he friendly to the Black Knight of the Road or is he not? Master T. feels that his hero's fate is in that toll-gate man's hands; he doesn't know if he should vastly admire him or regard him with the deadliest enmity. From the bottom of his heart he hopes that the toll-gate man may be friendly. He would cheerfully give up the only penny he has in his pocket to know that it were so. He would give a penny for a simple "yes" or "no," and all the while there are eight good letter-press pages along with the picture that would tell him all about it if he only were able to read! There is a scowl on his young face as he reflects on this, and bitterly he thinks of his hard-hearted father who sent him out to sell fusees when he should have been at school learning his A B C. Truly, he went for a short time to a Ragged School, but there the master kept all the jolly books to himself—the "Knight of the Road" and that sort of thing, and gave him to learn out of a lot of sober dry rubbish without the least flavour in it. Who says that he is a dunce and won't learn? Try him now. Buy a few numbers of the "Knight of the Road" and sit down with him, and make him spell out every word of it. Never was boy so anxious after knowledge. He never picked a pocket yet, but such is his present desperate spirit, that if he had the chance of picking the art of reading out of one, just see if he wouldn't precious soon make himself a scholar?

Thus it is with the neglected boy, blankly illiterate. It need not be supposed, however, that a simple and quiet perusal of the astounding adventures of his gallows heroes from the printed text would completely satisfy the boy with sufficient knowledge to enable him to spell through a "penny number." It whets his appetite merely. It is one thing to *read* about the flashing and slashing of steel blades, and of the gleam of pistol barrels, and the whiz of bullets, and of the bold highwayman's defiant "ha! ha!" as he cracks the skull of the coach-guard, preparatory to robbing the affrighted passengers; but to be satisfactory the marrow and essence of the blood-stirring tragedy can only be conveyed to him in bodily shape. There are many elements of a sanguinary drama that may not well be expressed in words. As, for instance, when Bill Bludjon, after having cut the throat of the gentleman passenger, proceeds to rob his daughter, and finding her in possession of a locket with some grey hair in it, he returns it to her with the observation, "Nay, fair lady, Bill Bludjon may be a thief: in stern defence of self he may occasionally shed blood, but, Perish the Liar who says of him that he respects not the grey hairs of honourable age!" There is not much in this as set down in print. To do Bill justice, you must see how his noble countenance lights as his generous bosom heaves with chivalrous sentiments; how defiantly he scowls, and grinds his indignant teeth as he hisses the word "*Liar!*"—how piously he turns his eyes heaven-ward as he alludes to "honourable old age." It is in these emotional subtleties that the hero rises out of the vulgar robber with his villanous Whitechapel cast of countenance, and his great hands, hideous with murder stains, must be witnessed to be appreciated. It is the gaff proprietor's high aim and ambition to effect this laudable object, and that he does so with a considerable amount of, at least, pecuniary success, is proved by his "crowded houses" nightly.

Now that the police are to be roused to increased vigilance in the suppression, as well as the arrest of criminality, it would be as well if those in authority directed their especial attention to these penny theatres. As they at present exist, they are nothing better than hot-beds of vice in its vilest forms. Girls and boys of tender age are herded together to witness the splended achievements of "dashing highwaymen," and of sirens of the Starlight Sall school; nor is this all. But bad as this is, it is really the least part of the evil. The penny "gaff" is usually a small place, and when a specially atrocious piece produces a corresponding "run," the "house" is incapable of containing the vast number of boys and girls who nightly flock to see it. Scores would be turned away from the doors, and their halfpence wasted, were it not for the worthy proprietor's ingenuity. I am now speaking of what I was an actual witness of in the neighbourhood of Shoreditch. Beneath the pit and stage of the threatre was a sort of large kitchen, reached from the end of the passage, that was the entrance to the theatre by a flight of steep stairs. There were no seats in this kitchen, nor furniture of any kind. There was a window looking toward the street, but this was prudently boarded up. At night time all the light allowed in the kitchen proceeded from a feeble and dim gas jet by the wall over the fire-place.

Wretched and dreary-looking as was this underground chamber, it was a source of considerable profit to the proprietor of the "gaff" overhead. As before stated, when anything peculiarly attractive was to be seen, the theatre filled within ten minutes of opening the besieged doors. Not to disappoint the late comers, however, all who pleased might pay and go downstairs until the performance just commenced (it lasted generally about an hour and a half) terminated. The prime inducement held out was, that "then they would be sure of good seats." The inevitable result of such an arrangement may be easier guessed than described. For my part, I know no more about it than was to be derived from a hasty glance from the stair-head. There was a stench of tobacco smoke, and an uproar of mingled youthful voices—swearing, chaffing, and screaming, in boisterous mirth. This was all that was to be heard, the Babel charitably rendering distinct pronouncing of blasphemy or indecency unintelligible. Nor was it much easier to make out the source from when the hideous clamour proceeded, for the kitchen was dim as a coal cellar, and was further obscured by the foul tobacco smoke the lads were emitting from their short pipes. A few were romping about—"larking," as it is termed—but the majority, girls and boys, were squatted on the floor, telling and listening to stories, the quality of which might but too truly be guessed from the sort of applause they elicited. A few—impatient of the frivolity that surrounded them, and really anxious for "the play"—stood apart, gazing with scowling envy up at the ceiling, on the upper side of which, at frequent intervals, there was a furious clatter of hobnailed boots, betokening the delirious delight of the happy audience in full view of Starlight Sall, in "silk tights" and Hessians, dancing a Highland fling. Goaded to desperation, one or two of the tormented ones down in the kitchen reached up with their sticks and beat on the ceiling a tattoo, responsive to the battering of the hobnailed boots before mentioned. This, however, was a breach of "gaff" rule that could not be tolerated. With hurried steps the proprietor approached the kitchen stairs, and descried me. "This ain't the theeater; you've no business here, sir!" said he, in some confusion, as I imagined. "No, my friend, I have no business here, but *you* have a very pretty business, and one for which, when comes the Great Day of Reckoning, I would rather you answered than me." But I only thought this; aloud, I made the gaff proprietor an apology, and thankfully got off his abominable premises.

CHAPTER V.

The Problem of Deliverance.

Curious Problem.—The Best Method of Treatment.—The "Child of the Gutter" not to be Entirely Abolished.—The Genuine Alley-Bred Arab.— The Poor Lambs of the Ragged Flock.—The Tree of Evil in Our Midst.— The Breeding Places of Disease and Vice.

The curious problem—"What is the best method of treatment to adopt towards improving the condition of neglected children, and to diminish their number for the future?" has been attempted for solution from so many points of attack, and by means so various, that a bare enumeration of the instances would occupy much more space than these limited pages afford.

We may never hope entirely to abolish the child of the gutter. To a large extent, as has been shown, he is a natural growth of vices that seem inseparable from our social system: he is of the world, the flesh, and the devil; and, until we purge our grosser nature, and become angelic, we must tolerate him as we must the result of all our ill-breeding. It is a thousand pities that it should be so, because, as I have endeavoured in these pages to show, the neglected child issuing from the source here hinted at, is by far the most unmanageable and dangerous. Blood is thicker than any water, not excluding ditch water; and the chances are that the unlucky "love-child" will not remain content to grovel in the kennel to which an accident of birth consigned him, but, out of his rebellious nature, conceive a deadly hatred against the world that has served him so shabbily, and do his best to be revenged on it. It is not of the neglected child of this breed that I would say a few concluding words, but of the genuine alley-bred Arab of the City; the worthy descendant of a tribe that has grown so used to neglect that it regards it as its privilege, and fiercely resents any move that may be taken towards its curtailment.

If ever a distressed creature had friends surely this one has. From time immemorial it has been the pet of the philanthropist. Unsavoury, unsightly bantling as it is, he is never tired of fondling

50

it, spending his time and money over it, and holding it up to the commiseration of a humane public, and building all manner of homes and asylums for it; but he still remains on hand. If he would grow up, and after being bound 'prentice to a wholesome trade cease to trouble us, there would be some satisfaction in the business; but it never grows up. It is like the borrowed beggar's brat, that, in defiance of the progress of time, never emerges from its bedgown, and never grows too big to be tucked under one arm, leaving the other at liberty to arrest the charitable passer-by.

To be sure it is a great consolation to know that despite our non-success, the poor little object of our solicitude is in no danger of being dropped in hopelessness and abandoned, but it would be encouraging to discover that we were making some progress with our main design, which can be nothing less than the complete extinction of children of the "gutter" tribe, such as we are now discussing.

As it is, we are making scarcely any progress at all. I am aware that statistics are against this statement, that the triumphant reports of this and that charity point to a different conclusion. This home has rescued so many little ones from the streets—that asylum can show a thousand decently clad and educated children that but for its efforts would at this moment be either prowling the streets, picking up a more precarious living than the stray dog picks up, or leading the life of a petty thief, and rapidly earning his right to penal servitude.

This, and much more, is doubtless true, but there remains the grim fact that our filthy byways still swarm with these dirty, ragged, disease-stricken little ones, and as plentifully as of yore they infest our highways, an eyesore and a shuddering to all decent beholders. If there has occurred any recent diminution in their number, I should rejoice to know it; but that such is in the least degree the fact, certainly I am not justified in assuming in the face of the urgent appeals daily put forth by the wise in such matters, and who never tire of urging on the benevolently disposed, that never was there such need as now to be up and stirring.

And it can never be otherwise while we limit our charitable doing to providing for those poor lambs of the ragged flock as fast as they are bred, and cast loose on the chance of their being mercifully kidnapped and taken care of. As with indiscriminate giving to beggars, it may be urged that we can never go wrong in ministering to the distress of the infantine and helpless. Opportunities of doing so should perhaps be joyfully hailed by us as affording wholesome exercise of our belief in the Christian religion, but we may rely on it that the supply of the essential ingredient towards the said exercise will never be unequal to the demand. Our charitable exertion flows in too narrow a channel. It is pure, and of depth immeasurable, but it is not broad enough. We have got into a habit of treating our neglected children as an evil unavoidable, and one that must be endured with kindly and pious resignation. We have a gigantic tree of evil rooted in our midst, and our great care is to collect the ripe seeds it drops and provide against their germinating, and we expend as much time and money in the process as judiciously applied would serve to tear up the old tree from its tenacious holding, and for ever destroy its mischievous power. No doubt it may be justly claimed by the patrons and supporters of homes and asylums, that by rescuing these children from the streets they are saved from becoming debased and demoralized as were the parents they sprang from, and so, in course of time, by a steady perseverance in their system, the breed of gutter prowlers must become extinct; but that is a tedious and roundabout method of reform that can only be tolerated until a more direct route is discovered, and one that can scarcely prove satisfactory to those who look forward to a lifetime return for some of their invested capital.

We may depend on it that we shall never make much real progress in our endeavours to check the growth of these seedlings and offshoots of ragged poverty and reckless squalor until we turn our attention with a settled purpose to the haunts they are bred in. Our present system compels us even in its first preliminary steps to do violence against nature. We cannot deal with our babies of the gutter effectually, and with any reasonable chance of success, until we have separated them entirely from their *home.* We may tame them and teach them to feed out of our hands, and to repeat after us the alphabet, and even words of two and three syllables. We may even induce them to shed their bedraggled feathers and adopt a more decent plumage; but they can never be other than restless and ungovernable, and unclean birds, while they inhabit the vile old parent nest.

It is these vile old nests that should be abolished. While they are permitted to exist, while Rosemary Lane, and Peter Street, Westminster, and Back Church Lane in Whitechapel, and Cow Cross and Seven Dials, and a hundred similar places are tolerated and allowed to flourish, it is utterly impossible to diminish the race of children of the gutter. Why should these breeding places of disease and vice and all manner of abomination be permitted to cumber the earth? There is but one opinion that these horrid dens are the sources from which are derived two-thirds of our neglected ragged urchin population. Further, it is generally conceded, that it is not because of the prevalence of extreme poverty there; the filthy little public-houses invariably to be found lurking in the neighbourhood of rags and squalor would not be so prosperous if such were the case. It is the pestilential atmosphere of the place that will let nothing good live in it. You may never purify it. It is altogether a rotten carcase; and if you stuff it to the mouth with chloride of lime, and whitewash it an inch thick, you will make nothing else of it. It is a sin and a disgrace that human creatures should be permitted to herd in such places. One and all should be abolished, and wholesome habitations built in their stead. Half measures will not meet the case. That has been sufficiently proved but recently, when, not for morality or decency sake, but to make room for a railway, a few score of these odious hole-and-corner "slums" were razed to the ground.

The result was to make bad worse. The wretched occupants of the doomed houses clung to them with as much tenacity as though each abode were an ark, and if they were turned out of it, it would be to drown in the surrounding flood. When the demolishers came with their picks and crows—the honest housebreakers,—and mounted to the roof, the garret lodgers retreated to the next floor, and so on, debating the ground step by step before the inexorable pickaxe, until they were driven into the cellar and could go no lower. Then they had to run for it; but, poor purblind wretches, they had lived so long in dungeon darkness, that the broad light of day was unbearable. Like rats disturbed from a drain, all they desired was to escape out of sight and hide again; and again, like rats, they knew of neighbouring burrows and scuttled to them with all speed.

Ousted from Slusher's Alley, they sought Grimes's Rents. Grimes's Rents were already fully occupied by renters, but the present was a calamity that might overtake anyone, and the desired shelter was not refused. It was a mere matter of packing a little closer. The donkey that lodged in the cellar was turned into the wash-house, and there was a commodious apartment for a large family, and nothing was easier than to rig up an old counterpane on an extended string, so converting one chamber into two. Hard as it is to believe, and in mockery of all our Acts of Parliament for the better ordering of lodging-houses, and our legal enactments regulating the number of cubic feet of air every lodger was entitled to and might insist on, in hundreds of cases this condition of things exists at the present writing. Within a stone's cast of the Houses of Parliament, where sit six hundred wise gentlemen empanelled to make what laws they please for improving the condition of the people, every one of the said six hundred being an educated man of liberal mind, and fully recognising the Christian maxim that godliness and cleanliness are identical, may be found human creatures housed in places that would ruin the health of a country-bred pig were he removed thereto. In these same places parents and grown up and little children herd in the same room night and day. Sickness does not break up the party, or even the presence of grim Death himself. Singularly enough, however, more ceremony is observed with new life than with old Death. A missionary friend related to me the case of a family of five inhabiting one small room, and the youngest boy, aged thirteen, died. The domestic arrangements, however, were not in the least disturbed by the melancholy event; the lad's coffin was laid against the wall, and meals were cooked and eaten and the two beds made and occupied as usual until the day of burial. A little while after, however, the mother gave birth to a child, and my friend visiting the family found it grouped on the landing partaking of a rough-and-ready tea. It was voted "undacent to be inthrudin'" until next day. However, the decent scruples of the head of the family did not hold out beyond that time, and by the evening of the next day the old order of things was quite restored.

How in the name of goodness and humanity can we, under such circumstances, hope to be delivered from the curse of neglected children?

II.

PROFESSIONAL THIEVES.

CHAPTER VI.

Their Number and Difficulties.

Twenty Thousand Thieves in London.—What it Means.—The Language of "Weeds."—Cleverness of the Pilfering Fraternity.—A Protest Against a Barbarous Suggestion.—The Prisoner's great Difficulty.—The Moment of Leaving Prison.—Bad Friends.—What Becomes of Good Resolutions and the Chaplain's Counsel?—The Criminal's Scepticism of Human Goodness.— Life in "Little Hell."—The Cow Cross Mission.

The happily ignorant reader, whose knowledge of the criminal classes is confined to an occasional glance through the police court and Sessions cases as narrated in his morning newspaper, will be shocked and amazed to learn that within the limits of the City of London alone, an army of male and female thieves, twenty thousand strong, find daily and nightly employment.

It is easy to write "twenty thousand," and easier still to read the words. Easier than all to pass them by with but a vague idea of their meaning, and perhaps a sympathetic shrug of the shoulders for the poor, hard-worked policemen who must have such a terrible time of it in keeping such an enormous predatory crew in anything like order. Still, and without the least desire to be "sensational," I would ask the reader, does he fully comprehend what twenty thousand thieves in London means? Roughly estimating the population of the metropolis as numbering three millions, it means that amongst us one person in every hundred and fifty is a forger, a housebreaker, a pickpocket, a shoplifter, a receiver of stolen goods or what not; a human bird of prey, in short, bound to a desperate pursuit of that terrible course of life into which vice or misfortune originally casts him; a wily, cunning man-wolf, constantly on the watch, seeking whom he may devour.

Almost every member of this formidable host is known to the "police," but unfortunately this advantage is almost counterbalanced by the fact that the police are as well known to the majority of the twenty thousand. To their experienced eyes, it is not the helmet and the blue coat that makes the policeman. Indeed, they appear to depend not so much on visual evidence as on some subtle power of scent such as the fox possesses in discovering the approach of their natural enemy. They can discover the detective in his innocent-looking smock-frock or bricklayer jacket, while he is yet distant the length of a street. They know him by his step, or by his clumsy affectation of unofficial loutishness. They recognise the stiff neck in the loose neckerchief. They smell "trap," and are superior to it.

There is a language current amongst them that is to be met with in no dictionary with which I am acquainted. I doubt if even the "slang dictionary" contains more than a few of the following instances that may be accepted as genuine. It will be seen that the prime essential of "thieves' latin" is brevity. By its use, much may in one or two words be conveyed to a comrade while rapidly passing him in the street, or, should opportunity serve, during a visit to him while in prison.

To erase the original name or number from a stolen watch, and substitute one that is fictitious—*christening Jack.*

To take the works from one watch, and case them in another—*churching Jack.*

Poultry stealing—*beak hunting.*

One who steals from the shopkeeper while pretending to effect an honest purchase—*a bouncer.*

One who entices another to play at a game at which cheating rules, such as card or skittle sharping—*a buttoner.*

The treadmill, *shin scraper* (arising, it may be assumed, on account of the operator's liability, if he is not careful, to get his shins scraped by the ever-revolving wheel).

To commit burglary—*crack a case,* or *break a drum.*

The van that conveys prisoners to gaol—*Black Maria.*

A thief who robs cabs or carriages by climbing up behind, and cutting the straps that secure the luggage on the roof—*a dragsman.*

Breaking a square of glass—*starring the glaze.*

Training young thieves—*kidsman.*

To be transported or sent to penal servitude—*lagged.*

Three years' imprisonment—*a stretch.*

Six months—*half stretch.*

Three months' imprisonment—*a tail piece.*

To rob a till—*pinch a bob.*

A confederate in the practice of thimble rigging—*a nobbler.*

One who assists at a sham street row for the purpose of creating a mob, and promoting robbery from the person—*a jolly.*

A thief who secretes goods in a shop while a confederate distracts the attention of the shopkeeper is—*a palmer.*

A person marked for plunder—*a plant.*

Going out to steal linen in process of drying in gardens—*going snowing.*

Bad money—*sinker.*

Passer of counterfeit coins—*smasher.*

Stolen property generally—*swag.*

To go about half-naked to excite compassion—*on the shallow.*

Stealing lead from the roof of houses—*flying the blue pigeon.*

Coiners of bad money—*bit fakers.*

Midnight prowlers who rob drunken men—*bug hunters.*

Entering a dwelling house while the family have gone to church —*a dead lurk.*

Convicted of thieving—*in for a vamp.*

A city missionary or scripture reader—*gospel grinder.*

Shop-lifting—*hoisting.*

Hidden from the police—*in lavender.*

Forged bank notes—*queer screens.*

Whipping while in prison—*scroby* or *claws for breakfast.*

Long-fingered thieves expert in emptying ladies' pockets—*fine wirers.*

The condemned call—*the salt box.*

The prison chaplain—*Lady Green.*

A boy thief, lithe and thin and daring, such a one as house-breakers hire for the purpose of entering a small window at the rear of a dwelling house—*a little snakesman.*

So pertinaciously do the inhabitants of criminal colonies stick to their "latin," that a well-known writer suggests that special religious tracts, suiting their condition, should be printed in the language, as an almost certain method of securing their attention.

There can be no question that that of the professional thief is a bitterly severe and laborious occupation, beset with privations that moral people have no conception of, and involves an amount of mental anxiety and torment that few human beings can withstand through a long lifetime. Some years ago a clergyman with a thorough acquaintance with the subject he was handling, wrote on "Thieves and Thieving," in the "Cornhill Magazine," and *apropos* of this benumbing atmosphere of dread, that constantly encompasses even the old "professional," he says:—

"But if an acquaintance with the thieves' quarters revealed to me the amazing subtlety and cleverness of the pilfering fraternity, it also taught me the guilty fear, the wretchedness, the moral guilt, and the fearful hardships that fall to the lot of the professional thief. They are never safe for a moment, and this unceasing jeopardy produces a constant nervousness and fear. Sometimes when visiting the sick, I have gently laid my hand on the shoulder of one of them, who happened to be standing in the street. The man would 'start like a guilty thing upon a fearful summons,' and it would take him two or three minutes to recover his self-possession sufficiently to ask me 'How are you to-day, sir?' I never saw the adage, 'Suspicion always haunts the guilty mind,' so painfully illustrated as in the thieves' quarter, by the faces of grey-haired criminals, whose hearts had been worn into hardness by the dishonouring chains of transportation. When, in the dusk of the evening, I have spoken to one of them as he stood idly on the public-house steps, I have spoken in a low and altered tone, so that he might not at first recognise me: again the guilty start as the man bent forward, anxiously peering into my face."

He is never at rest, the wretched professional thief. He goes about with the tools of war perpetually in his hands, and with enemies in the front and the rear, and to the right and the left of him. "Anybody, to hear 'em talk," a thief once remarked to me (he was a thief at present in possession of liberty; not an incarcerated rogue plying "gammon" as the incarcerated rogue loves to ply it), "anybody would think, to hear 'em talk, that it was all sugar with us while we were free, and that our sufferings did not begin until we were caught, and 'put away.' Them that think so know nothing about it. Take a case, now, of a man who is in for getting his living 'on the cross,' and who has got a 'kid' or two, and their mother, at home. I don't say that it is *my* case, but you can take it so if you like. *She* isn't a thief. Ask her what she knows about me, and she'll tell you that, wuss luck, I've got in co. with some bad uns, and she wishes that I hadn't. She wishes that I hadn't, p'raps —not out of any sort of Goody-two-shoes feeling, but because she loves me. That's the name of it; *we* haint got any other word for the feelin'; and she can't bear to think that I may, any hour, be dragged off for six months, or a year, p'raps. And them's my feelings, too, and no mistake, day after day, and Sundays as well as week-days. She isn't fonder of me than I am of her, I'll go bail for that; and as for the kids, the girl especially, why I'd skid a waggon wheel with my body rather than her precious skin should be grazed. Well, take my word for it, I never go out in the morning, and the young 'un sez 'good bye,' but what I think 'good bye— yes! p'raps it's good bye for a longer spell than you're dreaming about, you poor little shaver.' And when I get out into the street, how long am I safe? Why, only for the straight length of that street, as far as I can see the coast clear. I may find a stopper at any turning, or at any corner. And when you *do* feel the hand on your collar! I've often wondered what must be a chap's feelings when the white cap is pulled over his peepers, and old Calcraft is pawing about his throat, to get the rope right. It must be a sight worse than the *other* feeling, you'll say. Well, if it is, I wonder how long the chap manages to hold up till he's let go!"

I am the more anxious to remark on these lingering relics of humanity, and, I may almost say virtue, that, if properly sought, may be discovered in the most hardened criminals, because, of late, there appears to be a growing inclination to treat the habitual criminal as though he had ceased to be human, and had degenerated into the condition of the meanest and most irreclaimable of predatory animals, fit only to be turned over to the tender mercies of a great body of huntsmen who wear blue coats instead of scarlet, and carry staves and handcuffs in place of whips and horns, and to be pursued to death. I have already taken occasion in the public newspapers, and I have much pleasure in returning to the charge here, to exclaim against the barbarous suggestions of a gentleman holding high position in the police force, Colonel Fraser, Commissioner of the City Police.

Alluding to the Habitual Criminals Bill, Colonel Fraser says:—

"Parts 1 and 2 of the Bill are chiefly designed to ensure a clearer police supervision than now exists over convicts at large on licence, and to extend it to persons who have been, or may be convicted of felony; but all the pains and penalties to which such persons are liable are made to depend absolutely on proof being forthcoming that the alleged offenders are actual licence holders, or convicted felons, and the great difficulty which so frequently occurs in obtaining this proof will present serious obstacles to a satisfactory working of the statute.

"Organized as the English police forces are, it will be most difficult for them, notwithstanding the contemplated system of registration, to account satisfactorily for the movements of licence holders, or to obtain an effective supervision over them, if they are determined to evade it. But the number of these convicts at large is insignificant compared with the swarms of repeatedly-convicted thieves, who give infinitely greater trouble to the police than licence-holders, and who constantly escape with a light sentence, from the impossibility of obtaining ready proof of their former convictions."

Now comes the remedy for this unsatisfactory state of affairs!

"As a remedy for this, I would suggest that every convict, on being liberated on licence, and every person after a second conviction of felony, should be marked in prison, on being set free, in such manner as the Secretary of State might direct—as has been the practice in the case of deserters, and men dismissed for misconduct from the army: such marking to be accepted as sufficient proof of former convictions.

"The precise mode in which this should be effected is matter of detail; but, by a simple combination of alphabetical letters, similar to that employed in distinguishing postage-stamps, no two persons need bear precisely the same mark, and the arrangement of letters might be such as to show at a glance, not only the particular prison in which the offender had been last confined, but also the date of his last conviction. Copies of these marks, transmitted to the Central Office of Registration in London, would form an invaluable record of the history of habitual criminals, and enable the police to obtain that reliable information as to their antecedents, the want of which now so commonly enables practised offenders to escape the consequences of their misdeeds.

"Attempts might, and probably would, be made to alter the appearance of the tell-tale imprints; but it would be impossible to efface them, and any artificial discoloration of the skin appearing on the particular part of the arm, or body, fixed upon for the prison mark, should be considered as affording sufficient proof of former convictions; unless the person charged could show—to the satisfaction of the justice before whom he might be brought—that it was produced by legitimate means."

I have ventured to transcribe, in its integrity, the main portion of Colonel Fraser's "new idea," thinking that its importance demanded it. It is significant of much that is to be regretted, coming from such a source. It is somewhat excusable, maybe, in a common policeman—who yesterday may have been an agricultural labourer, or a member of a community of which no more in the way of education is expected—if he exhibits a kind of unreasoning, watch-dog antagonism towards the criminal classes. He is instructed in all sorts of manoeuvres, and paid a guinea a week to act *against* them—to oppose the weight of his officially-striped arm, and the full force of his handy staff against them, whenever he finds plausible excuse for doing so. And, possibly, this is a condition of affairs one should not be over eager to reform. The policeman, "too clever by half," is generally an instrument of injustice, and an impediment in the way of the law's impartial acting. So long as the common constable remains a well-regulated machine, and fulfils his functions without jarring or unnecessary noise, we will ask no more; but without doubt we expect, and we have a right to expect, some display of intelligence and humanity on the part of the chief engineer who directs and controls these machines. An official of polite education, and possessed of a thorough knowledge of the ways and means and the various resources of the enemy it is his duty to provide against, should be actuated by some more generous sentiment than that which points towards uncompromising extermination. Colonel Fraser should bear in mind that an act of criminality does not altogether change a man's nature. He is a human creature in which, perhaps through accident, perhaps through desperate, and to some extent deliberate culture, certain growths, injurious to the welfare of the commonwealth, have growth; but to brand, and destroy, and crush under the heel the said creature because of his objectionable affections, is much like smashing a set of valuable vases because stagnant water has been permitted to accumulate in them. It may be urged that if the said vases or men have secreted criminal vice and fouling until their whole substance has become saturated beyond possibility of cleansing, then the sooner they are utterly abolished the better. To this I answer that until the best known methods of cleansing have been tried on the foul vessels we are not in a position to say that they are irreclaimable; and again, even provided that you might discover certain such vessels fit for nothing but destruction, it would be a monstrous absurdity to issue an edict ordering the annihilation of every pot of a like pattern. And this is pretty much as Colonel Fraser would act.

Let the reader for a moment consider what would be the effect if such a law as that proposed by the Commissioner of Police for the City of London were passed. In the first place it would, in its immediate operation, prove immensely unjust to the milder sort of criminal. If we started anew with our army of twenty thousand to-morrow morning, and every member of it had been convicted but once, there would be fairness (admitting just for argument sake only that there is any fairness at all about it) in holding out the threat that the next man who committed himself should be branded. But, as the case stands, before a month had elapsed we should have hundreds of unlucky wretches against whose names but two felonious commitments stood, bearing the hateful brand, while thousands of the old and wary of the tribe acquainted with the interior of every prison in England would, as far as the tell-tale mark is concerned, appear as innocent as you or I. Nor would any "alphabetical postal system," however ingenious and cold-blooded, avoid this difficulty. The only way of doing full justice to the entire body of felons—the young beginners and the old practitioners—would be, whenever the latter were next taken to search all the prison records for convictions against them, and score them in regular order on the delinquents' writhing flesh. To do this, however, Colonel Fraser would have to abandon his idea of branding on the arm. That member would in many cases afford inadequate space, even if you brought the chronicle from the shoulder to the finger tips, and "turned over" and continued the length of the criminal's palm. As the newspaper reports frequently show, there are evil doers whose catalogues of crimes may scarcely be expressed in a century.

But these are the bad ones already so branded and seared in heart and mind that to prick and scorch an inch of their outward skin would be but to tickle their vanity, and give them to brag of another scar, got in their life-long war against society. Short of torturing them or killing them, it matters little what measures are provided against these case-hardened villains. But there are scores and hundreds who though they have earned for themselves the names of criminals, whom to class and force to herd with the before-mentioned set would be to incur the greatest responsibility, and one that under existing circumstances it would be utterly short of wanton brutality to engage in.

As regards the class last mentioned, that is to say, those members who have at present made no very desperate acquaintance with crime and its punishment, I believe that if they were but judiciously dealt with a very large number would be but too glad to escape from their present life of misery. "Many a thief," says a writer, whose able remarks are the more valuable, because they are founded on actual experience and conversation with the people he treats of; "many a thief is kept in reluctant bondage to crime from the difficulties he finds in obtaining honest employment, and earning honest bread. Many thieves are fond of their criminal calling. They will tell you plainly that they do not intend to work hard for a pound a week, when they can easily earn five times as much by thieving in less time and live like gentlemen. But others of them are utterly weary of the hazard, disgrace, and suffering attaching to their mode of life. Some of them were once pure, honest, and industrious, and when they are sick, or in prison, they are frequently filled with bitter remorse, and make the strongest vows to have done with a guilty life.

"Suppose a man of this sort in prison. His eyes are opened, and he sees before him the gulf of remediless ruin into which he will soon be plunged. He knows well enough that the money earned by thieving goes as fast as it comes, and that there is no prospect of his ever being able to retire on his ill-gotten gains. He comes out of prison, determined to reform. But where is he to go? What is he to do? How is he to live? Whatever may have been done for him in prison, is of little or no avail, if as soon as he leaves the gaol he must go into the world branded with crime, unprotected and un-helped. The discharged prisoner must be friendly with some one, and he must live. His criminal friends will entertain him on the understood condition that they are repaid from the booty of his next depredation. Thus the first food he eats, and the first friendly chat he has, becomes the half necessitating initiative of future crime. Frequently the newly discharged prisoner passes through a round of riot and drunkenness immediately on his release from a long incarceration, as any other man would do in similar circum-stances, and who has no fixed principles to sustain him. And so by reason of the rebound of newly acquired liberty, and the influence of the old set, the man is again demoralized. The discharged prisoner leaves gaol with good resolves, but the moment he enters the world, there rises before him the dark and spectral danger of being hunted down by the police, and being recognised and insul-ted, of being shunned and despised by his fellow workmen, of being everywhere contemned and forsaken."

There can be no doubt that to this utter want of friends of the right sort at the moment of leaving prison, may be attributed a very large percentage of the persistence in a career of crime by those who have once made a false step. In this respect we treat our criminals of comparatively a mild character with greater harshness and severity than those whose repeated offences have led to their receiving the severest sentences of the law. The convict who is dis-charged after serving a term of five years at Portland, receives ere he quits the gates of Millbank prison a money gratuity, varying in amount according to the character that was returned with him from the convict establishment. Nor do the chances that are afforded him of quitting his old course of life and becoming an honest man end here. There is the Prisoner's Aid Society, where he may obtain a little more money and a suit of working clothes, and if he really shows an inclination to reform, he may be even recom-mended to a situation. But for the poor wretch who has given society much less offence, who has become a petty thief, probably not from choice, but from hard necessity, and who bitterly repents of his offences, there is no one to take him by the hand and give or lend him so much as an honest half-crown to make a fair start with. It may be said that the convict is most in want of help because he *is* a convict, because he is a man with whom rob-beries and violence have become so familiar, that it is needful to provide him with some substantial encouragement lest he slide back into the old groove. Further, because he is a man so plainly branded that the most inexperienced policeman may know at a glance what he is; whereas, the man who has been but once convicted may, if he have the inclination, push his way amongst honest men, and not one of them be the wiser as to the slip he has made. And that would be all very well if he were assisted in rejoining the ranks of honest bread-winners, but what is his plight when the prison door shuts behind him? It was his poverty that urged him to commit the theft that consigned him to gaol, and now he is turned out of it poorer than ever, crushed and spirit-broken, and with all his manliness withered within him. He feels ashamed and disgraced, and for the first few hours of his liberty he would willingly shrink back for hiding, even to his prison, because, as he thinks, people look at him so. A little timely help would save him, but nothing is so likely as desperate "don't care" to spring out of this consciousness of guilt, and the suspicion of being shunned and avoided; and the army of twenty thousand gains another recruit.

This undoubtedly is frequently the case with the criminal guilty of but a "first offence." Be he man or lad, however, he will be subject to no such painful embarrassment on his leaving prison after a second or third conviction. By that time he will have made friends. He will have found a companion or two to "work with," and they will keep careful reckoning of the date of his incarceration as well as of the duration of his term of durance. Make no doubt that they will be on the spot to rejoice with him on his release. They know the exact hour when the prison gate will open and he will come forth, and there they are ready to shake hands with him. Ready to "stand treat." Ready to provide him with that pipe of tobacco for which he has experienced such frequent longing, and to set before him the foaming pot of beer. "Come along, old pal!" say they, "we thought that you'd be glad of a drink and a bit of bacca, and we've got a jolly lot of beef over some baked taters at home!"

What becomes of all his good resolutions—of the chaplain's wholesome counsel now! "Shut your eyes resolutely to the temptations your old companions may hold out to you," were the parting words of that good man; "if they threaten you, bid them defiance. Let it be the first test of your good resolves to tell them plainly and boldly that you have done with them and will have no more to do with them!" Most excellent advice truly! but how is the emancipated one to act on it? How can he find it in his heart to dash with cold ingratitude such warmth of generosity and good nature? What claim has he on them that they should treat him so? They owe him nothing, and can have no ulterior and selfish object in thus expending their time and their money on his comfort. All that they expect in return is, that should either of them fall into trouble similar to his, he will exert himself for him in the same manner, and surely that is little enough to ask. Perhaps with the chaplain's good advice still ringing in his ears, a sigh of lingering remorse is blended with the outpuffing of that first delicious pipe, but it is promptly swallowed down in the draught of free beer, with the grim reflection, perhaps, that if those professing to be his friends came to his timely assistance as promptly and substantially as did those his enemies, he might have been saved the ignominy of entering anew on the old crimeful path.

As I have endeavoured to show, the best time for treating with these unhardened criminals for their reform, is just before they leave the prison at the expiration of their sentence, or so soon as they have crossed its threshold and find themselves free men. But even if they are here missed and allowed to go their sinful way, it is not absolutely necessary to postpone the good work until the law lays hold on them again. The dens to which they retire are not impregnable. They do not live in fortified caves, the doors of which are guarded by savage dogs and by members of the gang armed with swords and pistols. It is wonderful how docile and respectful they will behave towards folk who visit them, treating them as nothing worse than fellow creatures suffering under a great misfortune, and not as savage creatures of prey who have forfeited all claim to human nature, and are fit only to be scourged and branded. A writer already quoted tells us that during two years in one of the largest towns in England he had unlimited access to the thieves' quarter at all hours and under any circumstances—weddings, midnight gatherings, "benefit nights," public houses, he has visited them all. "How I gained the confidence of the criminal fraternity I cannot say. I only sought their welfare, never went amongst them without some good errand, never asked questions about their affairs, or meddled with things that did not belong to me; and it is due to the thieves themselves to say that I never received from any of them, whether drunk or sober, an unkind look or a disrespectful word. . . . I had not pursued my quiet mission amongst the thieves many months without discovering the damning fact that they had no faith in the sincerity, honesty, or goodness of human nature; and, that this last and vilest scepticism of the human heart was one of the most powerful influences at work in the continuation of crime. They believe people in general to be no better than themselves, and that most people will do a wrong thing if it serves their purpose. They consider themselves better than many "square" (honest) people who practise commercial frauds. Not having a spark of faith in human nature their case is all but hopeless; and only those who have tried the experiment can tell how difficult it is to make a thief believe that you are really disinterested and mean him well. Nevertheless, the agencies that are at work for the arrest of crime are all more or less working to good purpose, and conducing to a good end. Had I previously known nothing of the zeal and labour that have been expended during the last few years in behalf of the criminal population, I should have learned from my intercourse with the thieves themselves, that a new spirit was getting amongst them, and that something for their good was going on outside thievedom. The thieves, the worst of them, speak gloomily of the prospects of the fraternity; just as a Red Indian would complain of the dwindling of his tribe before the strong march of advancing civilization."

In every essential particular can I corroborate the above account. There are few worse places in London than certain parts of Cow Cross, especially that part of it anciently known as Jack Ketch's Warren, or "Little Hell" as the inhabitants more commonly designate it, on account of the number of subjects it produced for the operations of the common hangman. Only that the law is more merciful than of yore, there is little doubt that the vile nests in question, including "Bit Alley," and "Broad Yard," and "Frying Pan Alley," would still make good its claim to the distinguishing title conferred on it. The place indicated swarms with thieves of every degree, from the seven-year old little robber who snatches petty articles from stalls and shop-fronts, to the old and experienced burglar with a wide experience of convict treatment, British and foreign. Yet, accompanied by a city missionary well known to them, I have many a time gone amongst them, feeling as safe as though I was walking along Cheapside. I can give testimony even beyond that of the writer last quoted. "I never asked questions about their affairs, or meddled with things that did not concern me," says the gentleman in question. I can answer for it that my pastor friend of the Cow Cross Mission was less forbearing. With seasoned, middle-aged scoundrels he seldom had any conversation, but he never lost a chance of tackling young men and lads on the evil of their ways, and to a purpose. Nor was it his soft speech or polished eloquence that prevailed with them. He was by no means a gloomy preacher against crime and its consequences; he had a cheerful hopeful way with him that much better answered the purpose. He went about his Christian work humming snatches of hymns in the liveliest manner. One day while I was with him, we saw skulking along before us a villanous figure, ragged and dirty, and with a pair of shoulders broad enough to carry sacks of coal. "This," whispered my missionary friend, "is about the very worst character we have. He is as strong as a tiger, and almost as ferocious. "Old Bull" they call him.

I thought it likely we would pass without recognising so dangerous an animal, but my friend was not so minded. With a hearty slap on his shoulder, the fearless missionary accosted him.

'Well, Old Bull!"

"Ha! 'ow do, Mr. Catlin, sir?"

"As well as I should like to see you, my friend. How are you getting along, Bull?"

"Oh, werry dicky, Mr. Catlin." And Bull hung his ears and pawed uncomfortably in a puddle, with one slip-shod foot, as though in his heart resenting being "pinned" after this fashion.

"You find matters going worse and worse with you, ah!"

"They can't be no worser than they is, that's *one* blessin'!"

"Ah, now there's where you are mistaken, Bull. They can be worse a thousand times, and they *will*, unless you turn over a fresh leaf. Why not, Bull? See what a tattered, filthy old leaf the old one is!"

(Bull, with an uneasy glance towards the outlet of the alley, but still speaking with all respect,) "Ah! it's all that, guv'nor."

"Well then, since you *must* begin on a fresh leaf, why not try the right leaf—the honest one, eh, Bull. Just to see how you like it."

"All right, Mister Catlin. I'll think about it."

"I wish to the Lord you would, Bull. There's not much to laugh at, take my word for that."

"All right, guv'nor, I ain't a larfin. I means to be a reg'lar model some day—when I get time. Morning, Mister Catlin, sir."

And away went "Old Bull," with a queer sort of grin on his repulsive countenance, evidently no better or worse for the brief encounter with his honest adviser, but very thankful indeed to escape.

"I've been up into that man's room," said my tough little, cheerful missionary, "and rescued his wife out of his great cruel hands, when three policemen stood on the stairs afraid to advance another step."

He would do more than in his blunt, rough-and-ready way point out to them what a shameful waste of their lives it was to be skulking in a filthy court all day without the courage to go out and seek their wretched living till the darkness of night. He would offer to find them a job; he made many friends, and was enabled to do so, earnestly exhorting them to try honest work just for a month, to find out what it was like, and the sweets of it. And many have tried it; some as a joke—as a whimsical feat worth engaging in for the privilege of afterwards being able to brag of it, and returned to their old practice in a day or two; others have tried it, and, to their credit be it spoken, stuck to it. In my own mind I feel quite convinced that if such men as Mr. C., of the Cow Cross Mission, who holds the keys not only of the houses in which thieves dwell, but, to a large extent, also, a key to the character and peculiarities of the thieves themselves, were empowered with proper facilities, the amount of good they are capable of performing would very much astonish us.

CHAPTER VII

Homes and Haunts of the British Thief.

The Three Classes of Thieving Society.—Popular Misapprehensions.—A True Picture of the London Thief.—A Fancy Sketch of the "Under-Ground Cellar."—In Disguise at a Thieves' Raffle.—The Puzzle of "Black Maria."—Mr. Mullins's Speech and his Song.

Although, as most people are aware, the great thief tribe reckons amongst its number an upper, and a middle, and a lower class, pretty much as corresponding grades of station are recognised amongst the honest community, it is doubtful, in the former case, if promotion from one stage to another may be gained by individual enterprise and talent and industry. The literature of the country is from time to time enriched by bragging autobiographies of villains confessed, as well as by the penitent revelations of rogues reclaimed, but, according to my observation, it does not appear that perseverance in the humbler walks of crime lead invariably to the highway of infamous prosperity. It seems to be an idea too preposterous even to introduce into the pages of Newgate romance, daring in their flights of fancy as are the authors affecting that delectable line. We have no sinister antithesis of the well-known honest boy who tramped from Bristol to the metropolis with twopence-halfpenny in his pocket, and afterwards became Lord Mayor of London. No low-browed ragged little thief, who began his career by purloining a halfpenny turnip from a costermonger's barrow, is immortalized in the page of the Newgate Calendar, as finally arrived at the high distinction of wearing fashionable clothes, and ranking as the first of swell-mobsmen. It is a lamentable fact, and one that should have weight with aspirants for the convict's mask and badge, that the poor, shabby, hard-working thief so remains, till the end of his days. There is no more chance of his carrying his shameful figure and miserable hang-dog visage into tip-top society of his order, than there is of his attaining the summit of that treadwheel, with the ever-recurring steps of which he is so painfully familiar.

And if there is a forlorn, abject, harassed wretch in the world it is the poor, threadbare, timid London thief. I believe the popular supposition to be that, to turn thief at least ensures for the desperate adventurer money to squander for the time being; that however severe may be the penalty paid for the luxury, while "luck" lasts the picker of pockets and purloiner of his neighbour's goods has ever at his command means wherewith to satisfy the cravings of his vices, however extravagant they may be—money to live on the fat of the land and get drunk and enjoy happy spells of ease and plenty. This, no doubt, is the tempting picture the devil holds up for the contemplation of heart-sick honesty, when patient integrity is growing faint with hunger and long privation; and truly it seems not an improbable picture. What inducement is there for a man to persist in a career of dishonesty with its certain and frequent penalties of prison and hard labour, unless his perilous avocation ensures him spells, albeit brief ones, of intoxicating enjoyment?

No wonder that the ignorant, sorely-tempted, out-o'-work labourer should take this view of the case, when men, who by station and education—men who profess to have gone out of their highly respectable paths in life to make such inquiries as should qualify them to discuss the matter in solemn Parliamentary conclave, declare that it is so. A curious exhibition of the lamentable credulity of our law makers occurred no longer ago than at the second reading of the Habitual Criminals Bill in the House of Lords. Naturally the subject was one concerning which their Lordships could know nothing, except by hearsay, and Earl Shaftesbury volunteered to put them in possession of such useful information as might guide them towards a decision as regarded the projected Bill.

It is only fair to state, however, that his Lordship was not personally responsible for his startling statements. He had them from a "practitioner," from a thief, that is to say. His Lordship did not reveal whether it was a thief at large who was his informant: but that is scarcely likely. Doubtless it was from some weeping villain, with an eye to a remission of his sentence, who so frankly confided to the soft-hearted Earl the various secrets of that terrible trade it was his intention never, *never* to work at again! At any rate, whoever the "practitioner" was, he succeeded in his design completely, as the horror-stricken visage of his lordship, as he delivered himself of the astounding revelations, fully attested.

They were to this effect, and the reader will please bear in mind that they were not tendered to be received at their worth, but as facts which might be relied on. Within the City of London, Lord Shaftesbury declared, "crucibles and melting-pots are kept going all day and all night. I believe that in a very large number of cases the whole of the plate is reduced within two or three hours of the robbery to ingots of silver. As for spoons, forks, and jewellery, they are not taken so readily to the melting-pot; but to well-known places where there is a pipe, similar to that which your lordships may have seen—I hope none may have seen it of necessity—in the shop of the pawnbroker. The thief taps, the pipe is lifted up, and in the course of a minute a hand comes out covered with a glove, takes up the jewellery, and gives out the money for it."

If that conscienceless "practitioner," who so scandalously gulled the good Earl, happened to be in enjoyment of liberty when the above quoted newspaper report was printed, how he must have grinned as he perused it? But what an unpleasant reversal of the joke it would be if the mendacious statements of the bare-faced villain lead to the passing of a bill imposing cruelly severe rules for the government of criminals, and the worthy in question should one fine day find himself groaning under the same! The most astounding part of the business however, is, that his lordship should have given credit to such a tissue of fudge. To his honour be it stated, he should know better. As an indefatigable labourer amongst the poor and afflicted, his name will be remembered and blest long after he has passed from among us. It is doubtful if any other man whose title gives him admission to the House of Lords, could have given nearly as much practical information on this painful subject, and there can be no question—and this is the most unfortunate part of the business—that all that his lordship stated was regarded as real. Every lord present to listen to and discuss the various clauses of Lord Kimberley's Bill, probably took to his vivid imagination the appalling picture of the underground cellars (to be reached only by known members of the burglarious brotherhood who could give the sign to the guardian of the cellar-door), where certain demon-men of the Fagin type presided constantly over crucibles and melting-pots, wherein bubbled and hissed the precious brew of gold and silver ornaments dissolved, the supply being constantly renewed by the bold "cracksmen" who numerously attended to bring the goods to market. Easier still even was it to conjure before the mind's eye the peculiar operations of the "pipe" that Lord Shaftesbury so graphically described. The deserted-looking house in the gloomy back street, with the street door always ajar so that customers might slip in and out at it in an instant—before even the policeman on beat could wink his sleepy eyes in amazement at the unexpected apparition; with the sliding panel in the dimly-lighted back kitchen, and the "spout" just like a pawnbroker's, and the "gloved hand," the fingers of it twitching with eager greed for the gold watch, still warm from the pocket of its rightful owner! How was it possible to deal with a subject bristling so with horrors with calmness and dignity? Their lordships had been given to understand by the mover of the bill that there were fifteen thousand thieves constantly busy in the Metropolis alone, and Lord Shaftesbury had informed them that the mysterious "spout" and the melting-pot were the chief channels for converting stolen goods into ready money. At this rate, London must be almost undermined by these gold-melting cellars—the midnight traveller through the great city might plainly hear and wonder at the strange tap-tapping that met his ears—the tapping at the "spout" that notified to the owner of the gloved hand that a new customer was in attendance? It would have been not very surprising if the Chief Commissioner of Police had been instantly communicated with, and given instructions at once to arrest every man and woman of the fifteen thousand, and hold them in safe keeping until their lordships had resolved on the most efficacious, and at the same time least painful way of exterminating them.

Seriously, it is impossible almost to exaggerate the amount of mischief likely to result from such false and inflammatory pictures of an evil that in its naked self is repulsive enough in all conscience. On the one hand, it excites amongst the people panic and unnecessary alarm, and furnishes the undeniable excuse of "self-defence" for any excess of severity we may be led into; and on the other hand, it tends to magnify the thief's importance in the eyes of the thief, and to invest his melancholy and everlastingly miserable avocations with precisely the same kind of gallows-glory as is preached by the authors of "Tyburn Dick" or the "Boy Highwayman." Curiously enough at the conclusion of his long and interesting speech, Lord Shaftesbury went a little out of his way to make mention of the literature of the kind just quoted, to remark on its intimate bearing on the crime of the country, and to intimate that shortly the whole question would be brought under their lordships' consideration. It is doubtful, however, and I say so with extreme regret, knowing as I well do how shocking even the suspicion of such a thing must be to Lord Shaftesbury, if in any dozen "penny numbers" of the pernicious trash in question, the young aspirant for prison fame would find as much stimulative matter as was provided in his lordship's speech, or rather speeches, on the Habitual Criminal question.

No, the affairs of those who affect the criminal walks of life are bad enough in all conscience, but they are much less romantic than his lordship has been led to believe. Shorn of the melo-dramatic "bandit" costume with which they have been temporarily invested they lose nothing in appalling effect.

Truly, it is hard to understand, but it is an undoubted fact, that the criminal who in police nomenclature is a "low thief" (to dis-tinguish him, it may be presumed, from "the respectable thief") is without exception of all men the most comfortless and miser-able; and should the reader be so inquisitive as to desire to be informed of the grounds on which I arrive at this conclusion, I beg to assure him that I do not rely on hearsay, neither do I depend on what thieves incarcerated for their offences have told me, holding it to be hardly likely that a prisoner in prison would vaunt his liking for crime and his eagerness to get back to it. I have mixed with thieves at liberty, an unsuspected spy in their camp, more than once. I will quote an example.

This was many years since, and as at the time I published a detailed account of the visit, I may be excused from more than briefly alluding to it here. It was at a thieves' raffle, held at a public-house in one of the lowest and worst parts of Westminster. I was young in the field of exploration then, and from all that I had heard and read made up my mind for something very terrible and desperate. I pictured to myself a band of rollicking desper-adoes, swaggering and insolent, with plenty of money to pay for bottles of brandy and egg-flip unlimited, and plenty of bragging discourse of the doughty deeds of the past, and of their cold-blooded and desperate intentions for the future. Likewise, my expectations of hope and fear included a rich treat in the shape of vocalization. It was one thing to hear play-actors on the stage, in their tame and feeble delineations of the ancient game of "high Toby," and of the redoubtable doings of the Knights of the Road, spout such soul-thrilling effusions as "Nix my Dolly Pals," and "Claude Duval," but what must it be to listen to the same bold staves out of the mouths of real "roaring boys," some of them, possibly, the descendants of the very heroes who rode "up Hol-born Hill in a cart," and who could not well hear the good words the attendant chaplain was uttering because of the noisy exchange of boisterous "chaff" taking place between the short-pipe smoking driver, whose cart-seat was the doomed man's coffin, and the glee-ful mob that had made holiday to see the fun!

But in all this I was dismally disappointed. I had procured a ticket for the raffle from a friendly police-inspector (goodness only knows how he came possessed of them, but he had quite a collection of similar tickets in his pocket-book), and, disguised for the occasion, I entered the dirty little dram shop, and exhibited my credential to the landlord at the bar. So far the business was promising. The said landlord was as ill-looking a villain as could be desired. He had a broken nose and a wooden leg, both of which deformities were doubtless symptomatic of the furious brawls in which he occasionally engaged with his ugly customers. As I entered he was engaged in low-whispered discourse with three ruffians who might have been brothers of his in a similar way of business, but bankrupt, and gone to the dogs. As I advanced to the bar the four cropped heads laid together in iniquity, separated suddenly, and the landlord affected a look of innocence, and hummed a harmless tune in a way that was quite melodramatic.

I intimated my business, and he replied shortly, "Go on through," at the same time indicating the back door by a jerk of his thumb over his shoulder. Now for it! On the other side of the back door I discovered a stone yard, at the extremity of which was dimly visible in the darkness a long, low, dilapidated building, with a light shining through the chinks. This, then was the robber's den! —a place to which desperate men and women who made robbery and outrage the nightly business of their lives, resorted to squander in riot and debauchery their ill-gotten gains! It would not have surprised me had I found the doorkeeper armed with a pair of "trusty barkers," and every male guest of the company with a life-preserver sticking out at the breast pocket of his coat.

The door was opened in response to my tap at it. I gave the pot-man there stationed my ticket, and I entered. I must confess that my first sensation as I cast my eye carelessly around, was one of disgust that I should have been induced to screw up my courage with so much pains for so small an occasion. The building I found myself in was a skittle-ground, furnished with forms and tables; and there were present about thirty persons. As well as I can remember, of this number a third were women, young generally, one or two being mere girls of sixteen, or so. But Jenny Diver was not there, nor Poll Maggot, nor Edgeworth Bess. No lady with ringlets curling over her alabaster shoulders found a seat on the knee of the gallant spark of her choice. No Captain Macheath was to be seen elegantly taking snuff out of a stolen diamond snuff-box, or flinging into the pink satin lap of his lady love a handful of guineas to pay for more brandy. Poor wretches! the female shoulders there assembled spoke rather of bone than alabaster, while the washed-out and mended cotton frocks served in place of pink satin, and hair of most humble fashion surmounted faces by no means expressive either of genuine jollity, or even of a desperate determination towards devil-may-careness, and the drowning of care in the bowl. There were no bowls, even, as in the good old time, only vulgar pewter porter pots, out of which the company thankfully swigged its fourpenny. There was no appearance of hilarity, or joviality even; no more of brag and flourish, or of affectation of ease and freedom, than though every man and woman present were here locked up "on remand," and any moment might be called out to face that damning piece of kept-back evidence they all along dreaded was in store for them. To be sure it was as yet early in the evening, and though the company may have assembled mainly for the purpose of drowning "dull care," that malicious imp being but recently immersed, may have been superior at present to their machinations, and able to keep his ugly head above the liquid poured out for his destruction. Or may be, again, being a very powerful "dull care," of sturdy and mature growth, he might be able to hold out through many hours against the weak and watery elements brought to oppose him.

Anyhow, so far as I was able to observe, there was no foreshadowing of the blue and brooding imp's defeat. His baneful wings seemed spread from one end of the skittle-alley to the other, and to embrace even the chairman, who being a Jew, and merely a receiver of stolen goods, might reasonably have been supposed to be less susceptible than the rest. There would seem to prevail, amongst a large and innocent section of the community, a belief that the thief is a creature distinguished no less by appearance than by character from the honest host he thrives by. I have heard it remarked more than once, by persons whose curiosity has led them to a criminal court when a trial of more than ordinary interest is proceeding, that really this prisoner or that did not *look* like a thief, or a forger, or stabber, as the case might be. "Lord bless us," I once heard an elderly lady exclaim, in the case of an oft-convicted scoundrel of the "swell mob" tribe, over whose affecting trial she had shed many tears, "Lord bless us!" said she, as the jury found him guilty, and sentenced him to two years' hard labour, "so thin, and genteel, and with spectacles on, too! I declare I should have passed that young man twenty times without dreaming of calling out for the police." On the other hand, there are very many persons less ingenuous than the old lady, who invariably regard a man through the atmosphere of crime, real or supposed, that envelopes him, and by means of its distorting influence make out such a villain as satisfies their sagacity. Had one of this last order been favoured with a private view of the company assembled to assist at Mr. Mullins's raffle, and have been previously informed that they were one and all thieves, in all probability they would have *appeared* thieves; but I am convinced that had they been shown to an unprepared and unprejudiced observer, his opinion would have been that the company gathered in the skittle-alley of the "Curly Badger" were no worse than a poor set of out-o'-work tailors, of French polishers, or weavers, or of some other craft, the members of which affect the gentility that black clothes and a tall hat is supposed to confer on the wearer; nor would an hour in their society, such as I spent, have sufficed to dissipate the innocent impression. Their expenditure was of the most modest sort, not one man in six venturing beyond the pot of beer. Their conversation, though not the most elegant, was least of all concerning the wretched trade they followed; indeed, the subject was never mentioned at all, except in melancholy allusion to Peter or Jerry, who had been recently "copped" (taken), and was expected to pass "a tail piece in the steel" (three months in prison). There was one observation solemnly addressed by one elderly man to another elderly man, the purport of which at the time puzzled me not a little. "Unlucky! Well you may say it. Black Maria is the only one that's doin' a trade now. Every journey full as a tuppenny omblibus!" I listened intently as prudence would permit for further reference to the mysterious female who was doing "all the trade," and "every journey" was "as full as a twopenny omnibus," but nothing in the conversation transpired tending to throw a light on the dark lady; so I mentally made a note of it for reference to my friend the inspector. He laughed. "Well, she has been doing a brisk stroke of business of late, I must say," said he. "Black Maria, sir, is our van of that colour that carries 'em off to serve their time."

But, as before observed, there was nothing in the demeanour of either the men or women present at Mullins's raffle to denote either that they revelled in the nefarious trade they followed, or that they derived even ordinary comfort and satisfaction from it. To be sure, it may have happened that the specimens of the thief class assembled before me were not of the briskest, but taking them as they were, and bearing in mind the spiritless, hang-dog, mean, and shabby set they were, the notion of bringing to bear on them such tremendous engines of repression as that suggested by the humane Commissioner of the City Police appears nothing short of ridiculous.

At the same time, I would have it plainly understood that my pity for the thief of this class by no means induces me to advise that no more effective means than those which at present exist should be adopted for his abolition. A people's respect for the laws of the country is its chief pillar of strength, and those who have no respect for the laws, act as so many rats undermining the said pillar, and although the rats assembled at Mullins's raffle were not of a very formidable breed, their hatred of the law, and their malicious defiance of it, was unmistakeable. For instance, the article to be raffled was a silk pocket handkerchief, and there it was duly displayed hanging across a beam at the end of the skittle-ground. The occasion of the raffle was, that Mr. Mullins had just been released after four months' imprisonment, and that during his compulsory absence from home matters had gone very bad, and none the less so because poor Mrs. Mullins was suffering from consumption. In alluding to these sad details of his misfortune, Mr. Mullins, in returning thanks for the charity bestowed on him, looked the picture of melancholy. "Whether she means ever to get on her legs again is more than I can say," said he, wagging his short-cropped head dolefully, "there ain't much chance, I reckon, when you're discharged from Brompton incurable. Yes, my friends, it's all agin me lately, and my luck's regler out. But there's one thing I must mention" (and here he lifted his head with cheerful satisfaction beaming in his eyes), "and I'm sure you as doesn't know it will be very glad to hear it—the handkerchief wot's put up to raffle here is the wery identical one that I was put away for." And judging from the hearty applause that followed this announcement, there can be no doubt that Mr. Mullins's audience were very glad indeed to hear it.

But even after this stimulant, the spirits of the company did not rally anything to speak of. Song singing was started, but nobody sung "Nix my Dolly Pals," or "Claude Duval." Nobody raised a roaring chant in honour of "ruby wine," or the flowing bowl, or even of the more humble, though no less genial, foaming can. There was a comic song or two, but the ditties in favour were those that had a deeply sentimental or even a funereal smack about them. The gentleman who had enlightened me as to Black Maria sang the Sexton, the chorus to which lively stave, "I'll provide you such a lodging as you never had before," was taken up with much heartiness by all present. Mullins himself, who possessed a fair alto voice, slightly damaged perhaps by a four months' sojourn in the bleak atmosphere of Cold Bath Fields, sang "My Pretty Jane," and a very odd sight it was to observe that dogged, jail-stamped countenance of his set, as accurately as Mullins could set it, to an expression matching the bewitching simplicity of the words of the song. I was glad to observe that his endeavours were appreciated and an encore demanded.

Decidedly the songs, taken as a whole, that the thieves sang that evening in the Skittle Saloon of the "Curly Badger" were much less objectionable than those that may be heard any evening at any of our London music halls, and everything was quiet and orderly. Of course I cannot say to what extent this may have been due to certain rules and regulations enforced by the determined looking gentleman who served behind the bar. There was one thing, however, that he could not enforce, and that was the kindliness that had induced them to meet together that evening. I had before heard, as everybody has, of "honour amongst thieves," but I must confess that I had never suspected that compassion and charity were amongst the links that bound them together; and when I heard the statement from the chair of the amount subscribed (the "raffle" was a matter of form, and the silk handkerchief a mere delicate concealment of the free gift of shillings), when I heard the amount and looked round and reckoned how much a head that might amount to, and further, when I made observation of the pinched and poverty-stricken aspect of the owners of the said heads, I am ashamed almost to confess that if within the next few days I had caught an investigating hand in my coat-tail pockets, I should scarcely have had the heart to resist.

CHAPTER VIII.

Juvenile Thieves.

The Beginning of the Downhill Journey.—Candidates for Newgate Honours.—
Black Spots of London.—Life from the Young Robber's Point of View.—
The Seedling Recruits the most difficult to reform.—A doleful Summing-
up.—A Phase of the Criminal Question left unnoticed.—Budding Burglars.—
Streams which keep at full flood the Black Sea of Crime.—The Promoters
of "Gallows Literature."—Another Shot at a Fortress of the Devil.—
"Poison-Literature."—"Starlight Sall."—"Panther Bill."

It is quite true that, counting prostitutes and receivers of stolen goods, there are twenty thousand individuals eating the daily bread of dishonesty within the city of London alone; there are many more than these. And the worst part of the business is, that those that are omitted from the batch form the most painful and repulsive feature of the complete picture. Shocking enough is it to contemplate the white-haired, tottering criminal holding on to the front of the dock because he dare not trust entirely his quaking legs, and with no more to urge in his defence than Fagin had when it came to the last—"an old man, my lord, a very old man;" and we give him our pity ungrudgingly because we are no longer troubled with fears for his hostility as regards the present or the future. It is all over with him or very nearly. The grave yawns for him and we cannot help feeling that after all he has hurt himself much more than he has hurt us, and when we reflect on the awful account he will presently be called on to answer, our animosity shrinks aside, and we would recommend him to mercy if it were possible. No, it is not those who have run the length of their tether of crime that we have to fear, but those who by reason of their tender age are as yet but feeble toddlers on the road that leads to the hulks. It would be instructive as well as of great service if reliable information could be obtained as to the beginning of the down-hill journey by our juvenile criminals. Without doubt it would be found that in a lamentably large number of cases the beginning did not rest in the present possessors at all, but that they were bred and nurtured in it, inheriting it from their parents as certain forms of physical disease are inherited.

In very few instances are they *trained* to thieving by a father who possibly has gone through all the various phases of criminal punishment, from the simple local oakum shed and treadmill to the far-away stone quarry and mineral mine, and so knows all about it. The said human wolf and enemy of all law and social harmony, his progenitor, does not take his firstborn on his knee as soon as he exhibits symptoms of knowing right from wrong, and do his best to instil into his young mind what as a candidate for Newgate honours the first principles of his life should be.

This would be bad enough, but what really happens is worse. To train one's own child to paths of rectitude it is necessary to make him aware of the existence of paths of iniquity and wrong, that when inadvertently he approaches the latter, he may recognise and shun them. So on the other hand, if by the devil's agency a child is to be made bold and confident in the wrong road, the right must be exhibited to him in a light so ridiculous as to make it altogether distasteful to him. Still a comparison is instituted, and matters may so come about that one day he may be brought to re-consider the judiciousness of his choice and perhaps to reverse his previous decision. But if he has received no teaching at all; if in the be-nighted den in which he is born, and in which his childish intellect dawns, no ray of right and truth ever penetrates, and he grows into the use of his limbs and as much brains as his brutish breeding affords him, and with no other occupation before him than to follow in the footsteps of his father the thief—how much more hopeless is his case?

Does the reader ask, are there such cases? I can answer him in sorrowful confidence, that in London alone they may be reckoned in thousands. In parts of Spitalfields, in Flower and Dean Street, and in Kent Street, and many other streets that might be enumera-ted, they are the terror of small shopkeepers, and in Cow Cross, with its horrible chinks in the wall that do duty for the entrance of courts and alleys—Bit Alley, Frying Pan Alley, Turk's Head-court, and Broad Yard, they swarm like mites in rotten cheese. As a rule, the police seldom make the acquaintance of this thievish small fry (if they did, the estimated number of London robbers would be considerably augmented); but occasionally, just as a sprat will make its appearance along with a haul of mackerel, one reads in the police reports of "Timothy Mullins, a very small boy, whose head scarcely reached the bar of the dock;" or of "John Smith, a child of such tender age that the worthy magistrate appeared greatly shocked," charged with some one of the hundred acts of petty pilfering by means of which the poor little wretches contrive to stave off the pangs of hunger. Where is the use of reasoning with Master Mullins on his evil propensities? The one propensity of his existence is that of the dog—to provide against certain gnawing pains in his belly. If he has another propensity, it is to run away out of dread for consequences, which is dog-like too. All the argument you can array against this little human waif with one idea, will fail to convince him of his guilt; he has his private and deeply-rooted opinion on the matter, you may depend, and if he screws his fists into his eyes, and does his earnest best to make them water—if when in the magisterial presence he contorts his countenance in affected agony, it is merely because he perceives from his worship's tone that he wishes to agonize him, and is shrewd enough to know that to "give in best," as he would express it, is the way to get let off easy.

But supposing that he were not overawed by the magisterial presence, and felt free to speak what is foremost in his mind unreservedly as he would speak it to one of his own set. Then he would say, "It is all very fine for you to sit there, you that have not only had a jolly good breakfast, but can afford to sport a silver toothpick to pick your teeth with afterwards, it is all very fine for you to preach to me that I never shall do any good, but one of these days come to something that's precious bad, if I don't cut the ways of thieving, and take to honest ways. There's so many different kinds of honest ways. *Yours* is a good 'un. I ain't such a fool as not to know that it's better to walk in honest ways like them *you've* got into, and to wear gold chains and velvet waistcoats, than to prowl about in ragged corduroys, and dodge the pleeseman, and be a prig: but how am I to get into them sorts of honest ways? Will you give me a hist up to 'em? Will you give me a leg-up—I'm such a little cove, you see—on to the bottom round of the ladder that leads up to 'em? If it ain't in your line to do so, p'raps you could recommend me to a lady or gentleman that would? No! Then, however am *I* to get into honest ways? Shall I make a start for 'em soon as I leaves this ere p'lice office, from which you are so werry kind as to discharge me? Shall I let the chances of stealing a turnip off a stall, or a loaf out of a baker's barrow, go past me, while I keep straight on, looking out for a honest way?—straight on, and straight on, till I gets the hungry staggers (*you* never had the hungry staggers, Mr. Magistrate), and tumble down on the road? I am not such a fool, thank'e. I don't see the pull of it. I can do better in dishonest ways. I'm much obliged to you. I'm sure of a crust, though a hard 'un, while I stick to the latter, and if I break down, you'll take care of me for a spell, and fatten me up a bit; but s'pose I go on the hunt after them honest ways you was just now preaching about, and I miss 'em, what am I then? A casual pauper, half starved on a pint of skilly, or 'a shocking case of destitution,' and the leading character in a coroner's inquest!" All this Master Timothy Mullins might urge, and beyond favouring him with an extra month for contempt of court, what could the magistrate do or say?

Swelling the ranks of juvenile thieves we find in large numbers the thief-born. Writing on this subject, a reverend gentleman of wisdom and experience says, "Some are thieves from infancy. Their parents are thieves in most cases; in others, the children are orphans, or have beenforsaken by their parents, and in such cases the children generally fall into the hands of the professional thief-trainer. In every low criminal neighbourhood there are numbers of children who never knew their parents, and who are fed and clothed by the old thieves, and made to earn their wages by dishonest practices. When the parent thieves are imprisoned or transported, their children are left to shift for themselves, and so fall into the hands of the thief-trainer. Here, then, is one great source of crime. These children are nurtured in it. They come under no good moral influence; and until the ragged-schools were started, they had no idea of honesty, not to mention morality and religion. Sharpened by hunger, intimidated by severe treatment, and rendered adroit by vigilant training, this class of thieves is perhaps the most numerous, the most daring, the cleverest, and the most difficult to reform. In a moral point of view, these savages are much worse off than the savages of the wilderness, inasmuch as all the advantages of civilization are made to serve their criminal habits. The poor, helpless little children literally grow up into a criminal career, and have no means of knowing that they are wrong; they cannot help themselves, and have strong claims on the compassion of every lover of his species."

Truly enough these seedling recruits of the criminal population are the most difficult to reform. They are impregnable alike to persuasion and threatening. They have an ingrain conviction that it is *you* who are wrong, not them. That you are wrong in the first place in appropriating all the good things the world affords, leaving none for them but what they steal; and in the next place, they regard all your endeavours to persuade them to abandon the wretched life of a thief for the equally poor though more creditable existence of the honest lad, as humbug and selfishness. "No good feeling is ever allowed to predominate; all their passions are distorted, all their faculties are perverted. They believe the clergy are all hypocrites, the judges and magistrates tyrants, and honest people their bitterest enemies. Believing these things sincerely, and believing nothing else, their hand is against every man, and the more they are imprisoned the more is their dishonesty strengthened."

This is, indeed, a doleful summing up of our present position and future prospects as regards so large a percentage of those we build prisons for. It is somewhat difficult to avoid a feeling of exasperation when, as an honest man, and one who finds it at times a sore pinch to pay rates and taxes, one contemplates the ugly, hopeless picture. Still, we should never forget that these are creatures who are criminal not by their own seeking. They are as they were born and bred and nurtured, and the only way of relieving society of the pest they are against it, is to take all the care we may to guard against the ravages of those we have amongst us, and adopt measures for the prevention of their breeding a new generation.

How this may be accomplished is for legislators to decide. Hitherto it has appeared as a phase of the criminal question that has attracted very little attention on the part of our law makers. They appear, however, to be waking up to its importance at last. Recently, in the House of Lords, Lord Romilly suggested that the experiment might be tried of taking away from the home of iniquity they were reared in the children of twice or thrice convicted thieves above the age of ten years; taking them away for good and all and placing them under State protection; educating them, and giving them a trade. If I rightly recollect, his lordship's suggestion did not meet with a particularly hearty reception. Some of his hearers were of opinion that it was setting a premium on crime, by affording the habitual thief just that amount of domestic relief he in his selfishness would be most desirous of. But Lord Romilly combatted this objection with the reasonable rejoinder, that by mere occupation the nature of the thief was not abased below that of the brute, and that it was fair to assume that so far from encouraging him to qualify himself for State patronage, his dread of having his children taken from him might even check him in his iniquitous career.

One thing, at least, is certain; it would come much *cheaper* to the country if these budding burglars and pickpockets were caught up, and caged away from the community at large, before their natures became too thoroughly pickled in the brine of rascality. Boy thieves are the most mischievous and wasteful. They will mount a house roof, and for the sake of appropriating the half-a-crown's worth of lead that forms its gutter, cause such damage as only a builder's bill of twenty pounds or so will set right. The other day a boy stole a family Bible valued at fifty shillings, and after wrenching off the gilt clasps, threw the book into a sewer; the clasps he sold to a marine store dealer for *twopence half-penny*! It may be fairly assumed that in the case of boy thieves, who are so completely in the hands of others, that before they can "make" ten shillings in cash, they must as a rule steal to the value of at least four pounds, and sometimes double that sum. But let us put the loss by exchange at its lowest, and say that he gets a fourth of the value of what he steals, before he can earn eighteen-pence a day, he must rob to the amount of two guineas a week—a hundred and nine pounds a year! Whatever less sum it costs the State to educate and clothe and teach him, the nation would be in pocket.

It would be idle to attempt to trace back to its origin the incentive to crime in the class of small criminals here treated of. Innocent of the meaning of the term "strict integrity," they are altogether unconscious of offending against it. They may never repent, for they can feel no remorse for having followed the dictates of their nature. No possible good can arise from piecing and patching with creditable stuff the old cloak of sin they were clothed in at their birth, and have worn ever since, till it has become a second skin to them. Before they can be of any real service as members of an honest community, they must be *reformed* in the strictest sense of the term. Their tainted morality must be laid bare to the very bones, as it were, and its rotten foundation made good from its deepest layer. The arduousness of this task it is hard to overrate; nothing, indeed, can be harder, except it be to weed out from an adult criminal the tough and gnarled roots of sin that grip and clasp about and strangle his better nature. And this should be the child criminal reformer's comfort and encouragement.

It must not be imagined, however, that the growth of juvenile criminality is altogether confined to those regions where it is indigenous to the soil; were it so, our prospects of relief would appear much more hopeful than at present, for, as before stated, all that is necessary would be to sow the baleful ground with the saving salt of sound and wholesome teaching, and the ugly vegetation would cease.

But there are other and more formidable sources from which flow the tributary streams that feed and keep at full flood our black sea of crime; more formidable, because they do not take the shape of irrepressible springs that make for the surface, simply because they are impelled thereto by forces they have not the strength to combat against, but rather of well planned artificial aqueducts and channels, and on the development of which much of intellect is expended. It is much harder to deal with the boy who, well knowing right from wrong, chooses the latter, than with the boy who from the beginning has been wrong from not knowing what right is.

Moreover, the boy who has been taught right from wrong, the boy who has been sent to school and knows how to read, has this advantage over his poor brother of the gutter—an advantage that tells with inexpressible severity against the community at large; he has trainers who, discovering his weakness, make it their profit and business to take him by the hand and bring him along in that path of life to which his dishonest inclination has called him.

I allude to those low-minded, nasty fellows, the proprietors and promoters of what may be truthfully described as "gallows literature." As a curse of London, this one is worthy of a special niche in the temple of infamy, and to rank first and foremost. The great difficulty would be to find a sculptor of such surpassing skill as to be able to pourtray in one carved stone face all the hideous vices and passions that should properly belong to it. It is a stale subject, I am aware. in my humble way, I have hammered at it both in newspapers and magazines, and many better men have done the same. Therefore it is stale. For no other reason. The iniquity in itself is as vigorous and hearty as ever, and every week renews its brimstone leaves (meanwhile rooting deeper and deeper in the soil that nourishes it), but unfortunately it comes under the category of evils, the exposure of which the public "have had enough of." It is very provoking, and not a little disheartening, that it should be so. Perhaps this complaint may be met by the answer: The public are not tired of this one amongst the many abuses that afflict its soul's health, it is only tired of being reminded of it. Explorers in fields less difficult have better fortune. As, for instance, the fortunate discoverer of a gold field is. Everybody would be glad to shake him by the hand—the hand that had felt and lifted the weight of the nuggets and the yellow chips of dust; nay, not a few would be willing to trim his finger nails, on the chance of their discovering beneath enough of the auriferous deposit to pay them for their trouble. But, to be sure, in a city of splendid commercial enterprise such as is ours, it can scarcely be expected that that amount of honour would be conferred on the man who would remove a plague from its midst as on the one whose magnificent genius tended to fatten the money-bags in the Bank cellars.

At the risk, however, of being stigmatized as a man with a weakness for butting against stone walls, I cannot let this opportunity slip, or refrain from firing yet once again my small pop-gun against this fortress of the devil. The reader may have heard enough of the abomination to suit his taste, and let him rest assured that the writer has written more than enough to suit *his*; but if every man set up his "taste" as the goal and summit of his striving, any tall fellow a tip-toe might, after all, see over the heads of most of us. The main difficulty is that the tens and hundreds of thousands of boys who stint a penny from its more legitimate use to purchase a dole of the pernicious trash in question, have *not* "had enough of it." Nothing can be worse than this, except it is the purveyors of letter-press offal have not had enough of it either, but, grown prosperous and muscular on the good feeding their monstrous profits have ensured them, they are continually opening up fresh ground, each patch fouler and more pestilent than the last.

At the present writing I have before me half-a-dozen of these penny weekly numbers of "thrilling romance," addressed to boys, and circulated entirely among them—and girls. It was by no means because the number of these poison pen'orths on sale is small that a greater variety was not procured. A year or so since, wishing to write a letter on the subject to a daily newspaper, I fished out of one little newsvendor's shop, situated in the nice convenient neighbourhood of Clerkenwell, which, more than any other quarter of the metropolis, is crowded with working children of both sexes, the considerable number of *twenty-three* samples of this gallows literature. But if I had not before suspected it, my experience on that occasion convinced me that to buy more than a third of that number would be a sheer waste of pence. To be sure, to expect honest dealing on the part of such fellows as can dabble in "property" of the kind in question, is in the last degree absurd, but one would think that they would, for "business" reasons, maintain some show of giving a pen'orth for a penny. Such is not the case, however. In three instances in my twenty-three numbers, I found the self-same story published *twice* under a different title, while for at least half the remainder the variance from their brethren is so very slight that nobody but a close reader would discover it.

The six-pen'orth before me include, "The Skeleton Band,"

"Tyburn Dick,", "The Black Knight of the Road," "Dick Turpin," "The Boy Burglar," and "Starlight Sall." If I am asked, is the poison each of these papers contains so cunningly disguised and mixed with harmless-seeming ingredients, that a boy of shrewd intelligence and decent mind might be betrayed by its insidious seductiveness? I reply, no. The only subtlety employed in the precious composition is that which is employed in preserving it from offending the blunt nostrils of the law to such a degree as shall compel its interference. If it is again inquired, do I, though unwillingly, acknowledge that the artful ones, by a wonderful exercise of tact and ingenuity, place the law in such a fix that it would not be justified in interfering? I most distinctly reply, that I acknowledge nothing of the kind; but that, on the contrary, I wonder very much at the clumsiness of a legislative machine that can let so much scoundrelism slip through its cogs and snares.

The daring lengths these open encouragers of boy highwaymen and Tyburn Dicks will occasionally go to serve their villanous ends is amazing. It is not more than two or three years since, that a prosperous member of the gang, whose business premises were in, or within a few doors of Fleet Street, by way of giving a fair start to his published account of some thief and murderer, publicly advertised that the buyers of certain numbers would be entitled to a chance of a Prize in a grand distribution of *daggers.* Specimens of the deadly weapons (made, it may be assumed, after the same fashion as that one with which "flash Jack," in the romance, pinned the police officer in the small of his back) were exhibited in the publisher's shop window, and in due course found their way into the hands of silly boys, with minds well primed for "daring exploits," by reading "numbers 2 and 3 given away with number 1."

It is altogether a mistake, however, to suppose that the poison publisher's main element of success consists in his glorification of robbers and cut-throats. To be sure he can by no means afford to dispense with the ingredients mentioned in the concoction of his vile brew, but his first and foremost reliance is on lewdness. Everything is subservient to this. He will picture to his youthful readers a hero of the highway, so ferocious in his nature, and so reckless of bloodshed, that he has earned among his comrades the flattering nick-name of "the Panther." He will reveal the bold panther in all his glory, cleaving the skull of the obstinate old gentleman in his travelling carriage, who will not give up his money, or setting an old woman on the kitchen fire, as a just punishment for hiding her guineas in the oven, in fishing them out of which the panther burns his fingers; he will exhibit the crafty "panther" wriggling his way through the floor boards of his cell, into a sewer beneath, and through which he is to make his escape to the river, and then by a flourish of his magic pen, he will convey the "panther" to the "boudoir" of Starlight Sall, and show you how weak a quality valour is in the presence of "those twin queens of the earth," youth and beauty! The brave panther, when he has once crossed the threshold of that splendid damsel (who, by the way, is a thief, and addicted to drinking brandy by the "bumper") is, vulgarly speaking, "nowhere." The haughty curl of his lip, the glance of his eagle eye, "the graceful contour of his manly form," a mere gesture of which is sufficient to quell rising mutiny amongst his savage crew, all fall flat and impotent before the queenly majesty of Sall. But there is no fear that the reader will lose his faith in Panther Bill, because of this weakness confessed. As drawn by the Author (does the pestiferous rascal so style himself, I wonder?) Starlight Sall is a creature of such exquisite loveliness, that Jupiter himself might have knelt before her. She is such a matchless combination of perfection, that it is found necessary to describe her charms separately, and at such length that the catalogue of the whole extends through at least six pages.

It is in this branch of his devilish business that the author of "Starlight Sall" excels. It is evident that the man's mind is in his work, and he lingers over it with a loving hand. Never was there such a tender anatomist. He begins Sall's head, and revels in her auburn tresses, that "in silken, snaky locks wanton o'er her shoulders, white as eastern ivory." He is not profound in foreheads, and hers he passes over as "chaste as snow," or in noses, Sall's being described briefly as "finely chiselled;" but he is well up in the language of eyes—the bad language. He skirmishes playfully about those of Sall, and discourses of her eyebrows as "ebon brow," from which she launches her excruciating shafts of love. He takes her by the eye-lashes, and describes them as the "golden fringe that screens the gates of paradise," and finally he dips into Sall's eyes, swimming with luscious languor, and pregnant with tender inviting to Panther Bill, who was consuming in ardent affection, as "the rippling waves of the bright blue sea to the sturdy swimmer." It is impossible here to repeat what else is said of the eyes of Starlight Sall, or her teeth, "like rich pearls," or of her "pouting coral lips, in which a thousand tiny imps of love are lurking." Bear it in mind that this work of ours is designed for the perusal of thinking men and women; that it is not intended as an amusing work, but as an endeavour to pourtray to Londoners the curses of London in a plain and unvarnished way, in hope that they may be stirred to some sort of absolution from them. As need not be remarked, it would be altogether impossible to the essayer of such a task, if he were either squeamish or fastidious in the handling of the material at his disposal; but I *dare* not follow our author any further in his description of the personal beauties of Starlight Sall. Were I to do so, it would be the fate of this book to be flung into the fire, and every decent man who met me would regard himself justified in kicking or cursing me; and yet, good fathers and mothers of England—and yet, elder brothers and grown sisters, tons of this bird-lime of the pit is vended in London every day of the Christian year.

Which of us can say that *his* children are safe from the contamination? Boys well-bred, as well as ill-bred, are mightily inquisitive about such matters, and the chances are very clear, sir, that if the said bird-lime were of a sort not more pernicious than that which sticks to the fingers, we might at this very moment find the hands of my little Tom and your little Jack besmeared with it. Granted, that it is unlikely, that it is in the last degree improbable, even; still, the remotest of probabilities have before now shown themselves grim actualities, and just consider for a moment the twinge of horror that would seize on either of us were it to so happen! Let us for a moment picture to ourselves our fright and bewilderment, if we discovered that our little boys were feasting off this deadly fruit in the secrecy of their chambers! Would it then appear to us that it was a subject the discussion of which we had "had enough of"? Should we be content, *then,* to shrug our shoulders after the old style, and exclaim impatiently against the barbarous taste of writers who were so tiresomely meddlesome? Not likely. The pretty consternation that would ensue on the appalling discovery!—the ransacking of boxes and cupboards, to make quite sure that no dreg of the poison, in the shape of an odd page or so, were hidden away!—the painful examination of the culprit, who never till now dreamt of the enormity of the thing he had been doing!—the reviling and threatening that would be directed against the unscrupulous news-agent who had supplied the pernicious pen'orth! Good heavens! the tremendous rumpus there would be! But, thank God, there is no fear of *that* happening.

Is there not? What are the assured grounds of safety? Is it because it stands to reason that all such coarse and vulgar trash finds its level amongst the coarse and vulgar, and could gain no footing above its own elevation? It may so stand in reason, but unfortunately it is the unreasonable fact that this same pen poison finds customers at heights above its natural low and foul water-line almost inconceivable. How otherwise is it accountable that at least a *quarter of a million* of these penny numbers are sold weekly? How is it that in quiet suburban neighbourhoods, far removed from the stews of London, and the pernicious atmosphere they engender; in serene and peaceful semi-country towns where genteel boarding schools flourish, there may almost invariably be found some small shopkeeper who accommodatingly receives consignments of "Blue-skin," and the "Mysteries of London," and unobtrusively supplies his well-dressed little customer with these full-flavoured articles? Granted, my dear sir, that your young Jack, or my twelve years old Robert, have minds too pure either to seek out or crave after literature of the sort in question, but not un-frequently it is found without seeking. It is a contagious disease, just as cholera and typhus and the plague are contagious, and, as everybody is aware, it needs not personal contact with a body stricken to convey either of these frightful maladies to the hale and hearty. A tainted scrap of rag has been known to spread plague and death through an entire village, just as a stray leaf of "Panther Bill," or "Tyburn Tree" may sow the seeds of immorality amongst as many boys as a town can produce.

CHAPTER IX

The Thief Non-professional.

*The Registered and the Unregistered Thieves of the London Hunting-ground.
—The Certainty of the Crop of Vice.—Omnibus Drivers and Conductors.—
The "Watchers."—The London General Omnibus Company.—The Scandal
of their System.—The Shopkeeper Thief.—False Weights and Measures.—
Adulteration of Food and Drink.—Our Old Law, "I am as honest as I can
afford to be!"—Rudimentary Exercises in the Art of Pillage.*

There are unregistered as well as "registered" thieves. How many of
the former make London their hunting-ground, it were much more
difficult to enumerate. Nor is it so much out of place as might at
first appear, to class both phases of rascality under one general
heading. We have to consider the sources from which are derived
our army of London thieves. It is not as though the plague of
them that afflicts was like other plagues, and showed itself mild or
virulent, according to well-defined and ascertained provocatives.
On the contrary, the crop of our crime-fields is even more un-
deviating than our wheat or barley crops. A grain of corn cast into
the ground may fail, but the seeds of vice implanted in kindly soil
is bound to germinate, unless the nature of the soil itself is altered.
As already stated, the number of our London thieves has somewhat decreased of late years, but it is merely to the extent of six
or seven per cent. If it is twenty thousand at the present time, this
day twelvemonths, allowing for the increased population, it will be
nineteen thousand, say.

Appalling as are the criminal returns for the city of London, it
would be a vain delusion to imagine that when the "twenty
thousand" have passed in review before us, the whole of the
hideous picture has been revealed. The Government statistics deal
only with "professional criminals;" that class of persons, that is to
say, who have abandoned all idea of living honestly, and who,
weighing the probable consequences, resign themselves to a life of
systematic depredation, and study existing facilities, and likely
new inventions, just as the ingenious joiner or engineer does in an
honest way.

The all-important question being, what are the main sources from which are derived with such steadiness and certainty, recruits for the great criminal army, it would be as well to inquire how much of dishonesty is permitted amongst us unchecked, simply because it does not take precisely that shape and colour it must assume before it so offends us that we insist on the law's interference. It should perhaps tend to make us more tender in our dealings with thieves denounced as such, and convicted, and sent to prison, when we consider the thousands of men of all grades who know honesty by name only, and who would at the merest push of adversity slip off the straight path on which for years past they have been no better than barefaced impostors and trespassers, and plunge at once into the miry ways of the professed thieves. It ceases to be a wonder how constantly vacancies in the ranks of crime are filled when we reflect on the flimsy partition that screens so many seemingly honest men, and the accidental rending of which would disclose a thief long practised, and cool, and bold through impunity. There are whole communities of men, constituting complete branches of our social economy, on whom the taint of dishonesty rests, and their masters are fully aware of it, and yet year after year they are allowed to continue in the same employment. Nay, I think that I may go as far as to assert that so complete is the disbelief in the honesty of their servants by these masters, that to the best of their ability they provide against loss by theft by paying the said servants very little wages. A notable instance of this is furnished by the omnibus conductors in the service of the General Omnibus Company. It is not because the company in question conducts its business more loosely than other proprietors of these vehicles that I particularize it, but because it is a public company in the enjoyment of many privileges and monopolies, and the public have an undoubted right to expect fair treatment from it. I don't know how many omnibuses, each requiring a conductor, are constantly running through the streets of London, but their number must be very considerable, judging from the fact that the takings of the London General Omnibus Company alone range from nine to ten thousand pounds weekly. Now it is well known to the company that their conductors rob them. A gentleman of my acquaintance once submitted to the secretary of the company an ingenious invention for registering the number of passengers an omnibus carried on each journey, but the secretary was unable to entertain it. "It is of no use to us, sir," said he. "The machine we want is one that will make our men *honest,* and that I am afraid is one we are not likely to meet with.

They *will* rob us, and we can't help ourselves." And knowing this, the company pay the conductor four shillings a day, the said day, as a rule, consisting of *seventeen hours*—from eight one morning till one the next. The driver, in consideration it may be assumed of his being removed from the temptation of handling the company's money, is paid six shillings a day, but his opinion of the advantage the conductor still has over him may be gathered from the fact that he expects the latter to pay for any reasonable quantity of malt or spirituous liquor he may consume in the course of a long scorching hot or freezing cold day, not to mention a cigar or two and the invariable parting glass when the cruelly long day's work is at an end.

It would likewise appear that by virtue of this arrangement between the omnibus conductor and his employers, the inter-ference of the law, even in cases of detected fraud, is dispensed with. It is understood that the London General Omnibus Com-pany support quite a large staff of men and women watchers, who spend their time in riding about in omnibuses, and noting the number of passengers carried on a particular journey, with the view of comparing the returns with the conductor's receipts. It must, therefore, happen that the detections of fraud are numerous; but does the reader recollect ever reading in the police reports of a conductor being prosecuted for robbery?

To be sure the Company may claim the right of conducting their business in the way they think best as regards the interests of the shareholders, but if that "best way" involves the countenancing of theft on the part of their servants, which can mean nothing else than the encouragement of thieves, it becomes a grave question whether the interests of its shareholders should be allowed to stand before the interests of society at large. It may be that to prosecute a dishonest conductor is only to add to the pecuniary loss he has already inflicted on the Company, but the question that much more nearly concerns the public is, what becomes of him when suddenly and in disgrace they turn him from their doors? No one will employ him. In a few weeks his ill-gotten savings are exhausted, and he, the man who for months or years, perhaps, has been accustomed to treat himself generously, finds himself without a sixpence, and, what is worse, with a mark against his character so black and broad that his chances of obtain-ing employment in the same capacity are altogether too remote for calculation. The respectable barber who declined to shave a coal-heaver on the ground that he was too vulgar a subject to come under the delicate operations of the shaver's razor, and who was reminded by the grimy one that he had just before shaved a baker, justified his conduct on the plea that his professional dignity compelled him to draw a line *somewhere,* and that he drew it at bakers. Just so the London General Omnibus Company. They draw the line at thieves rash and foolish. So long as a servant of theirs is content to prey on their property with enough of discretion as to render exposure unnecessary, he may continue their servant; but they make it a rule never again to employ a man who has been so careless as to be found out.

As has been shown, it is difficult to imagine a more satisfactory existence than that of an omnibus conductor to a man lost to all sense of honesty; on the other hand it is just as difficult to imagine a man so completely "floored" as the same cad disgraced, and out of employ. It is easy to see on what small inducements such a man may be won over to the criminal ranks. He has no moral scruples to overcome. His larcenous hand has been in the pocket of his master almost every hour of the day for months, perhaps years past. He is not penitent, and if he were and made an avowal to that effect, he would be answered by the incredulous jeers and sneers of all who knew him. The best that he desires is to meet with as easy a method of obtaining pounds as when he cheerfully drudged for eighteen hours for a wage of four-shillings. This being the summit of his ambition, presently he stumbles on what appears even an easier way of making money than the old way, and he unscrupulously appears not in a new character, but in that he has had long experience in, but without the mask.

I should wish it to be distinctly understood, that I do not include *all* omnibus conductors in this sweeping condemnation. That there are honest ones amongst them I make no doubt; at the same time I have no hesitation in repeating that in the majority of cases it is expected of them that they will behave dishonestly, and they have no disinclination to discredit the expectation. I believe too, that it is much more difficult for a man to be honest as a servant of the company than if he were in the employ of a "small master." It is next to impossible for a man of integrity to join and work harmoniously in a gang of rogues. The odds against his doing so may be calculated exactly by the number that comprise the gang. It is not only on principle that they object to him. Unless he "does as they do," he becomes a witness against them every time he pays his money in. And he does as they do. It is so much easier to do so than, in the condition of a man labouring hard for comparatively less pay than a common road-scraper earns, to stand up single handed to champion the cause of honesty in favour of a company who are undisguisedly in favour of a snug and comfortable compromise, and has no wish to be "bothered."

It is a great scandal that such a system should be permitted to
exist; and a body of employers mean enough to connive at such
bargain-making, can expect but small sympathy from the public if
the dishonesty it tacitly encourages picks it to the bones. What are
the terms of the contract between employer and employed? In
plain language these: "We are perfectly aware that you apply to us
well knowing our system of doing business, and with the deliberate intention of robbing us all you safely can; and in self-defence,
therefore, we will pay you as what you may, if you please, regard
as wages, *two-pence three farthings an hour,* or four shillings per
day of seventeen hours. We know that the probabilities are, that
you will add to that four shillings daily to the extent of another
five or six. It is according to our calculation that you will do so.
Our directors have arrived at the conclusion, that as omnibus conductors, of the ordinary type, you cannot be expected to rob us of
a less sum than that, and we are not disposed to grumble so long
as you remain so moderate; but do not, as you value your situation with all its accompanying privileges, go beyond that. As a
man who only robs us of say, five shillings a day, we regard you as
a fit and proper person to wait on our lady and gentleman passengers; to attend to their convenience and comfort, in short, as a
worthy representative of the L.G.O.C. But beware how you outstrip the bounds of moderation as we unmistakably define them
for you! Should you do so, we will kick you out at a moment's
notice, and on no consideration will we ever again employ you."

Taking this view of the case, the omnibus conductor, although
entitled to a foremost place in the ranks of thieves non-professional, can scarcely be said to be the least excusable amongst the
fraternity. There are many who, looking down on the "cad" from
their pinnacle of high respectability, are ten times worse than he
is. Take the shopkeeper thief for instance. He is by far a greater
villain than the half-starved wretch who snatches a leg of mutton
from a butcher's hook, or some article of drapery temptingly
flaunting outside the shop of the clothier, because in the one case
the crime is perpetrated that a soul and a woefully lean body may
be saved from severance, and in the other case the iniquity is made
to pander to the wrong-doer's covetous desire to grow fat, to wear
magnificent jewellery, and to air his unwieldly carcase annually at
Margate.

He has enough for his needs. His deservings, such as they are,
most liberally attend him; but this is not enough. The "honest

penny" is very well to talk about; in fact, in his cleverly assumed
character of an upright man, it is as well to talk about it loudly
and not unfrequently, but what fudge it is if you come to a downright blunt and "business" view of the matter to hope ever to
make a fortune by the accumulation of "honest pennies!" Why,
thirty of the shabby things make no more than half-a-crown if you
permit each one to wear its plain stupid face, whereas if you plate
it neatly and tender it—backed by your reputation for respectability, which your banking account of course proves beyond a
doubt—it will pass as genuine silver, and you make two and fivepence at a stroke! You don't call it "making," you robbers of the
counter and money-till, that is a vulgar expression used by "professional" thieves; you allude to it as "cutting it fine." Neither do
you actually plate copper pennies and pass them off on the unwary as silver half-crowns. Unless you were very hard driven indeed, you would scorn so low and dangerous a line of business.
Yours is a much safer system of robbery. You simply palm off on
the unwary customer burnt beans instead of coffee, and ground
rice instead of arrowroot, and a mixture of lard and turmeric
instead of butter. You poison the poor man's bread. He is a drunkard, and you are not even satisfied to delude him of his earnings
for so long a time as he may haply live as a wallower in beer and
gin, that is beer and gin as originally manufactured; you must, in
order to screw a few halfpence extra and daily out of the poor
wretch, put grains of paradise in his gin and coculus indicus in his
malt liquor! And, more insatiable than the leech, you are not content with cheating him to the extent of twenty-five per cent by
means of abominable mixtures and adulteration, you must pass
him through the mill, and cut him yet a little finer when he comes
to scale! You must file your weights and dab lumps of grease
under the beam, and steal an ounce or so out of his pound of
bacon. If you did this after he left your premises, if you dared
follow him outside, and stealthily inserting your hand into his
pocket abstracted a rasher of the pound he had just bought of
you, and he caught you at it, you would be quaking in the grasp of
a policeman in a very short time, and branded in the newspapers as
a paltry thief, you would never again dare loose the bar of your
shop shutters. But by means of your dishonest scales and weights,
you may go on stealing rashers from morning till night, from
Monday morning till Saturday night that is, and live long to adorn
your comfortable church pew on Sundays.

  I must be excused for sticking to you yet a little longer, Mr.
Shopkeeper Thief, because I hate you so. I hate you more than

ever, and you will be rejoiced when I tell you why. A few months since, there seemed a chance that your long career of cruel robbery was about to be checked. An excellent lord and gentleman, Lord E. Cecil, made it his business to call the attention of the House of Commons to the state of the law with respect to false weights and measures, and the adulterations of food and drinks. His lordship informed honourable members that the number of convictions for false weights and measures during the past year amounted to the large number of *thirteen hundred,* and this was exclusive of six districts, namely: Southwark, Newington, St. George's, Hanover Square, Paddington, and the Strand, which for reasons best known to the local authorities, made no return whatever. In Westminster alone, and within six months, a hundred persons were convicted, and it was found that of these twenty-four or nearly one-fourth of the whole were licensed victuallers, and forty-seven were dairymen, greengrocers, cheesemongers, and others, who supplied the poor with food, making in all seventy per cent. of provision dealers. In the parish of St. Pancras, the convictions for false weights and measures exceed those of every other parish. But in future, however much the old iniquity may prevail, the rogue's returns will show a handsome diminution. This has been managed excellently well by the shrewd vestrymen themselves. When the last batch of shopkeeper-swindlers of St. Pancras were tried and convicted, the ugly fact transpired that not a few of them were gentlemen holding official positions in the parish. This was serious. The meddlesome fellows who had caused the disagreeable exposure were called a "leet jury," whose business it was to pounce on evil doers whenever they thought fit, once in the course of every month. The vestry has power over this precious leet jury, thank heaven! and after sitting in solemn council, the vestrymen, some of them doubtless with light weights confiscated and deficient gin and beer measures rankling in their hearts, passed a resolution, that in future the leet jury was to stay at home and mind its own business, until the vestry clerk gave it liberty to go over the ground carefully prepared for it.

Alluding to the scandalous adulteration of food, Lord E. Cecil remarked, "The right hon. gentleman, the President of the Board of Trade, in one of his addresses by which he had electrified the public and his constituents, stated that the great panacea for the ills of the working class was a free breakfast table. Now he, Lord E. Cecil, was the last person in the world to object to any revision of taxation if it were based upon really sound grounds. But with all due deference to the right hon. gentleman, there was one thing of even more importance, namely, a breakfast table free from all impurities." And then his lordship proceeded to quote innumerable instances of the monstrous and dangerous injustice in question, very much to the edification of members assembled, if reiterated "cheers," and "hear, hear," went for anything. This was promising, and as it should be. As Lord Cecil remarked, "when I asked myself why it is that this great nation which boasts to be so practical, and which is always ready to take up the grievances of other people, has submitted so tamely to this monstrous and increasing evil, the only answer I could give was that what was everybody's business had become nobody's business." Doubtless this was the view of the case that every member present on the occasion took, and very glad they must have been when they found that what was everybody's business had become somebody's business at last.

And what said the President of the Board of Trade when he came to reply to the motion of Lord Cecil: "That in the opinion of the House it is expedient that Her Majesty's Government should give their earliest attention to the wide spread and most reprehensible practice of using false weights and measures, and of adulterating food, drinks, and drugs, with a view of amending the law as regards the penalties now inflicted for those offences, and of providing more efficient means for the discovery and prevention of fraud"? Did the right hon. President promptly and generously promise his most cordial support for the laudable object in view? No. Amazing as it may appear to the great host of working men that furnish the shopkeeping rogue with his chief prey, and who to a man are ready to swear by the right hon. gentleman, he did nothing of the kind. He started by unhesitatingly expressing his opinion that the mover of the question, quite unintentionally of course, had much exaggerated the whole business. And further, that although there might be particular cases in which great harm to health and much fraud might possibly be shown, yet general statements of the kind in question were dangerous, and almost certain to be unjust.

"Now, I am prepared to show," continued the hon. gentleman, "that the exaggeration of the noble lord—I do not say intentional exaggeration, of course—is just as great in the matter of weights and measures as in that of adulteration. Probably he is not aware that in the list of persons employing weights that are inaccurate—I do not say fraudulent; no distinction is drawn between those who are intentionally fraudulent and those who are accidentally inaccurate, and that the penalty is precisely the same and the offence is just as eagerly detected. Now the noble lord will probably be surprised to hear that many persons are fined annually, not because their weights are too small, but because they are too large."

Probably, however, his lordship, who has evidently given much attention to the subject, is master of this as well as all other branches of it, and is not so much surprised as it may be assumed the less knowing President of the Board of Trade was when the anomaly was brought under his notice. Probably Lord Cecil is aware, that in a very large number of businesses, articles are bought as well as sold by weight by the same shopkeeper and at the same shop, in such case it is nothing very wonderful to discover a weight of seventeen ounces to the pound. Moreover, it may be unknown to Mr. Bright, but it is quite a common trick with the dishonest shopkeeper to have means at hand for adjusting his false weights at the very shortest notice. It is not a difficult process. Weights are, as a rule, "justified" or corrected by means of adding to, or taking from, a little of the lead that is for this purpose sunk in the hollow in which the weight-ring is fixed. This leaden plug being raised by the point of a knife, nothing is easier than to add or withdraw a wedge of the same material. The knife point raises the leaden lid, the knife handle forces it down at a blow, and the trick is done. At the same time, the coolest rogue with a knowledge that the "leet" is only next door, cannot always manage his conjuring deftly, and this may in not a few instances account for the weight *more* than just. Besides, taking the most liberal view of the matter, it would be manifestly dangerous to allow a system of "averages" to do duty for strict and rigid justice. The relations between customer and shopkeeper would speedily fall into a sad muddle if the latter were permitted to excuse himself for selling fifteen ounces instead of a full pound of butter to-day, on the ground that he has a seventeen ounce weight somewhere about, and the probability that what he is short to-day the customer had over and above in the pound of lard he bought yesterday.

Again, let us listen to Mr. Bright as an advocate of self-protection. "If the corporations and the magistrates have not sufficient interest in the matter, if the people who elect the corporation care so little about it, I think that is fair evidence that the grievance is not near so extensive and injurious and burdensome as it has been described by the noble lord. My own impression with regard to adulteration is, that it arises from the very great and, perhaps, inevitable competition in business; and that to a large extent it is prompted by the ignorance of customers. As the ignorance of customers generally is diminishing, we may hope that before long the adulteration of food may also diminish. It is quite impossible that you should have the oversight of the shops of the country by inspectors, and it is quite impossible that you should have persons going into shops to buy sugar, pickles, and cayenne pepper, to get them analysed, and then to raise complaints against shopkeepers and bring them before magistrates. If men in their private business were to be tracked by government officers and inspectors every hour in the day, life would not be worth having, and I should recommend them to remove to another country where they would not be subject to such annoyance."

With a knowledge of the source from which this expression of opinion as to commercial morality emanates, one is apt to mistrust once reading it. Surely a line has been inadvertently skipped, a line that contains the key of the puzzle, and reveals the refined sarcasm that lurks beneath the surface. But no—twice reading, thrice reading, fails to shed any new lights on the mystery. Here is Mr. John Bright, the President of the Board of Trade, the working man's champion, and the staunch upholder of the right of those who sweat in honest toil, to partake plentifully of untaxed food and drink, putting forth an extenuation for those who, under guise of honest trading, filch from the working man, and pick and steal from his loaf, from his beer jug, from his sugar bason, from his milk-pot, in short, from all that he buys to eat or drink. "My own impression is," says the Right Hon. President, "that adulteration arises from competition in business." Very possibly, but does *that* excuse it? We are constantly reminded that "competition is the soul of trade," but we should be loth to think that such were the fact if the term "competition" is to be regarded as synonymous with adulteration, or, in plain language, robbery. "It is quite impossible that you should have persons going about endeavouring to detect the dishonest tradesman in his peculations, with a view to his punishment." Why is it impossible? Must not the repose of this sacred "soul of business" be disturbed, on so trivial a pretext as the welfare of the bodies of a clodhopping people, who are not commercial? So far from its being "impossible" to substitute vigilant measures for the detection of the petty pilferer who robs the poor widow of a ha'porth of her three penn'orth of coals, or the fatherless child of a slice out of its meagre allowance of bread, it should be regarded by the Government as amongst its chief duties. Other nations find it not impossible. In France a commissary of police has the right to enter any shop, and seize any suspected article, bearing of course all the responsibility of wrongful seizure. In Prussia, as Lord Cecil informed the House, "whoever knowingly used false weights and measures was liable to imprisonment for three months, to be fined from fifty to a thousand thalers, and to suffer the temporary loss of his rights of citizenship. Secondly, where false weights and measures were not regularly employed, a fine of thirty thalers may be imposed, or the delinquent sent to prison for four weeks. Thirdly, the adulteration of food or drink is punishable with a fine of 150 thalers, or six weeks' imprisonment. Fourthly, if poisonous matter or stuff be employed, the offender is liable to imprisonment for a term not exceeding ten years. Fifthly, where adulteration was proved to have caused severe physical injury, a sentence of from ten to twenty years' imprisonment might be passed. And yet in this country offences of this nature could only be punished by the imposition of a penalty of a fine of £5, with costs." These are not laws of yesterday. They have stood the test of many years, and French and Prussians find it not "impossible" to continue their salutary enforcement. But it is curious the extraordinary view men in authority amongst us at times take of the licence that should be permitted the "trader." I remember once being present at a County Court, and a case tried was that between a wholesale mustard dealer and a cookshop keeper. The cookshop keeper declined to pay for certain mustard delivered to him on the ground that his customers would not eat it. Indeed, it could hardly be called mustard at all, being little else than flour coloured with turmeric, and, backed by medical testimony, the defendant mainly relied on this point, *i.e.*, that it was not mustard at all, for a verdict. But the judge would not hear of this; in his summing up he remarked that it was idle to contend that the stuff was *not* mustard; *it was mustard in a commercial sense*, whatever might be its quality, and thereon gave a verdict for the plaintiff, and for the amount claimed.

I must confess that at the time I had my doubts as to this being sound law, but after the declaration of the President of the Board of Trade, I am bound to admit the possibility of my being mistaken. "Competition is the soul of commerce; competition is the parent of adulteration; adulteration is theft as a rule,—murder as an exception. The loaf that is composed of inferior flour, rice, potatoes, and alum, is the "wheaten bread" of "commerce." The poisonous liquid composed of a little malt and hops, eked out with treacle and *coculus indicus*, is the beer of "commerce." And, according to the same ruling, a lump of lard stuck under the butter-shop scale, or the inch snipped off the draper's yard, or the false bottom to the publican's pot, constitute the weights and measures of "commerce." All thse little harmless tricks of trade are, it seems, within the scope of a tradesman's "private business," and according to the President of the Board of Trade, if a tradesman in pursuit of his private business is to be watched and spied over for the malicious purpose of bringing him within the grasp of the law, why the sooner he quits the country, and settles amongst a more easy-going people, with elbow-room proper for his commercial enterprise, the better for him.

Undoubtedly, the better for him and the better for us. I would make this difference, however. When his iniquity was discovered, he should not go altogether unrewarded for his past services. He should be assisted in his going abroad. He should not be called on to pay one penny for his outward passage, and, what is more, he should be supplied with substantial linsey-wolsey clothing, and his head should be cropped quite close, so that the scorching sun of Bermuda or Gibraltar might not upset his brain for future commercial speculation.

It needs, however, something more persuasive than the "mustard of commerce" to induce us to swallow with satisfaction the President's assertion, that "to a large extent adulteration is promoted by the ignorance of customers," nor are we immensely consoled by the suggestion that "as the ignorance of the customer diminishes, the adulteration of food will also diminish." Decidedly this is a bright look out for the ignorant customer! There is to be no help for him, no relief. He must endure to be cheated in weight and measure, and slowly poisoned in the beer he drinks, and the bread he eats, until he finds time and money to provide himself with a scientific education, and becomes an accomplished scholar in chemistry, able to detect adulteration at sight or smell. Is this what the President of the Board of Trade means, or what is it? He cannot mean that the imposture is endured because the consumer will not take the trouble to avail himself of the laws made for his protection, because he is distinctly informed that although there are such laws, they are rendered inoperative because of the "impossibility" of having inspectors and detectives going about prying into the "private business" of the shopkeeper, and annoying him. If the ignorance of the honest man is to be regarded as the fair opportunity of the rogue, then there appears no reason why the immunity enjoyed by the fraudulent shopkeeper should not likewise be the indulgence allowed to the professional thief. It is the "ignorance of the customer" that enables the cheat to impose on him bad money for good, or a forged signature for one that is genuine. It is the ignorance of the green young man from the country as regards the wicked ways of London, that enables the skittle sharper to fleece him with ease and completeness. Undoubtedly, if we were all equally "wide awake," as the vulgar saying is, if no one had the advantage of his neighbour as regards cunning, and shrewdness, and suspicion, and all the other elements that constitute "a man of the world," then the trade of cheating would become so wretched a one that even ingrain rogues would for their life-sake cultivate the sort of honesty that was prevalent as the best policy, though very much against their natural inclination; but it might possibly be found that there are thousands and tens of thousands of simple people who would prefer to remain in "ignorance," having no desire to become "men of the world" in the sense above indicated, and electing for their soul's-sake to be lambs with a fleece to lose, than ravening wolves, whose existence depends on the fleecing of lambs.

Apropos of the practice of cheating by means of the adulteration of foods and drinks, it may not be out of place here to mention that during the discussion a member in whom Mr. Bright expressed great confidence announced that the use of alum in bread, so far from being injurious, was *positively beneficial.* Doctor Letheby, however, is of a somewhat different opinion. Recently, at the Society of Arts, he read a paper on the subject. Here are his opinions on the matter: "By the addition of alum, inferior and even damaged flour may be made into a tolerable looking loaf. It is the property of alum to make the gluten tough, and to prevent its discoloration by heat, as well as to check the action of the yeast or ferment upon it. When, therefore, it is added to good flour, it enables it to hold more water, and so to yield a larger number of loaves; while the addition of it to bad flour prevents the softening and disintegrating effect of the yeast on the poor and inferior gluten, and so enables it to bear the action of heat in the progress of baking. According to the quality of flour, will be the proportion of alum, and hence the amount will range from 2 ozs. to 8 ozs. per sack of flour. These proportions will yield from 9 to 37 grains of alum in the quartern loaf, quantities which are easily detected by chemical means. Indeed, there is a simple test by which much smaller quantities of it may be readily discovered. You have only to dip a slice of the bread into a weak solution of logwood in water, and if alum be present, the bread will speedily acquire a red or purplish tint. Good bread should not exhibit any black specks upon its upper crust; it should not become sodden and wet at the lower part by standing; it should not become mouldy by keeping in a moderately dry place; it should be sweet and agreeable to the taste and smell; it should not give, when steeped, a ropy, acid liquor; and a slice of it taken from the centre of the loaf should not lose more than forty-five per cent. by drying."

Again, speaking of the cruelty and dishonesty of the various "sophistications" practised by the vendors of food as regards the inefficacy of the laws made for its suppression, the good doctor says:

"Parliament has attempted to deal with the matter by legislation, as in the 'Act for Preventing the Adulteration of Articles of Food or Drink' of 1860; but as the Act is only permissive, little or no effect has been given to it. Even in those places, as in the City of London, where it has been put into operation, and public analysts have been appointed, no good has resulted from it; in fact, it stands upon the statute-book as a dead letter. Speaking of the City, I may say that every inducement has been offered for the effective working of the Act, but nothing has come of it. In olden times, the remedies for such misdemeanours were quick and effectual. In the *Assisa panis,* for example, as set forth in *Liber Albus,* there are not only the strictest regulations concerning the manner in which the business of the baker is to be conducted, but there are also penalties for failing in the same, 'If any default,' it says, 'shall be found in the bread of a baker in the City, the first time, let him be drawn upon a hurdle from the Guildhall to his own house through the great streets where there be most people assembled; and through the great streets which are most dirty, with the faulty loaf hanging about his neck. If a second time he shall be found committing the same offence, let him be drawn from the Guildhall, through the great street of Chepe in manner aforesaid to the pillory, and let him be put upon the pillory and remain there at least one hour in the day; and the third time that such default shall be found, he shall be drawn, and the oven shall be pulled down, and the baker made to forswear the trade within the City for ever.' It further tells us, that William de Stratford suffered this punishment for selling bread of short weight, and John de Strode 'for making bread of filth and cobwebs.' One hoary-headed offender was excused the hurdle on account of his age and the severity of the season; and it would seem that the last time the punishment was inflicted was in the sixteenth year of the reign of Henry VI., when Simon Frensshe was so drawn. A like punishment was awarded to butchers and vintners for fraudulent dealings; for we are told that a butcher was paraded through the streets with his face to the horse's tail for selling measly bacon at market, and that the next day he was set in the pillory with two great pieces of his measly bacon over his head, and a writing which set forth big crimes. In the judgments recorded in *Liber Albus* there are twenty-three cases in which the pillory was awarded for selling putrid meat, fish, or poultry; thirteen for unlawful dealings of bakers, and six for the misdemeanours of vintners and wine dealers. Verily we have degenerated in these matters."

And while we are on the subject of thieves non-professional, and their easy conversion to the article legally stamped and recognised, it may not be amiss briefly to remark on the odd ideas of honesty entertained and practised by thousands of our hard-fisted, and except for the singular weakness hinted at, quite worthy and decent "journeymen." It is curious how much of hallucination prevails amongst us on the subject of "common honesty." It is as though there were several qualities of that virtue, "common," "middling," and "superfine," as there are in house-hold bread; and that, carrying out the simile, although the "super-fine" is undoubtedly nicer, and what one would always use if he could afford it, the honesty dubbed "common" is equally whole-some, and on the whole the only sort on which it is possible for a working man to exist.

"I am as honest as I can afford to be," is an observation com-mon in the mouth of those who really and truly earn their bread and acquire a creditable reputation by the sweat of their brow. It never seems to occur to them that such an admission is equal to a confession of dishonesty, and since it is simply a matter of degree, that the common thief on the same grounds may claim the privi-lege of shaking them by the hand as their equal. The man who fixes the standard of his honesty at no greater height becomes an easy prey to temptation. "If he is as honest as he can afford to be," and no more, it simply means that his means not being equal to his necessities he has already admitted the thin end of the wedge of dishonesty to make good the gap, and that should the said gap unhappily widen, the wedge must enter still further in until a total splitting up of the system ensues, and the wedge itself becomes the only stedfast thing to cling to.

That this melancholy consummation is not more frequently attained is the great wonder, and would tend to show that many men adopt a sort of hobbling compromise, walking as it were with one foot on the path of rectitude, and the other in the miry way of petty theft, until they get to the end of life's tether and both feet slip into the grave.

It is a fact at once humiliating, but there it stands stark and stern, and will not be denied, that there are daily pursuing their ordinary business, and passing as honest, hundreds and thousands of labouring folk, who, if their various malversations were brought to light, and they were prosecuted, would find themselves in prison ere they were a day older. Nor should this startle us very much, as we are well aware of it, and mayhap are in no small degree responsible for it, since it is mainly owing to our indolent disregard that the evil has become so firmly established; at the same time it should be borne in mind, that this no more excuses those who practise and profit on our indifference to small pilferings than a disinclination to prosecute a professional pickpocket mitigates the offence of the delinquent.

The species of dishonesty alluded to, as not coming within the official term "professional," has many aliases. Ordinary it is called by the cant name of "perks," which is a convenient abbreviation of the word "perquisites," and in the hands of the users of it, it shows itself a word of amazing flexibility. It applies to such unconsidered trifles as wax candle ends, and may be stretched so as to cover the larcenous abstraction by our man-servant of forgotten coats and vests. As has been lately exposed in the newspapers, it is not a rare occurrence for your butler or your cook to conspire with the roguish tradesman, the latter being permitted to charge "his own prices," on condition that when the monthly bill is paid, the first robber hands over to the second two-shillings or half-a-crown in the pound. It is not, however, these sleek, and well-fed non-professional thieves that I would just now speak of, but rather of the working man—the journeyman tailor for example.

Did anyone ever yet hear of a working tailor who was proof against misappropriation of his neighbour's goods, or as he playfully designates it, "cabbage?" Is it not a standard joke in the trade this "cabbage?" Did one ever hear of a tailor being shunned by his fellow-workmen, or avoided by his neighbours, on account of his predilection for "cabbage?" Yet what is it but another word for "theft?" If I entrust a builder with so much timber, and so much stone, and so many bricks, to build me a house, and I afterwards discover that by clever dodging and scheming he has contrived to make me believe that all the material I gave him has been employed in my house, whereas he has managed to filch enough to build himself a small cottage, do I accept his humorous explanation that it is only "cabbage," and forgive him? No. I regard it as my duty to afford him an opportunity of explaining the matter to a magistrate. But if I entrust my tailor with stuff for a suit, and it afterwards comes to my knowledge that he has "screwed" an extra waistcoat out of it, which he keeps or sells for his own benefit, do I regard it as a serious act of robbery? I am ashamed to say that I do not; I may feel angry, and conceive a contempt for tailors, but I take no steps to bring the rogue to justice. I say to myself, "It is a mean trick, but they all do it," which is most unjust to the community of tailors, because though I may suspect that they all do it, I have no proof of the fact, whereas I have proof that there is a dishonest tailor in their guild, and I have no right to assume but that they would regard it as a favour if I would assist them in weeding him out.

And it is almost as good a joke as the calling downright theft by the comical name of "cabbage," that the tailor will do this and all the time insist on his right to be classed with honest men. He insists on this because he was never known to steal anything besides such goods as garments are made out of. As he comes along bringing your new suit home he would think it no sin to call at that repository for stolen goods, the "piece broker's," and sell there a strip of your unused cloth for a shilling, but you may safely trust him in the hall where the hats and umbrellas and overcoats are. He would as soon think of breaking into your house with crowbars and skeleton keys, as of abstracting a handkerchief he saw peeping out of a pocket of one of the said coats.

As with the tailor, so it is with the upholsterer, and the dressmaker, and the paperhanger, and the plumber, and all the rest of them. I don't say that every time they take a shred of this, or a pound weight of that, that they have before their eyes the enormity of the offence they are about to commit. What they do they see no great harm in. Indeed, point out to them and make it clear that their offence has but to be brought fairly before the criminal authorities to ensure them a month on the treadmill, and they would as a rule be shocked past repeating the delinquency. And well would it be if they were shocked past it, ere misfortune overtake them. It is when "hard up" times set in, and it is difficult indeed to earn an honest penny, that these rudimentary exercises in the art of pillage tell against a man. It is then that he requires his armour of proof against temptation, and lo! it is full of holes and rust-eaten places, and he falls at the first assault of the enemy.

CHAPTER X.

Criminal Suppression and Punishment.

Lord Romilly's Suggestion concerning the Education of the Children of Criminals.—Desperate Criminals.—The Alleys of the Borough.—The worst Quarters not, as a rule, the most Noisy.—The Evil Example of "Gallows Heroes," "Dick Turpin," "Blueskin," &c.—The Talent for "Gammoning Lady Green."—A worthy Governor's Opinion as to the best way of "Breaking" a Bad Boy.—Affection for "Mother."—The Dark Cell and its Inmate.— An Affecting Interview.

No less an authority than Lord Romilly, discoursing on the alarming prevalence and increase of crime, especially amongst the juveniles of the criminal class, remarks: "It is a recognised fact, that there is a great disposition on the part of children to follow the vocation of their father, and in the case of the children of thieves there is no alternative. They become thieves because they are educated in the way, and have no other trade to apply themselves to. To strike at the root of the evil, I would suggest, that if a man committed felony, all his children under the age, say of ten, should be taken from him, and educated at the expense of the State. It might perhaps be said, that a man who wanted to provide for his children, need in that case only to commit felony to accomplish his object, but I believe that the effect would be just the contrary. I believe that no respectable person would commit felony for such a purpose, and that if we knew more about the feelings of thieves, we should find that they had amongst them a species of morality, and displayed affection for their children. My opinion is, that to take their children away from them would be an effectual mode of punishment; and though the expense might be great, it would be repaid in a few years by the diminution in crime."

Although Lord Romilly's opinions on this subject may be somewhat in advance of those commonly prevalent, there can be no question that they tend in the right direction. Crime may be suppressed, but it can never be exterminated by simply lopping the flourishing boughs and branches it puts forth; it should be attacked at the root, and the thief child is the root of the adult growth, tough, strong-limbed, and six feet high. Precisely the same argument as that used as regards the abolition of neglected children applies in the case of the infant born in crime. The nest in which for generations crime has bred should be destroyed. It is only, however, to the initiated that the secluded spots where these nests may be found is known. A correspondent of the *Times* lately made an exploration, from the report of which the following is an extract.

"I was shown in the east and south sides of London what I may almost say were scores of men, about whom the detectives, who accompanied me, expressed grave doubts as to my life being safe among them for a single hour, if it were known I had £20 or £30 about me; and above all, if the crime of knocking me on the head could be committed under such circumstances as would afford fair probabilities of eluding detection. I don't mean to say that these desperate criminals are confined to any particular quarter of London; unfortunately they are not, or if they were, there is only one particular quarter in which we should wish to see them all confined, and that is Newgate. But no matter how numerous they may be elsewhere, there is certainly one quarter in which they are pre-eminently abundant, and that is around the alleys of the Borough. Here are to be found, not only the lowest description of infamous houses, but the very nests and nurseries of crime. The great mass of the class here is simply incorrigible. Their hand is against every man; their life is one continuous conspiracy against the usages of property and safety of society. They have been suckled, cradled, and hardened in scenes of guilt, intemperance, and profligacy. Here are to be found the lowest of the low class of beershops in London, and probably in the world, the acknowledged haunts of "smashers," burglars, thieves, and forgers. There is hardly a grade in crime, the chief representatives of which may not be met among the purlieus of the Borough. There are people who have been convicted over and over again, but there are also hundreds of known ruffians who are as yet unconvicted, and who, by marvellous good luck, as well as by subtle cunning, have managed up to the present time to elude detection. It is the greatest error to suppose that all, or even a majority of the criminal classes are continually passing through the hands of justice. Griffith, the bank-note forger, who was tried, I think, in 1862, stated in prison that he had carried on the printing of counterfeit notes for more than 15 years. Of course this man was sedulous in concealing his occupation from the police, but there are hundreds of others who almost openly follow equally criminal and far more dangerous pursuits with whom the police cannot interfere. Our present business should be to lock up these vagabonds, and our future vocation to destroy their recognised haunts. It is no good killing one wasp when we leave the nest untouched. Thieves, it must be remembered, are a complete fraternity, and have a perfect organization among themselves. The quarter round Kent Street, in the Borough, for instance, is almost wholly tenanted by them, and the houses they occupy are very good property, for thieves will pay almost any amount of rent, and pay it regularly, for the sake of keeping together. The aspect of this quarter is low, foul and dingy. Obscurity of language and conduct is of course common to all parts of it, but it is not as a rule a riotous neighbourhood. Thieves do not rob each other, and they have a wholesome fear of making rows, lest it should bring the police into their notorious territory. These haunts are not only the refuges and abiding places of criminals, but they are the training colleges for young thieves. Apart from the crimes which arise, I might say almost naturally from passion or poverty—apart also from the mere relaxation of moral culture, caused by the daily exhibition of apparent success in crime, it is known that an organized corruption is carried on by the adult thieves among the lads of London.''

It is by laying hands on these children, and providing them with employment, the pleasurable exercise of which shall of itself convince them how infinitely superior as a "policy" honesty is to be preferred to that which consigned their father to Portland, that we may do more good than by the concoction of as many legislative enactments as have had birth since Magna Charta. Of the children who are not the progeny of thieves, but who somehow find their way into the criminal ranks, it is undoubtedly true that pernicious literature, more than once alluded to in these pages, does much to influence them towards evil courses. This is a belief that is justified, not alone by observation and inference, but by the confession of juvenile prisoners themselves. It is a fact that at least fifty per cent. of the young thieves lodged in goal, when questioned on the subject, affect that it was the shining example furnished by such gallows heroes as "Dick Turpin" and "Blueskin," that first beguiled them from the path of rectitude, and that a large proportion of their ill-gotten gains was expended in the purchase of such delectable biographies.

This, however, is ground that should be trod with caution. Useful as such revelations may be in guiding us towards conclusions on which vigorous action may be based, it should be constantly borne in mind that it is not all pure and untainted truth that proceeds from the mouths of the juvenile habitual criminal in gaol any more than from his elders under the same conditions. A talent for gammoning "Lady Green," as the prison chaplain is irreverently styled, is highly appreciated amongst the thieving fraternity. Boys are as quick-witted as men in their way, and on certain matters much quicker. They are less doggedly obstinate than most adults of the same class, and more keenly alive to mischief, especially when its practice may bring them some benefit. I have witnessed several instances of this, and many others have been brought under my notice by prison officials. As, for instance, in a certain gaol that shall be nameless, the governor has a fixed conviction that the one huge fountain head of juvenile depravity is the tobacco pipe. And ample indeed are his grounds for such conclusion, since almost every boy that comes into his custody testifies to his sagacity. His old customers never fail. He invariably questions the male delinquent on the subject, and as invariably he gets the answer he expects, and which favours his pet theory: "It is all through smoking, sir; I never knowed what bad 'abits was afore I took to 'bacca.'" The probabilities, however, are that the little villains are aware of the governor's weakness, and humour it.

It would seem so the more, because these same boys when quartered in another gaol, the master of which rode a hobby of another pattern, alter their tune so as to meet the emergency. There is a prison in the suburbs of London, one of the largest, and as far as I have had opportunity of judging, one of the best managed and conducted; but the governor of it has his boy-weakness. He is quite convinced in his own mind that the main spring of crime is the perusal of the sort of literature herein alluded to. This is a fact generally known among the juvenile criminal population, and they never fail to make the most of it when the time comes. I went the rounds of his gaol with this governor on one occasion, when the "boy wing" was occupied by about forty tenants, and in each case was the important question put, and in the majority of cases it was answered, "It was them there penny numbers what I used to take in, sir," or words to that effect, and the little humbug was rewarded by a pat on the head, and an admonition "always to speak the truth."

The same gentleman has another peculiarity; it does not deserve to be stigmatised a weakness, its nature is so amiable. He has a firm belief that the best way of "breaking" a bad boy, is to appeal to his bygone affection for his mother. "The boy who is callous to an appeal of that sort is past hope in my opinion," said the worthy governor, and in justice to the lads at the time in his keeping, I must confess that there was not a callous one amongst them, for they all most dutifully wept, in some cases bellowed as loudly as the stern restriction of the silent system would permit, as soon as the delicate subject was broached.

The effect of this talisman was curiously exhibited in the case of a boy, about as depraved and hardened a little wretch as it is possible to imagine. He had only been admitted the previous day, and already he was incarcerated in a dark cell for outrageous conduct.

I had never before seen a dark cell, and therefore had no idea of the horrible place it was. A cell within a cell. The interior of the first is so black that when the governor entered it I speedily lost sight of him, and I was only made aware of his opening an inner door by hearing the key clicking in the lock.

"Come out here, lad," he exclaimed firmly, but kindly.

The lad came out, looming like a small and ragged patch of twilight in utter blackness until he gradually appeared before us. He was not a big lad, not more than thirteen years old, I should say, with a short-cropped bullet-head, and with an old hard face with twice thirteen years of vice in it.

The prison dress consisted of a sort of blouse and trousers, both of a stout woollen material of slate colour. It was evening, and evidently, the captive, hopeless of release that night, had, previously to our disturbing him, composed himself for slumber. His method, doubtless derived from frequent experience of so disposing his attire as to get as much warmth out of it as possible, was somewhat curious: he had released his trousers of their braces, so that they descended below his feet, and the collar of his blouse was pulled up high over his ears. Owing to his embarrassed habiliments, he shambled out of the pitchy blackness at a snail's pace, his white cotton braces trailing behind like a tail, and completing his goblin-like appearance.

"This is a very bad lad, sir," remarked the governor sternly; "he only came in yesterday, and to-day while out for exercise with the others, he must misconduct himself, and when the warder reproved him, he must swear some horrible oath against him. It is for that he is here. How many times have you been here, lad?"

Lad (gulping desperately). "Three times, sir!"

Governor (sternly). "What! speak the truth, lad."

Lad (with a determined effort to gouge tears out of his eyes with his knuckles). "Four times, sir."

Governor. "Four times! and so you'll go on till you are sent away, I'm afraid. Can you read, lad?"

Lad (with a penitential wriggle). "Yes, sir; I wish as I couldn't, sir."

Governor. "Ah! why so?"

Lad (with a doleful wag of his bullet head). "Cos then I shouldn't have read none of them highwaymen's books, sir; it was them as was the beginning of it."

Governor. "Ah!" (a pause) "Have you a mother, my lad?"

Lad. "Boo-oh!"

Governor. "Answer me, my lad, have you a mother?"

Lad (convulsively clasping the corners of his collars, and hiding his eyes in them). "Ye-ye-ess, sir!"

Governor. "Ah, I thought so! where does she live?"

Lad. "Man-manchester, please, sir!" (a tremulous sniff, indicative of the impending explosion).

Governor. "And what do you think would be her feelings could she see you as you now are?"

Lad. "Boo-ooh" (here a writhe so agonized that a hand had to be spared from his eyes to save his trousers from slipping down). "Boo-ooh! I was just a thinkin' on her when you opened the cell, sir! Boo-oo-ooh!"

Governor. "You were thinking of your mother, eh? Well, well, I'm glad to hear that. If I let you go back to your own cell, will you promise never to swear again?"

Lad. "Booh! yes, sir."

Governor. "You may go, then."

And with a countenance almost radiant with his unexpected stroke of good luck, the incorrigible young thief grasped his trouser legs, and scuttled up the long dim corridor till, except for his white tail, he was lost in the darkness.

"They don't like the dark cell," remarked the humane governor, as he gazed after the retreating figure; "anything rather than that."

"The younger prisoners especially, I should say," I returned.

"Oh, I don't know that," said the governor, at the same time, however, shaking his head rather as a man who *did* know, but did not care to say.

CHAPTER XI

Adult Criminals and the New Law for their Better Government.

Recent Legislation.—Statistics.—Lord Kimberley's "Habitual Criminals" Bill.—The Present System of License-Holders.—Colonel Henderson's Report.—Social Enemies of Suspected Men.—The Wrong-Headed Policeman and the Mischief he may Cause.—Looking Out for a Chance.—The Last Resource of Desperate Honesty.—A Brotherly Appeal.—"Ginger will Settle Her."—Ruffians who should be Imprisoned for Life.

Regarding the terms professional thief and habitual criminal as synonymous, now that we come to consider briefly what are at present the means adopted for the reformation of criminals and the suppression and punishment of crime, and what the most recent and plausible suggestions for amendment and improvement, we find the work already done to our hand, and naught remains but to cull from the shoals of evidence *pro* and *con* that have been lately set before the public.

The total cost of our prisons and prisoners for the year 1867, was £657,129, distributed as follows: (1) Extra-ordinary charges for new buildings, &c., £177,553 19s. 9d. (2) Ordinary charges £108,218 15s. 11d. (3) Officers' salaries, &c., £213,285 15s. 5d., and (4) Prisoners' diet, sick allowances, clothing, &c., £158,071 5s. 3d. The average yearly charge per prisoner under each head of costs, was as follows:—(1) Extraordinary charges £9 17s. 4d. (2) Ordinary annual charges £6 0s. 3d. (making together £15 17s. 7d.). (3) Officers and attendants £11 17s. 1d. (4) Prisoners' diet £6 11s. 1d., and clothing £2 4s. 7d. (together £8 15s. 8d.), making a total per prisoner of £36 10s. 4d., or omitting the extraordinary charge for buildings, &c., £26 13s. The average of £36 10s. 4d. is higher than the corresponding average for 1865-6 by £2 1s. 8d. The average of £26 13s. is higher than the corresponding average by 15s. 1d. These averages are calculated upon the total amounts under each head of expenditure, and the total daily average number in all the prisons. The average cost per prisoner naturally shows great variation in different prisons. The highest is at Alnwick, viz.: £114 3s. 2d. against £110 1s. 2d. in 1865-6, £108 2s. 5d. in 1864-5, and £88 15s. 11d. in 1863-4, *with a daily average of one prisoner in each year*! At Oakham, the average cost for 1866-7 is £80 13s. 3d., with a daily average of 10 prisoners against £93 16s. 2d. in 1865-6, and £87 1s. 9d. in 1864-5, with the daily average of 8 prisoners in each of those years; at Appleby £70 2s. with a daily average of 6 prisoners; at Ilford £51 6s. with a daily average of 20 prisoners. The lowest averages are as follows: At Hull £16 17s., with a daily average of 173 prisoners; at Salford £16 17s. 8d., with a daily average of 568 prisoners; at Liverpool £18 8s. 9d. with a daily average of 952 prisoners; at Devonport £18 12s. 4d., with a daily average of 58 prisoners; at Durham £18 16s. 9d., with a daily average of 433 prisoners; and at Manchester £19 1s. 3d., with a daily average of 631 prisoners. The following are the comparative costs per prisoner for the whole of the prisons for each of the last six years:—£24 3s. 4d., £23 7s. 5d., £23 7s. 10d., £24 3s. 3d., £25 17s. 11d., and £26 13s.

The total number of police and constabulary for the same year, is set down at 24,073 as against 23,728 in the year preceding. The total cost for the year is £1,920,505 12s. 2d. as against £1,827,105 16s. 7d. in 1866, an increase of upwards of 5 per cent. following an increase of £78,647 17s. 1d., or 4.5 per cent. upon the amount for 1864-5. As compared with the total costs for 1856-7, the first year for which returns were made under the Act; the increase in 1866-7 amounts to £654,926, or upwards of 51 per cent. The increase in the number of the police and constabulary during the same period is 4,886, or upwards of 25 per cent.

The number of persons committed for trial in 1867 was less than the number for any of the four years immediately preceding 1866. The increase in 1867, as compared with 1866, is in the number of males, viz., 328. In the number of females there is a *decrease* of 206. The following are the numbers committed for trial in each of the last 20 years:—

1848	.. 30,349	1855	.. 25,972	1862	.. 20,001
1849	.. 27,816	1856	.. 19,437	1863	.. 20,818
1850	.. 26,813	1857	.. 20,269	1864	.. 19,506
1851	.. 27,960	1858	.. 17,855	1865	.. 19,614
1852	.. 27,510	1859	.. 16,674	1866	.. 18,849
1853	.. 27,057	1860	.. 15,999	1867	.. 18,971
1854	.. 29,359	1861	.. 18,326		

As already intimated in these pages, Lord Kimberley is responsible for introducing the broad and important subject of Criminal Law Reform to the legislature for its reconsideration and reformation. In introducing this bill for the suppression of crime, his lordship reminded the peers assembled that in the year 1853, after a very full discussion with respect to transportation it was resolved, partly on account of the evils of the system, and partly on account of the strong remonstrances of our Australian colonists to whom our convicts had been sent, that it should, to a considerable extent cease, and that accordingly an Act was passed imposing for the first time the sentence of penal servitude as a substitute for transportation in the greater number of cases. From that time transportation was limited to Western Australia and the Bermudas. The numbers sent to Western Australia did not average more than 460 per annum. The colonists, however, despite this moderate consignment, felt by no means flattered by the distinction conferred on them, and in consideration of their strong remonstrances, in the course of a few years transportation to Australia entirely ceased.

Penal servitude was the arrangement substituted, and the chief feature of it was the ticket-of-leave. The system promised well, but no sooner was it fairly at work than the public took alarm at the number of convicts scattered over the country holding these tickets, and then another change was resolved on. A commission, presided over by Lord Carnarvon, was appointed to examine the whole question of penal servitude, and the result was a report containing several important recommendations. Foremost of these was that sentences of penal servitude which had been as short as three years, should not, in future, be passed for shorter terms than seven years. Another, almost equally important, was to the effect that convicts sentenced to penal servitude should be subjected in the first place to nine months' separate imprisonment, and then to labour on public works for the remainder of the term for which they were sentenced, but with a power of earning by industry and good conduct an abridgment of this part of punishment. The provision under which police supervision has since been carried out, and the conditions under which licences should be earned by good conduct, were also laid down. As further stated by his lordship, when the Act of 1864 was under consideration, great doubts were expressed whether it was possible to carry out a satisfactory system by which the good conduct of convicts and their industry when employed on public works could be so measured that they should earn an abridgment of their sentences. Experience, however, showed that the system in its working was to a great extent successful, especially when the management of the business in question fell into the hands of Colonel Henderson, who succeeded the late Sir Joshua Jebb. Under Colonel Henderson's supervision it has been found possible to exact from convicts the really hard and patient industry which is necessary before they can obtain a remission of their sentences. The value of the work performed by convicts at the three convict prisons—Portsmouth, Portland, and Chatham—was during the year 1868, £106,421; while the cost of maintaining those establishments was £110,532, so that the earnings nearly equalled the whole expense to which the country was put; indeed, as regards Chatham, where there are great facilities for remunerative work in making bricks for public works, there was an actual profit. In 1867 the average daily number of convicts at Chatham was 990, and the value of their labour was £40,898 7s., while the cost of their maintenance and supervision was £35,315 18s., there being thus a surplus of £5,582 9s. Under this new and improved system, in which the feature last quoted shows so satisfactorily, crime decreased. In 1865-6 the indictable offences committed numbered 50,549, and in 1866-7 they were 55,538, showing an increase of 4,989, or something under 10 per cent. From 1856 to 1862, the convictions excluding summary ones, the annual average was 13,859, while in 1867 the number was 14,207. His lordship explained that he began with 1856, because in the previous year the Criminal Jurisdiction Act was passed, enabling a considerable number of crimes to be dealt with summarily. Although this shows an apparent increase from 13,859 to 14,207, it must be remembered that in the interval the population increased by nearly two and a-half millions, so that there is a decrease rather than an increase in proportion to the population. Satisfactory, however, as was this result, it appeared to Lord Kimberly that, as we naturally obtain fresh experience from year to year, fresh opportunities of committing crime being discovered and fresh means of meeting these offences, it is necessary from time to time to re-adjust our system, and make it more complete. Another reason for carefully scrutinising, and seeing whether we cannot improve our system, is the complete cessation of transportation; for though during the last few years we have not sent out to our colonies any very large number of convicts, it is obvious that for 500 convicts a year to remain in this country involves a considerable increase of the convict population. The number of males now on licence is 1,566, and of females 441, in 1870 it will probably be 1,705, and about ten years hence it will probably be something under 3,000.

These, however, form but a small portion of the great criminal class. Of this latter the average of 1865-6, 1864-5 and 1863-4, shows the following results:

Known thieves and depredators, 22,959, receivers of stolen goods 3,095, prostitutes 27,186, suspected persons 29,468, vagrants and tramps 32,938, making a total of 122,646. In the metropolis alone there were in 1866-7, 14,648 persons living by dishonest means, and 5,628 prostitutes. The number in 1865-6 being 14,491 and 5,554.

The above being in the main Lord Kimberley's grounds of justification for bringing forward his "Habitual Criminals' Bill," let us take its first provision, that applying to convicts, who on the strength of a ticket-of-leave are in the enjoyment of conditional liberty, and inquire what is precisely the system it is intended to supersede, and what are the practical results of the workings of this last mentioned system, viz.: that which on the recommendation of the committee, under the presidency of Lord Carnarvon, became law in 1864. The following memorandum as to the present system of licence holders reporting themselves to the police, under the Penal Servitude Amendment Act, 1864, was issued recently by Colonel Henderson, Commissioner of Police of the Metropolis:—

"A male licence holder is required personally to report himself at the principal police-station of the district in which he resides within three days of his liberation. A printed descriptive form of the licence holder is sent from the prison to the police with the address where the man, previous to his liberation, stated he intended to reside. The officer on duty, when the licence holder reports himself, instructs him in what he is required to do, and also delivers to him a printed notice. No further steps are then taken by the police for a month from that date, when, if the licence holder again reports himself, he is considered as complying with the law.

"After inquiry to ascertain if the address given is a correct one, no further supervision is kept over him by the police, and his lodgings are not again visited.

"If a licence holder neglects to report himself as above, or is seen, or suspected of leading an irregular life, then the police make quiet inquiry, and, as is frequently the case, if it is found that he has left the address he was living at, his description is inserted in the *Police Gazette,* with directions for apprehension.

"The employers are never informed by the police that they are employing a licence holder.

"Licence holders apprehended for offences have complained to the magistrates that the police harass them, but on investigation such statements have always proved to be without foundation.

"No case has ever been known of police levying black mail on licence holders.

"The Discharged Prisoners' Aid Society, 39, Charing Cross, with the sanction of the Secretary of State, undertakes the care of licence holders.

"The licence holders who wish to place themselves under the care of this Society are required to report themselves, on liberation, at the King Street Police Station, Westminster, where they are served with a notice.

"A messenger from Millbank Prison accompanies the licence holders to the police-station, and after this form is gone through, all local police supervision ceases until a report is made from the Society to the Commissioner.

"Of 368 male licence holders discharged into the Metropolitan Police district in 1969, 290 placed themselves under the care of the Discharged Prisoners' Aid Society, either on discharge or subsequently.

"There have been difficulties in consequence of this divided jurisdiction, but in the event of this bill passing, the supervision of convicts who place themselves in charge of the Prisoners' Aid Society, will be carried on by the police, in conjunction with the officers of the Society, and can be so arranged as to avoid any undue interference with the men; in fact, it is quite as much the interest of the police to endeavour to assist licence holders to get honest work, as to arrest them if they misconduct themselves, and for this purpose it would be quite sufficient if the licence holder were bound by the conditions of his licence to report change of residence and employment, the monthly report being of no particular value, so long as proper supervision is exercised by the police.

"As regards the arrest of licence holders, or of persons who have been twice convicted of felony, it is clear all must depend on the personal knowledge of the police constable of the person and antecedents of the suspected person.

"Under ordinary circumstances, no constable interferes with any licence holder, nor would he arrest any man on suspicion, without previously reporting the circumstances to the Commissioner, who would order quiet inquiry to be made, and give instructions, if necessary, for the man's arrest.

"Identification would be rendered more easy than at present, by the proposed central registration."

As the law at present stands, then, in the event of a ticket of leave man failing to comply with the police regulations, and on his being conveyed before a magistrate, it is provided that if the magistrate is satisfied that he is not earning an honest living, he may be committed to undergo his original term of imprisonment. Under the restrictions of the proposed new Bill, however, much more stringent arrangements are suggested. The onus of proving his honesty will rest with the man who holds the ticket. "A licence holder may at any time be summoned by a police constable before a magistrate, and called upon to show that he is earning an honest livelihood, the burden of proof resting on him; if he cannot prove his honesty, he may be committed to undergo his original sentence of Penal Servitude."

Now it is evident on the face of it that the above quoted clause of the proposed "Habitual Criminals Bill" is beset by many grave objections. In the first place, to vest such an amount of irresponsible power in the police is a step hardly warranted by one's experience of the intelligence and integrity of the "force," satisfactory on the whole as it may be. There can be no question that as a rule the superintendents and inspectors and sergeants are in every respect equal to the duties imposed on them; only for the unenviable notoriety lately achieved by a functionary still higher in command, commissioners also might have been included in the favourable list.

It is equally true, too, that the great majority of the men of the "force" discharge their duty with efficiency; at the same time it is undeniable that there are exceptions to the good rule. But too frequently do our criminal records remind us that virtue's perfect armour is not invariably represented by the helmet and the coat of blue. Only lately there occurred an alarming instance of this. A gang of plunderers and receivers of stolen goods was apprehended, and presently there appeared on the scene an individual, then an inspector of railway detective police, and formerly holding a responsible position in the Metropolitan force, taking on himself, with a coolness that bespoke his long experience, the office of screening the thief and arranging his escape from the law's righteous grasp. Richards is this fellow's name, and he was evidently well known to a large circle of acquaintance, whose fame is recorded in the records of the Old Bailey. With amazing audacity Mr. Richards addressed himself to the two detective policemen who had the case in hand, and offered them ten pounds each if they would accommodate his clients by committing perjury when the day of trial came. Happily the integrity of the two officers was proof against the tempting bribe, and the unfortunate negotiator found himself even deeper in the mire than those his disinterested good nature would have aided. At the same time one cannot refrain from asking, is this the first time that Mr. Richards has evinced his obliging disposition, and the still more important question, does he stand alone, or are there others of his school? As is the case with all large communities, the police force must include in its number men malicious, prejudiced, wrong-headed and foolish. Probably there are no serious grounds for the alarm that under the convenient cloak the clause in question provides, the policeman, unscrupulous and dishonest, might by levying black mail on the poor wretches so completely in his power, reap a rich and iniquitous harvest, and render nugatory one of the Bill's prime provisions. This is an objection that carries no great weight. No law that could be passed could put the criminal, the burglar, and the housebreaker more at the mercy of the dishonest policeman that he now is. As repeatedly appears in our criminal reports, the sort of odd intimacy that commonly exists between the thief and his natural enemy, the policeman, is very remarkable; the latter is as well acquainted with the haunts of the former as he is with the abodes of his own friends and relatives. Should the enemies meet in the street, the acquaintance is acknowledged by a sort of confident "I-can-have-you-whenever-I-want-you" look on the one part, and a half devil-may-care, half deprecatory glance on the other. When the crisis arrives, and the thief is "wanted," he is hailed as Jack, Tom, or Bill, and the capture is effected in the most comfortable and business-like manner imaginable.

Under such an harmonious condition of affairs, nothing could be easier, were they both agreed, than bribery and corruption of the most villanous sort, and, taking Colonel Henderson's word, "that no case has ever been known of police levying black mail on licence holders," and further, considering the inadequate pay the policeman receives for the amount of intelligent and vigilant service required of him, the country may be congratulated on possessing, on the whole, such an almost unexceptionally good servant.

It is the wrong-headed policeman, probably, who would work the greatest amount of mischief in this direction. The busy, over-zealous man, neither malicious, dishonest, nor vindictive, but simply a little too anxious to win for himself a character for "shrewdness and intelligence." This would probably be the young policeman, desirous of making up for his lack of experience by a display of extraordinary sagacity. To such a man's home-bred, unofficially cultivated ideas of right and wrong, it would appear of small use "suspecting" an individual, unless he immediately set about testing him with the utmost severity to know the extent to which the suspicion was justified.

To be sure, an attempt is made in the Bill, as it passed the Lords, to guard against the weaknesses and shortcomings of constables by making it incumbent on them to obtain the written authority of a superior before they arrest and take a man before a magistrate; but really this may mean just nothing at all. It may be assumed that all the evidence a director of police would require before he granted a written authority, would be the declaration of the policeman applying for it that he had fair grounds for making the application. Undoubtedly he would be expected to make out a good case; but that, as an over-zealous and prejudiced man, he would be sure to do. The superintendent, or whoever it was that had power to issue a written warrant for a "suspect's" apprehension, could not, by examination of the prisoner, convince himself of the justice of the act of his subordinate, to do which would be to usurp the magisterial office. And the process would probably be attended with this disadvantage,—that the said written order for arrest would wear an importance that really did not belong to it. If a man were arrested simply on the authority of a common policeman, the chances are that the magistrate would scrutinise the case narrowly, and be guided to a conviction solely by the evidence and his own discretion; but the case would come under the new act before him to a large extent prejudiced. He is instructed that the warrant that legalised the man's apprehension was not issued in vague supposition that it might be justifiable: an official of the law —a man high in authority—has sanctioned the arrest, and here is his written testimony that he considered the step expedient.

Again, let us for a moment contemplate the difficulties that must always attend the proving of his honesty by a man who, according to the high authority of the Lord Chancellor, has "no character to lose." "As to what was said about the injury done to a man's character by supervision, he must observe that a man's character was gone after two convictions. It was idle to say that after two convictions a man had a character."

In the case of a man against whom nothing criminal was ever suspected, it might be easy enough for him to prove his honesty any day, or any hour of the day, he might be called on to do so; but it is altogether different with the individual who dare not even lay claim to a character for honesty, to prove that the suspicions entertained against him are unfounded. It should be borne in mind that the difficulties of the poor wretch's condition almost preclude the possibility of his making a show of earning his bread in a worthy manner. In the majority of cases he will be found to be a man without a trade, or, if he has one, he will probably sink it, and endeavour to keep out of sight of all who knew him and the story of his downfall, by hiding amongst the great multitude who turn their hands to any rough-and-ready labour that will bring them a shilling. There are hundreds and thousands of men in London, and indeed in all great cities, who "pick up" a living somehow—anyhow, and who, though they all the time are honest fellows, would find it difficult to account for, and bring forward evidence to show, how they were engaged last Monday, and again on Wednesday, and what they earned, and whom they earned it of. Such men "job about," very often in localities that, in the case of a man under police supervision, to be seen there would be to rouse suspicions as to his intentions. For instance, many a shilling or sixpence is "picked up" by men who have nothing better to do, by hanging about railway stations and steamboat wharves, and looking out for passengers who have luggage they wish carried. But supposing that a man, a "ticket-of-leave," was to resort to such a means of obtaining a livelihood, and that he was seen "hanging about" such places day after day by a watchful detective who knew who and what he was,—with what amount of credulity would the authorities receive his statement that he was "looking out for a chance to carry somebody's trunk or carpet-bag"! In all probability the naive assertion would provoke a smile on the face of the magistrate who heard the case, and there would be "laughter" in court.

Again, as is well known, hundreds of men seek work at the docks. It might be supposed by their innocent lordships that nothing could be easier than for a man to prove his employment at such gigantic and sternly-regulated establishments as the London or St. Katherine Docks, with their staff of liveried officials and responsible gate-keepers. The dock-labourer, on his admittance, is furnished with a ticket, and when he leaves he is searched so as to make sure that he has stolen none of the valuable goods scattered in every direction. But it is a fact that no system can be looser or more shambling or shabbier than that which rules in the drudgery departments of these great emporiums for ship-loading and warehousing. Every morning the dock-gates are besieged by a mob clamorous as that which in the old time swarmed about the door of the casual-ward; and if rags and patches and hunger-pinched visages go for anything, the quality of both mobs is much of a sort. It is only men who can find nothing else to do who apply at the docks for work, for the pay is but threepence an hour, and the labour, hoisting-out and landing goods from the holds of ships, is cruelly hard; and it is not uncommon to employ a man for an hour and a half or two hours, and then discharge him. But it is better than nothing, and it is the "ready penny"—emphatically the penny—that the miserable, shamefaced, twice-convicted man, with some remnant of conscience and good intent remaining in him, would seek as the last resource of desperate honesty, all other sources failing him. But it would be next to impossible for him to prove that he had been working at the docks; no one knows him there. He might be there employed twenty times, and each time in a different gang, and under a different ganger. His workmates for the time are strangers, bearing not names, but numbers. Were it to save his life, he would find it hard to prove that he occasionally found a "job" at the docks, and, despite all his honest exertions, he would be liable to have his ticket revoked, and be sent back to finish to its full length his original sentence.

Again, it might even happen that a suspected man able to prove his honesty would find himself almost in as complete a fix as the one who, through circumstances over which he had no control, was unable to do so. Under the existing system, we have Colonel Henderson's word for it, masters are never informed by the police that they are employing a license-holder; but he would cease to be assured this immense advantage if Lord Kimberley has his way with him. As Earl Shaftesbury pertinently remarks: "A holder of the ticket-of-leave goes before a magistrate; and what happens? He proves that he is earning an honest livelihood, and the magistrate dismisses him. He returns to his work, and his employer dismisses him also. It has occurred before now that men have been dismissed by their employers under somewhat similar circumstances. How can you compensate a man for such a loss as that? You cannot do it; and yet you expose men who may be earning an honest livelihood to the danger of that happening to them if they refuse a demand for hush-money, or in any other way give offence to a dishonest police-constable. I know at the present moment a young man who, though convicted, is now in respectable employment, and in the receipt of good wages. He is living in terror, lest, under the circumstances to which I have referred, he may be brought before a police-magistrate. Depend on it that hundreds of men in that position are now watching the progress of this Bill.

"On the authority of the late Sir Richard Mayne it has been stated that the police have, through the clause that insists on convicts reporting themselves monthly, been enabled to furnish employment to a good many of the ticket-of-leave men; this, however, is very doubtful. That some situations may have been obtained for these men through the exertions of the police and the Discharged Prisoners' Aid Society may be true; but of this I am certain, that whatever returns the police may make of the places they have obtained for released convicts, they have not obtained anything like the number that those men obtained for themselves before the adoption of so stringent a provision."

There is undoubtedly a depth of criminality to which it is possible for a man to descend, putting himself utterly beyond reach of anything but human compassion. His conversion is quite hopeless, and he is no better than a predatory wild-beast, whose ferocity will endure just as long as his brute-strength remains; he would probably bite his best friend at his dying gasp. The sort of ruffian here alluded to will perhaps be better understood by aid of the following illustration, "drawn from life" not many months since. It is a case of a ruffian committed for trial for "garotting" and nearly murdering a gentleman. The delectable epistle was written by garotter "Bill" to his brother; and was intrusted to a prisoner, who had served his time and was about to quit the gaol, for hand-delivery. Either out of fear or forgetfulness, however, the letter was left behind and discovered by the authorities.

"Dundee Prison, July 18th, 1868.—Dear Brother, the only thing I am afraid of is that moll; if you can manage to square her I fear nothing; but if she swears she saw me have him by the throat it will not go well with me, for they are most d—d down on garotting. Then again, if she says she saw him with that amount of money, by ——! they might put me in for the robbery too; and there is seven years dead certain. You don't know what a b— like that will say. It can surely to God be squared between so many of you, and only the moll to come against me. If the bloke is in town he could be easily squared, I think; you could get him sweet, put the gloves on him, and things like that, and get him to say he cannot swear to me in court; that would be all that was wanted; or it is very easy giving that moll a dose. Put Ginger up to it; who the h— would take notice of a w— kicking the bucket? I would do it for you. If any of them is squared, tell Ginger to just sign M. H. at the bottom of her letter, so as I may know. I think it would be a good idea for my mother to get the bloke privately, and make an appeal to him; he would have a little feeling for her, I think; if you was getting him into the Garrick the wifey could talk to him so fine. If you only had one of them squared that's all that is wanted; for I am certain there is no more against me than them two. Set your brains to work, and stick at nothing; tell them not to be afraid of perjury in this case; they can't be brought in for it nohow; swear black is white; I must get off if they do the right thing; swear to anything; swear the b— wigs off their heads; there is no danger of being brought in for perjury in this case, not a d—d bit.—Bill." At the head of the letter the following was written across the page: "Poison the moll if she will not do what's right; by C—! I would think d—d little of doing it to save my brother! Ginger will fix her if you tell her to." The following was written inside the envelope of the letter: "They must not forget about me having a sore hand; that might help me too, as it would not be very likely I could seize him by the throat and compress the same, as it is stated in my indictment. That will be a good point, I think, he being a stout man. Tell them to be sure and stick to not seeing the bloke, and that I slept in the house that night; not likely that I could hold him with one hand; they can swear that my right hand was very sore, not fit to be used anyhow, as it was, and no mistake."

It came out in the course of the evidence that the meaning of the word "bloke" was "a man whom a woman might pick up in the street;" that "moll" was the name for a woman; and that "Ginger" was a nickname for one of the female witnesses.

To ruffians of this school, if to any, applies Lord Carnarvon's terrible suggestion of imprisonment for life, without hope, or possibility even, of release.

"It is idle to say that the subject of so many convictions is not absolutely and hopelessly hardened: they belong to a class of persons on whom punishment is only wasted, and the only thing is to shut them up for the rest of their lives, and keep them out of the possibility of doing any harm to society. I believe that such a course is best for them and for society, and that no objection to it can be reasonably urged. The convict-establishments of this country are already paying their way, and the surplus cost is very light; on the other hand, if you look at the cost which a criminal puts the State to in his detection, trial, and other criminal pro-ceedings, it is perfectly clear that the cheapest course for the country would be to shut him up. As far as the man himself is con-cerned it is also the most humane and the kindest course. He ex-changes a most miserable state of life outside the prison-walls, for one of comparative cleanliness and order inside. And if you calcu-late the time which such a man has spent in prison—broken only by the shorter intervals during which he has been let loose and again recaptured—it will be found that the difference between the period actually spent in prison and a lifelong sentence would really be very slight in amount."

As need not be mentioned, however, habitual criminals of the type above quoted are by far the exception, and not the rule. Experience teaches us that to become a ticket-of-leave man is not invariably to be converted from a human creature to a callous brute,—blind and deaf in vice, and doggedly determined so to continue to the last; give him a fair chance to amend, and in very many cases he will embrace it, thankfully even. The statistics of the Prisoners' Aid Society encourage us to hope better of even the worst of the criminal class. As has already been shown, the convicts themselves recognise and gratefully appreciate the advantages held out to them by the humanitarians whose head-quarters are by Charing Cross. Of 368 male convicts discharged in one year, only 78 neglected to make application for the bounty. It appears from the Society's most recent return that the total number of discharged prisoners assisted by the association since May 1857 was 5,798, but the average number had recently decreased, because fewer prisoners had of late been released on license. The number of those who had applied to the Society during the first six months of last year (1868) was 145, of whom 26 had emigrated; 44 had found good and constant employment in the metropolis; 15 had gone to sea; 25 had been sent to places beyond the Metropolitan Police-district, and placed under the supervision of the local police, and 35 had been classed as unsatisfactory and bad: but these included all those who were known to be in honest employment, but were so classed because they failed to report themselves to the police, as required by the Act.

It remains to be seen whether the Commons will give countenance to the new and severe measures sought by the Lords to be adopted against the convicted man at liberty under ticket-license. One thing is certain, it would be better to do away altogether with tickets-of-leave than use them as stumbling-blocks to a man's reformation. The only object of a ticket-of-leave is to give the holder a chance of returning to honest courses some months earlier than, under the rigid term of his sentence, he would be enabled to. Undoubtedly it is necessary to guard against, as far as possible, an abuse of the privilege. Full and sufficient opportunity should be allowed a man to follow honest pursuits, if he be so inclined; but it is only fair that the authorities should reserve to themselves the power of holding him in tether, so to say, so as to be able to haul him back to fast anchorage, should his ill-behaviour make such a step desirable; but meanwhile the tether-line should run slack and free—it should by no means be wound about a man's hands so as to impede his honest use of them, or about his neck so as to strangle him. At Wakefield we are informed there is an organisation by which every prisoner on his discharge—whether on a ticket-of-leave or otherwise—could find a home for six or twelve months, till he is able to find employment for himself, or till an employer came to look for him. Eighty per cent of the persons attached to the Wakefield establishment had engaged in, and settled down to, honest employment. Surely such a result should encourage those in authority to found similar institutions in other parts of the country.

To return, however, to the projected Habitual Criminals' Bill. It is not the ticket-of-leave man alone who has reasons for quaking lest it should become law; quaking for fear of injustice, not justice, that is to say. The class its stern provisions chiefly, and, as I venture to opine, cruelly affect are those unfortunates who have suffered two distinct terms of imprisonment. From the date of his second conviction a man is to be subject to police supervision for a term of seven years. They have the advantage over the ticket-of-leave man, that they are not required to report themselves periodically at a police-station; but, like the criminal of deeper dye, any day within their seven years of supervision they are liable to be arrested by the police and taken before a magistrate, to prove that they are not deriving a livelihood from dishonest sources. Should they fail in doing so, they are to be committed to prison for a year. Of the question itself, "What is an habitual criminal?" remarks the *Times,* commenting on the communication of its correspondent, "we say, take a walk with the police, and they will show you the class in all its varieties as easily as you could be shown the animals in the Zoological Gardens. Here they are,—men about whose character and calling nobody would ever pretend to entertain a doubt. We have been all perplexing ourselves with the possible fate of some contrite convict disposed to become respectable, but thwarted in his efforts by the intervention of the police. Why, among the real genuine representatives of crime—among the people described by our correspondent—there is not a man who dreams, or ever would dream, of any honest calling. . . . The profession has its grades, like any other; and so here is a company of first-class thieves, and another company representing the opposite end of the scale. At one establishment they are fashionably attired, and not altogether ill-mannered; at another the type is that of Bill

Sykes himself, even to his bulldog. But through all these descriptions, whether of house or inmate, host or guest, high or low, thief or receiver, there runs one assumption which we press upon our readers as practically decisive of the question before us. It is this: that about 'the habitual criminality' of the whole class there is not, in the mind of any human creature concerned, the smallest doubt whatever. ... The practice of the past generation was simple: some petty offence commonly began, then as now, a criminal career. It was detected and punished, and the criminal was sent back to his place in society. A second, and perhaps a third, act of deeper guilt followed, and the graduate in crime was condemned to transportation beyond seas. As long as this punishment retained any terrors it may have been efficient; but long before it was abandoned it had come to be recognised as an acknowledged benefit rather than a penalty by those who were sentenced to it. The result was the constant secretion of a criminal class on one hand, and the removal on the other to another sphere when they became ripe for the voyage—the removal being viewed as an encouragement to the commission of similar offences. We must make the painful acknowledgment that part of this dismal cycle cannot be materially altered. When a man is convicted of his first criminal act, we cannot know whether it is an isolated deed or whether it is the first-fruit of a lifetime. When he has gone from less to greater, and has proved himself indurated in crime, we are forced to protect society by removing him from it. ... Nor does the proposal involve that extensive and minute system of police *espionage* of which some people have been apprehensive. An honest man can always keep out of such questionable circumstances; and unless he places himself within them, he is as independent of the police as any unconvicted Englishman. When a man has been twice convicted, it is surely no great hardship to deprive him of the privilege of attempting and plotting crime with impunity."

III.

PROFESSIONAL BEGGARS.

CHAPTER XII

The Beggar of Olden Time.

"Only a Beggar"—The Fraternity 333 Years ago—A Savage Law—Origin of the Poor-Laws—Irish Distinction in the Ranks of Beggary—King Charles's Proclamation—Cumberland Discipline.

Were it not that the reader's sound and simple sense renders it quite unnecessary, it might be of importance to premise that to be "only a beggar" does not constitute a human being a curse against his species. There are those amongst the greatest and most famous who have been beggars, and many of the mightiest, groaning under the crushing burden of distracting power and unruly riches, have bemoaned their fate and envied the careless beggar whose dwindled strength was at least equal to carrying his slender wallet, whose heart was as light as his stomach, and whose wildest dreams of wealth never soared vastly above a cosy barn to sleep in, a warm old cast-off coat, and a sixpence. To be sure, in many instances these dissatisfied ones may not have given any stedfast consideration as regards such a decided change of state as might happen to suit them. It is related of a King of Scotland that, wearying of the cares of government, he slipped away from his palace and its cloying luxuries, to taste the delights that attach to the existence of ragged roving mendicants; but though his majesty affected to have enjoyed himself very much, and discoursed afterwards gravely of the great moral profit it brought him, it is not recorded that he persevered for any very long time in the pursuit of the newly-discovered blessing, or that he evinced any violent longing to return to it. Perhaps, having convinced himself of the advantages of poverty, he generously resolved to leave it to his subjects, contenting himself with such occasional glimpses of it as might be got by looking out o' window.

It is now 333 years ago since the beggar ceased to be dependent on voluntary charity, and the State insisted on his support by the parishes. In the year 1536 was passed an Act of Parliament abolishing the mendicant's right to solicit public alms. Under a

135

penalty of twenty shillings a month for every case of default, the parochial authorities were bound to provide work for the able-bodied. A poor's-rate, as we now understand the term, was not then thought of, the money required for pauper relief being chiefly derived from collections in the churches, a system that to a limited extent enabled the clergy to exercise their pious influences as in the old times, and before the destruction of monasteries and religious houses by Henry VIII. It was the wholesale spoliation in question, that occurred immediately after the Reformation, that first made known to the people at large the vast numbers of beggars that were amongst them. The Act of 27 Henry VIII. c. 25, prohibited indiscriminate almsgiving.

What the charitable townsman had to give, he was bound to distribute within the boundaries of the parish in which he resided. Under the old and looser condition of affairs the beggar derived the greater part of his gettings from the traveller; but the obnoxious Act effectually cut off from him this fruitful source of supply, since it provided that any parishioner or townsman who distributed alms out of his proper district, should forfeit to the State ten times the amount given. Whether the recipient of the bounty was in a position to act as "informer," with the customary advantage of receiving half the penalty, is not stated.

Against sturdy beggars the law was especially severe. On his first conviction he was whipped, the second led to the slicing-off of his right ear, and if after that he was deaf to the law's tender admonitions, sentence of death was executed on him.

This savage law, however, remained in force not more than ten years; one of the earliest Acts of Edward VI. was to mitigate the penalties attaching to beggary. Even under this humane King's ruling, however, a beggar's punishment was something very far beyond a joke. Every person able to work, and not willing, and declining a "job," though for no more tempting wages than his bare meat and drink, was liable to be branded on the shoulder, and any man willing to undertake the troublesome charge might claim the man as his slave for two years. His scale of diet during that time was more meagre than that allotted to the pauper in our own times. If the slave's master was a generous man, he might bestow on him the scraps from his table, or such meat-offal as his dogs had no relish for; but in law he was only bound to provide him with a sufficiency of bread and water. If such hot feeding did not provoke him to arouse and set to work with a will, his master might chain him and flog him to death's door; and so long as he did not drive him beyond that, the law would hold him harmless.

Sometimes the poor wretch so goaded would run away, but in the event of his being recaptured, he was branded on the cheek, and condemned to lifelong servitude; and if this did not cure his propensity for "skedaddling," he was hanged offhand. Any employer having a fancy for such a commodity as an incorrigible runaway might have the man so condemned as his slave for life; but if no one offered, he was chained at the legs and set to work to keep the highways in repair.

It was speedily found, however, that under such mild laws it was impossible to keep the begging fraternity in a proper frame of mind; and after a trial of it for three years the old Act of Henry was restored in full force.

In 1551 there dawned symptoms of the system that has taken more than three hundred years to develop and even now can scarcely lay claim to perfection. Collectors were appointed whose duty it was to make record of the name, residence, and occupation of all who apparently were able to give, as well as of those whose helpless distress entitled them to relief. In the words of the ancient enactment, the said collectors were to "gently ask every man and woman, that they of their charity will give weekly to the relief of the poor." To give, however, was optional, and not compulsory; no more severe pressure was brought to bear against a grudger than that the minister or churchwardens were sent to him to exhort him to charity; but so many curmudgeons remained inexorable that the voluntary system remained in force no longer than twelve years; and then the statute regulating poor's relief was remodelled, and it was declared good law that any person able to contribute, and declining to do so, might be summoned before a justice, who would tax him according to his discretion, and commit him to gaol if he still remained obdurate.

This last Act was passed in 1563, but nine years afterwards, we find the Government once again urged to repair what evidently had all this time remained an unsatisfactory business. It is evident that the arrangements made for the support of the impotent poor tended to loosen the shackles invented for the suppression of the professional beggar. The last-mentioned individual was found to be flourishing again, and it was deemed advisable to make still shorter his restricted tether. A law was passed enacting that "all persons whole and mighty in body, able to labour, not having land or master, nor using any lawful merchandise, craft, or mystery, and all common labourers, able in body, loitering and refusing to work for such reasonable wage as is commonly given, should for the first offence be grievously whipped, and burned through the gristle of the right ear with a hot iron of the compass of an inch about."

This mild and moderate mandate was promulgated under the sanction of the virgin Queen Elizabeth, and it is to be observed that during the same beneficent reign were passed laws in connection with labour and labourers that, were they revived, would go hard with trade-unionists and strikers in general. By the statutes 39 of Elizabeth, cap. 3 and 4 (1598), to refuse to work at the recognised and ordinary wages subjected the malcontent to be "openly whipped until his body should be bloody, and forthwith sent from parish to parish, the most straight way to the parish where he was born, there to put himself to labour, as a true subject ought to do." Under the same Acts of Elizabeth, the overseers of the poor in every parish were empowered to raise by "taxation of every inhabitant, parson, vicar, and other, and of every occupier of lands, houses, tithes, mines, &c., such sums of money as they shall require for providing a sufficient stock of flax, hemp, wool, and other ware or stuff to set the poor on work, and also competent sums for relief of lame, blind, old, and impotent persons." By virtue of the Acts in question, justices were empowered to commit to prison the able-bodied who would not work; and church-wardens and overseers were charged to build suitable houses, at the cost of the parish, for the reception of the impotent poor only.

As, however, is observed by Mr. Halliday (to whose excellent account of the *Origin and History of the Poor-Laws* I stand indebted for much of the material employed in this summary) "these simple provisions were in course of time greatly perverted, and many abuses were introduced into the administration of the poor-law. One of the most mischievous practices was that which was established by the justices for the county of Berks in 1795, when, in order to meet the wants of the labouring population—caused by the high price of provisions—an allowance in proportion to the number of his family was made out of the parish fund to every labourer who applied for relief. This allowance fluctuated with the price of the gallon loaf of second flour, and the scale was so adjusted as to return to each family the sum which in a given number of loaves would cost beyond the price, in years of ordinary abundance. This plan was conceived in a spirit of benevolence, but the readiness with which it was adopted in all parts of England clearly shows the want of sound views on the subject. Under the allowance-system the labourer received a part of his means of subsistence in the form of a parish-gift, and as the fund out of which it was provided was raised from the contributions of those who did not employ labourers as well as of those who did, their employers, being able in part to burden others with the payment for their labour, had a direct interest in perpetuating the system. Those who employed labourers looked upon the parish contribution as part of the fund out of which they were to be paid, and accordingly lowered their rate of wages. The labourers also looked on the fund as a source of wage. The consequence was, that the labourer looked to the parish, and as a matter of right, without any regard to his real wants; and he received the wages of his labour as only one and a secondary source of the means of subsistence. His character as a labourer became of less value, his value as a labourer being thus diminished under the combined operation of these two causes."

In the olden time, as at present, it appears that the Irish figured conspicuously in the ranks of beggary. As is shown by the recent returns, there are haunting the metropolis nearly three mendicants hailing from the Emerald Isle to one of any other nation; and that it was so so long ago as the reign of King Charles II. the following proclamation will sufficiently attest:

"A Proclamation for the speedy rendering away of Irishe Beggars out of this Kingdome into their owne Countrie and for the Suppressing and Ordering of Rogues and Vagabonds according to the Laws.

"Whereas this realme hath of late been pestered with great numbers of Irishe beggars who live here idly and dangerously, and are of ill example to the natives of this Kingdome; and whereas the multitude of English rogues and vagabonds doe much more abound than in former tymes—some wandering and begging under the colour of soldiers and mariners, others under the pretext of impotent persons, whereby they become a burden to the good people of the land—all which happeneth by the neglect of the due execution of the lawes formerly with great providence made for relief of the true poor and indigent and for the punishment of sturdy rogues and vagabonds: for the reforming thereof soe great a mischiefe, and to prevent the many dangers which will ensue by the neglect thereof; the King, by the advice of his Privy Council and of his judges, commands that all the laws and statutes now in force for the punishment of rogues and vagabonds be duly putt in execution; and more particularly that all Irishe beggars which now are in any part of this Kingdome, wandering or begging under what pretence soever, shall forthwith depart this realme and return to their owne countries and there abide."

The authorities of Cumberland and Westmoreland appear to

have hit on an expedient that has proved successful in diminishing the number of tramps that formerly infested those counties. A recently published report states: "In consequence of frequent and general complaints from the people of these two counties, as to the numerous robberies committed by tramping vagrants, it was determined, at the end of the year 1867, to enforce the Vagrant Act strictly. The result has been that, in the year ending at Michaelmas 1868, 524 persons were apprehended in the two counties for begging from house to house, and 3.74 of them were committed to prison. The effect has been, to a certain extent, like that which occurred in the time of the cattle-plague; when the police told the tramps at the frontier that they must either stop or must be disinfected, and they turned back. The daily average number of tramps and vagrants in the two counties in the year ending at Michaelmas 1868 was only 150, making a total decrease of 6935 in the year; and various petty larcenies, burglaries, and other crimes decreased remarkably. The chief constable has reported that the course adopted has been attended with most beneficial results, in checking professional mendicancy and preventing crime; and he is persuaded that if the law were generally and uniformly carried into effect, tramping vagrancy, as a trade, would be very soon put an end to. He says that, as a rule, the condition of the hands will enable the police to judge between the professional tramp and the working man really travelling in search of work, and that all difficulty might be removed by requiring the latter to procure a certificate from the head of the police of the starting-place, which would protect him against apprehension, and which might also guarantee certain relief at appointed places along his route."

CHAPTER XIII.

The Work of Punishment and Reclamation.

The Effect of "The Society for the Suppression of Mendicity"—State Business carried out by Individual Enterprise—"The Discharged Prisoners' Aid Society"—The quiet Work of these Societies—Their Mode of Work—Curious Statistics—Singular Oscillations—Diabolical Swindling.

The Society for the Suppression of Mendicity has done more towards checking imposture, and bringing evildoers to punishment, than the Government itself, notwithstanding all the elaborate and expensive machinery at its command. Nor, by the way, is this a solitary instance of business peculiarly its own being shirked by the State, and handed over to be dealt with by the skill, energy, and perseverance of a few private individuals. A kindred association to that, the province of which is the better government of the beggars of London, is that which devotes its energies to the reclamation of returned convicts. Anyone at all acquainted with the matter is aware of the immense amount of lasting and substantial good that the "Discharged Prisoners' Aid Society" has accomplished. That the individuals chiefly concerned—the returned convicts themselves—fully appreciate the advantages held out by the said Society is sufficiently proved by the fact, that out of 368 licence-holders discharged into the metropolis, 290 placed themselves in its hands. No doubt such arrangements do prove as convenient as economical as regards the Government; but whether it is just to inflict a responsibility of such magnitude on private individuals is another question; or whether the easement it confers is cheaply purchased by our rulers at the cost of so unmistakable a confession of their incapacity.

So quietly and unobtrusively do these self-constituted guardians of public morality perform the arduous duties they undertake, that it may be safely assumed not one person in a thousand is aware what their prime objects are, let alone the means by which they are accomplished. As regards the Mendicity Society, there can be no doubt what is the popular impression. It is commonly regarded as a sort of amateur detective association for the discovery of fraudulent begging,—a Society that has in its employ certain cunning individuals of the detested breed of "spies," who earn their wages by lurking in shady places, and peeping over men's shoulders, and covertly listening to their private conversation. The full extent of the Society's usefulness, according to vulgar prejudice, is represented by the unfortunate "cadger" pounced on in the act of receiving alms, and carried before a magistrate to account for that enormous iniquity. People, however, who know no more of the Society than this, know only of the smallest and least important of its functions. It is a poor's-relief association on an extensive scale. It has its labour-sheds for testing the genuineness of the mendicants that apply at the office, to say nothing of a real treadmill of its own. Moreover it proclaims its ability to offer suitable employment to *every* able-bodied mendicant referred to it. The following is the Society's method of dealing. The plan of the institution is to provide subscribers with tickets, which are intended to be distributed to street-beggars only, and which will insure admission to the Society's office, where the applicant is examined by the sitting or assistant manager, who directs such immediate relief as in his judgment may appear proper.

If the applicant appears deserving, and is without lodging, money sufficient to procure one for the night is given. In cases where the applicant appears to have an immediate claim on any London parish, the pauper is referred to the overseers of such parish. If, as in some cases, it is requisite for the applicant to return on a subsequent day, he is furnished with a return-ticket, which introduces him again to the office for further relief. In the mean time inquiry is made, if practicable, into the character of the pauper, by which the sitting manager is governed in awarding proper relief. Men are sent to the Society's premises to chop wood, and women and children to the oakum-room. During the time they are employed, men receive eightpence, and women fourpence per day, for lodging-money, and two meals, and one meal for each member of the family; and on Saturdays double allowance of money, with an extra meal to take home for each, that they may have no excuse for begging on Sunday. Each meal in winter consists of a pint of nutritious soup, and a sixth of a four-pound loaf of good bread; and in summer one quarter of a pound of cheese, and the same proportion of bread. At the end of a week, if they apply, the order for work may be renewed, until they have been employed a month, when the case is discharged, unless the sitting manager considers an extension of employment desirable; in which case it is laid before the committee, who renew the order for another month, or give such other relief as they think most likely to prevent the necessity of a recurrence to street-begging. In order to check repeated applications from the same persons, those who habitually resort to the refuges for the house-less, or the metropolitan workhouses, for lodging, and to the Society for food, if males, have to perform three hours' work at the mill; if females, three hours' work at oakum-picking, before food is given them; and the men may also, if practicable, have three days' work at stone-breaking. Applicants of this description making more than six applications within one year are refused further relief, unless on investigation they are found deserving of assistance.

Persons who have not been six months in London are not con-sidered objects of the charity; but food is given to persons passing through London in search of work, to assist them on their way. In the case of mendicants incapable of labour, the amount of daily allowance is 6*d*. for a single man, 9*d*. for a man, his wife, and young child, and 1*s*. in any other case; but this allowance may be doubled on Saturday night, at the discretion of the sitting or assistant-manager. Labourers at the mill receive 6*d*. per day, and the wife and children of persons employed may receive a meal. The wives of men employed either at the mill or stoneyard may also have work, and receive wages, provided that their joint earn-ings do not exceed one shilling per day.

The Society's "Report" recently issued shows the kind and the extent of the business transacted through its officials up to the close of the year 1867. It contains much that is interesting as well as instructive, and not a little that is puzzling. We are informed that within the year 644 vagrants were arrested and taken before a magistrate, and that of this number 311 were committed, and 333 discharged. From the commencement to the close of the year 1867, upwards of 10,000 cases of "casual" relief passed through the hands of the Society, as well as between 400 and 500 cases that are alluded to as "registered"—a term, it may be assumed, that distinguishes the ordinary casual case from that which demands investigation and private inquiry. Amongst the whole number, 44,347 meals were distributed, and a considerable sum of money and some clothes; it being no uncommon occurrence for the management to rig-out the ragged, hard-up unfortunate applying for relief, and to start him in the world in a way that, if he has the intention, gives him a fair chance of recovering a decent position.

The most curious part of the affair, however, appears in the plain and simple tabulated statement that represents the yearly number of vagrants relieved and set to work, and consigned to proper punishment, since the time of the Mendicity Society's first establishment. In the first year of the Society's existence, when the scheme was new, and the vagrant crop dead-ripe for gathering, and the officers eager to get at their new and novel employment, 385 "sturdy beggars" were caught and sent to gaol. It is consoling to know that in the last year (1967) this number was decreased considerably, and that no more than 311 were sentenced. This may appear no vast reduction, but when we consider not only the enormously-increased population since 1818, and, what is of equal significance, the advance of intellect and cleverness and cunning amongst this as every other community doomed to live by the exercise of its wits, the result is one on which the country may be congratulated.

When, however, we come to regard the long column that at a glance reveals the figures that pertain to vagrant committals for fifty successive years, a decided damper is thrown on one's hopes that the trade of the shiftless roving vagabond is becoming surely though slowly extinguished. As might be expected of a class so erratic in its movements, it would be difficult to measure them by any fixed standard; but one is scarcely prepared to discover the awful amount of uncertainty that prevails as regards the going and coming of these impostor tramps, when there is a dearth of them, and when their swarming may be expected. They are like cholera or plague, and have their seasons of sloth, and again of general prevalence and virulence. The laws that govern the movements of the professional beggar are inscrutable. You may make war on him and thin his ranks, and prosecute him and persecute him, and by the end of the year be able to show in plain unmistakable figures that he is not half the formidable fellow he was last year; that you have blunted his sting and decreased his dimensions. You still prosecute the war of extermination, and next year you are in a position to reveal in black-and-white further glorious results. The thousand has become seven hundred, and again the seven hundred four. At this rate, ere two more years are elapsed, you may strip the rags from your last beggar's back, and hang them on the city gate as a scarecrow and a caution against a revival of the detestable trade.

But alas for our delusive hopes! Come another year—that which showed our seven hundred beggars dwindled down to four—and without any apparent cause the enemy, crippled and more than half killed as it seemed, reappears on the stage hale and sound, and with years of life in him yet. The four hundred has grown to six. There are no means of accounting for it. Depression of trade and poverty widely prevailing will not do so, for such are times of prosperity and fattening with the professional beggar. When "giving" is the order of the day, and benevolence, sickening at the sight of privation and distress that seems endless, shuts her eyes and bestows her gifts on all comers, then is the cadger's harvest, then he may pursue his shameful avocation with comparative impunity. If we required evidence of this, it is furnished by the Society's statistics. In 1865, which was an ordinarily fair year with the working man, the number of vagrant committals reached 586, while in the year following, when destitution prevailed so enormously, and the outcries of famine were so generously responded to through the length and breadth of the land, the number of begging impostors who got into trouble were only 372.

It will be as well, perhaps, that the reader should have set before him the figures for the various years precisely as they stand in the Society's last issued Report. As will be seen, for some reason that is not explained, there are no returns for the four years 1830 to 1833 inclusive. Appended to the "committed vagrant list" is a record of the number of cases specially inquired into and "registered," as well as a statement of the number of meals that were in each year distributed.

Years.	Cases registered.	Vagrants committed.	Meals given.
1818	3,284	385	16,827
1819	4,682	580	33,013
1820	4,546	359	46,407
1821	2,336	324	28,542
1822	2,235	287	22,232
1823	1,493	193	20,152
1824	1,441	195	25,396
1825	1,096	381	19,600
1826	833	300	22,972
1827	806	403	35,892
1828	1,284	786	21,066
1829	671	602	26,286
1830	848	—	105,488
1831	1,285	—	79,156
1832	1,040	—	73,315

Years.	Cases registered.	Vagrants committed.	Meals given.
1833	624	—	37,074
1834	1,226	652	30,513
1835	1,408	1,510	84,717
1836	946	1,004	68,134
1837	1,087	1,090	87,454
1838	1,041	873	155,348
1839	1,055	962	110,943
1840	706	752	113,502
1841	997	1,119	195,625
1842	1,223	1,306	128,914
1843	1,148	1,018	167,126
1844	1,184	937	174,229
1845	1,001	868	165,139
1846	980	778	148,569
1847	910	625	239,171
1848	1,161	979	148,661
1849	1,043	905	64,251
1850	787	570	94,106
1851	1,150	900	102,140
1852	658	607	67,985
1853	419	354	62,788
1854	332	326	52,212
1855	235	239	52,731
1856	325	293	49,806
1857	354	358	54,074
1858	329	298	43,836
1859	364	305	40,256
1860	430	350	42,912
1861	446	335	73,077
1862	542	411	47,458
1863	607	451	45,477
1864	413	370	55,265
1865	774	586	52,137
1866	481	372	38,131
1867	488	311	44,347
	54,767	27,609	3,713,726

Assuming that the Society constantly employs the same number of officers, and that they are always maintained in the same condition of activity, it is difficult to account for the disparity displayed by the above-quoted figures. It would almost seem that the mendicity constabulary were gifted with a prescience of what was about to happen; that they know, by the barking of dogs or some other unmistakable token, when "the beggars are coming to town," and sallied out, as fishermen do at the approach of herrings or mackerel, prepared, and fully determined to make a good haul.

It is a pity that, despite the good work it accomplishes, the Society for the Suppression of Mendicity should have weighty reasons for lamenting the falling-off of public support it has of late experienced. Nothing could be more promising than its launching. It took the field with a staff of eight constables only, and an income of 4,384*l.*; nor could it be said to disappoint the expectations of its patrons. In its first year of operation it prosecuted 385 professional vagrants. Its success progressed. After a lapse of twenty-five years, in 1842 we find it with an income of 6,576*l.*; and that prosperity had not dulled its energy appears from the fact that in the year last mentioned there occurred, in the deep waters where that slippery and voracious fish, the incorrigible beggar, lurks for prey, the splendid catch of over thirteen hundred. Encouraged by so fair a stroke of business, and the kindness and generosity of an appreciative public, the Society then added a new branch to their business—the begging-letter branch; which, it should be understood, did not originally come within the scope of its operations in any shape.

At the expiration of another quarter of a century, however, we find that, instead of an increase of income to the extent of one-third, as occurred in the first quarter of a century of the Society's existence, its resources have fallen off to the extent of nearly one-half, as compared with the income of 1842.

This is as it should not be. As has been shown, feeding the deserving poor as well as punishing the inveterate vagrant comprises a prominent feature of the Society's business, and this it is impossible to do without adequate funds. It might be supposed that the passing of the Houseless Poor Act would have diminished the number of applicants to this and other charitable societies; but there is a large class of persons temporarily thrown out of work to whom the casual wards of workhouses are useless, and who do not apply for assistance there. The number of this class who applied with tickets at the Society's office during the past year was more *than double the number of such applicants in the preceding year,* being, in 1866, 4,378; but in 1867, 10,532. Among these poor persons 44,347 meals, consisting of 7,389 four-pound loaves, upwards of four tons of cheese and 785 gallons of soup, have been distributed. In addition to this amount of food, 65*l.* 7*s.*, in small sums of money, has been given to those whose cases seemed suitable for such relief.

The apprehended cases were 644, as compared with 693 such

cases in 1866, but though a diminished constabulary force was employed for part of the year, yet nearly as large a number of old offenders was committed by the magistrate, being 311 compared with 372 in 1866. The number of begging-letters referred to the office for inquiry during the past year was 2,019, being somewhat fewer than the return of such applications for the year 1866. Of the 2,019 letters 790 were from unknown applicants; 620 from persons previously known to the Society's officials, but requiring a more recent investigation; and 609 from persons too well known to require any investigation.

The following cases that have occurred during the past year will show the mode in which the Society deals with the very different classes of applicants brought within the sphere of its operations:

"No. 617. F. J.—This young man, 24 years of age, came to the office with a subscriber's ticket. He stated that he had been employed last as a bookkeeper at Manchester, and left that situation in April, and had since been in London seeking a situation, in which he had failed, and having no friends here, had become destitute. He was a well-spoken single man, and appeared to be truthful in his statements and anxious to return to Manchester, where he had relatives who would assist him. At the instance of the presiding manager some old clothes were given him, which improved his appearance, and thirty shillings were handed to a constable to pay his fare, which was done, and the balance was given to him. A few days after he wrote from Manchester a letter, in which he stated that he had every prospect of obtaining employment, and expressed much gratitude for what had been done for him at this office."

"No. 883. S. F.—This woman, 37 years of age, applied to the Society with a subscriber's ticket, alleging her distress to have been caused by the desertion of her husband and her own inability to procure employment, owing to the want of decent clothing. She was sent to the Society's oakum-room to work, and while there saved enough money to purchase several articles of wearing apparel. Inquiry was made; and it being found that her statements were true and her character good, a situation was found her, in which she still is, apparently giving satisfaction to her employers, and likely to obtain a respectable living for the future."

"No. 169,150. S. W. G.—This poor woman, the widow of a labourer, and aged 45 years, had done her best to bring up her family in credit, by keeping a small coal and greengrocery shop, making ginger-beer, &c. during the summer months; and several of the children were nearly providing for themselves, when she lost her sight, and was found in a state of distress. Her eldest daughter had been obliged to leave her situation to look to the house; but having a knowledge of the sewing-machine and a prospect of obtaining work at home, it was decided to recommend the case for liberal relief, in order that a machine might be obtained and the daughter thus enabled to assist in rearing the younger children at home, which object there is reason to hope has been accomplished."

"No. 54,494. C. T., *alias* S.—A well-dressed woman was apprehended on a warrant, charging her with obtaining charitable contributions by false pretences; she had been known to the Society's officers for years, and a number of complaints had been lodged at the office against her during that time; when apprehended on previous occasions no one could be found willing to appear against her. In the present instance she had applied to a lady residing at Rutland-gate for a loan of 2*l.* to enable her to take her brother to Scotland, whom she represented as having just left the Brompton Hospital very ill, and that she had been advised to get him to his native air, where they had friends. To strengthen her appeal she mentioned the names of two or three persons known to the lady to whom she was applying, and as having been sent by one of them to her; on the faith of the representations made she was assisted with 2*l.* 6*s.*; but subsequent inquiry convinced this lady that the statement was false. At the time the prisoner was taken into custody she had 5*l.* 8*s.* 5½*d.* on her person; and being made acquainted with the charge confessed herself guilty of these offences, and offered to repay the money; but on the case being stated to the magistrate he sentenced her to three months' imprisonment, and the money found in her possession to be applied to her maintenance while there."

"No. 42,064. T. B., with a number of aliases, was again apprehended by one of the Society's constables; he had been known as a begging-letter impostor for upwards of twenty years, and during that period had been three times transported, and as many times liberated on tickets-of-leave. On this occasion (in company with a woman whom he represented as a district visitor) he applied to a gentleman residing in Eaton-square, stating he was 'Mr. Bond,' one of the overseers of St. Marylebone parish, and gave in his card to that effect. On obtaining an interview, he said he and the lady with him had interested themselves on behalf of a 'Mrs. Cole,' a widow with six children, a native of Ledbury in Herefordshire, who wished to return home, where she would be able to obtain a living for herself and family, and he was seeking subscriptions to purchase the family a little clothing and funds to defray the expense of their transit. The gentleman knowing Ledbury well, and believing the prisoner's statement to be true, gave him 10*s*.; but afterwards finding that he had been imposed on, obtained a warrant for his apprehension, and the case being clearly proved, he was sentenced to three months' imprisonment; and the magistrate remarked that a more hardened criminal had never been brought before him, and that the Home Secretary should be applied to to cause him to finish his unexpired term of two years and three months."

"No. 54,889. M. W.—A woman with an infant in her arms was apprehended by one of the Society's constables for endeavouring to obtain money by false pretences from a gentleman residing in Portland-place, by stating that her husband was at the Bournemouth Sanatorium, and produced a letter purporting to be from the medical officer of the institution, which was as follows: 'National Sanatorium, Bournemouth, Hants.—The resident surgeon wishes to inform Mrs. W. that her husband, having ruptured a blood-vessel, is in a very precarious state. James W. is very desirous of seeing his wife, and begs she will come as early as possible.' This note was signed as by the resident medical officer. She stated to the prosecutor that having no means of paying her railway fare, she had applied to him for assistance, as he had been kind to her husband on previous occasions. Being apprehended and detained for inquiries, she admitted the truth of the charge made against her; and the case being clearly proved, she was sentenced to three months' imprisonment. The prisoner and her husband had been carrying on this system of imposition for a long time, but owing to parties declining to come forward to prosecute, had not previously been convicted."

But there remains yet to notice one member of the begging-letter-writing fraternity, compared with whom all the rest are mere innocent and harmless scribblers. After an experience so long and varied, and so many conflicts sharp and severe with their natural enemies the officers of the "Society," and so many exposures and defeats, it might be reasonably hoped that the professional beggar whose genius takes an epistolary turn must find his ingenuity well-nigh exhausted; but, as recent revelations have disclosed, the machinery brought against him for this suppression has but sharpened his wits and rendered him more formidable than ever. Although but recently discovered, it is hard to say for how long a time this diabolical desire for swindling the unwary has existed. Very possibly, many a "dodge" of minor calibre has been invented and run the length of its tether, and died the death of all dodges, while the one in question has lurked in the dark, and grown fat and prospered.

It would be next to impossible for the imagination most fertile in wicked invention to conceive anything more devilish and mischievous, or an evil that might be perpetrated with less fear of detection. The mainspring of the pretty scheme is not to impose on the benevolence and credulity of the living, but to blast and vilify the character of the dead. To obliterate from the hearts of those who were nearest and dearest to him—the husband dead and buried—all kindly remembrance of him; to tear, as it were, from his poor honest body the white shroud in which tender hands had enveloped it, and show him to have lived and died a traitor, a hypocrite, and an impostor, false to that very last breath with which he bade his wife, his "only darling," farewell; and this that some cold-blooded ruffian may extort from the wronged man's duped indignant survivors a few miserable pounds or shillings, as the case may be.

The process by which the villany in question may be accomplished is much more simple than would at first appear. The prime condition of the impostor's success is that he must reside at a long distance from those it is his intention to dupe. The swindler lives in France or Germany, sometimes as far away as America. The first "move" is to look into the newspaper obituary notices for a likely victim. A gentleman who dies young, leaving a wife and a numerous family to bemoan their bitter bereavement, is not uncommonly the case fixed on. If, during his lifetime, he was a man who, from his station in life, must have been tolerably well known, so much the better. It is a woman who writes the letter. She writes of course to the individual as though not in the least suspecting that he is dead. The following *genuine* copy of such a letter will, better than anything, illustrate the cold, cruel, subtle villany essential to the success of the "Dead-man's lurk," as in the profession it is styled:

"My ever-dearest Robert,—It is only after enduring the sickening disappointment that has attended my last three letters sent to the old address, that I venture to write to your private abode, in the fervent hope that this my desperate appeal to your oft-tried generosity may fall into no other hands but your own.

"I cannot think that my boy's father can have grown cold towards her whose whole life is devoted to him, who fled from home and friends, and took up her abode in a foreign land and amongst strangers, that her darling might not be troubled,—that his *home* might be peace. Alas! what is *my* home? But I will not upbraid you. Were I alone, I would be content to die rather than cause you a single pang of uneasiness; but, as my dear Robert knows, I am *not* alone. God still spares our boy to me, though I much fear that the doctor's prediction that he would get the better of his ailments when he had turned the age of ten will not be verified. Sometimes as I sit of nights—long, weary, thoughtful nights—watching my sick darling, and thinking of those old times of brief bitter sweetness, I wish that you could see him, so like your own dear self; but the thought is at once hushed, when I reflect on the pain it would cause you to contemplate our poor *fatherless* boy. I am almost tempted to thank God that he cannot remain much longer on earth; but it is hard, cruelly hard, to see him suffer from *want* as well as from his painful malady. Do, for the sake of the *old times,* send me a little money, though only a few pounds. There is no other resource for us but the work-house. At any rate, pray send me an answer to this, and relieve the dreadful suspense that haunts me.

"P.S. As I have been, from reasons too painful to disclose to you, compelled to quit the lodgings in V.-street, please direct Post-office,——. Yours, ever true and faithful,　　Elizabeth——."

As it happened, the gentleman to whom this villanous epistle was addressed had, till within a few years of his demise, resided in a far-away quarter of the globe, and under such conditions as rendered a ten-years-ago intimacy with any English Elizabeth utterly impossible; but unfortunately his survivors were content to treat the attempted imposture with silent contempt, and a likely opportunity of bringing to proper punishment one of a gang of the most pestiferous order of swindlers it is possible to conceive was lost. It was probably only the *very* peculiar and exceptionally con-clusive evidence that the letter could not apply to Mr. Robert ——, that saved his friends from painful anxiety, and perhaps robbery. It is so much less troublesome to hush-up such a matter than to investigate it. To be sure, no one would have for a moment suspec-ted, from the precise and proper behaviour of the man dead and gone, that he could ever have been guilty of such wickedness and folly; but it is so hard to read the human heart. Such things have happened; and now that one calls to mind—

That is the most poisonous part of it,—"now that one calls to mind!" What is easier than to call to mind, out of the ten thousand remembrances of a man whose society we have shared for twenty years or more, one or two acts that at the time were regarded as "strange whims," but now, regarded in the light that the damnable letter sheds on them, appear as parts of the very business so unexpectedly brought to light? Perhaps the man was privately charitable, and in benevolent objects expended a portion of his income, without making mention of how, when, and where, or keeping any sort of ledger account. How his means so mysteriously dwindled in his hands was a puzzle even to his most intimate friends—*now* it is apparent where the money went! But there, it is no use discussing that now; he has gone to answer for all his sins, and it is to be devoutly wished that God, in the infinite stretch of His mercy, will forgive him even this enormous sin. Meanwhile it will never do to have this base creature coming as a tramping beggar, perhaps with her boy, and knocking at the door, desperately determined on being cared for by the man who was the cause of her ruin and her banishment. Better to send her ten pounds, with a brief note to the effect that Mr. —— is now dead, and it will be useless her troubling again.

This is what did *not* happen in the case quoted, and for the reasons given; but it might, and in very many cases it doubtless has happened; and it would be worth a whole year's catch of common begging-letter impostors if the Society for the Suppression of Mendicity could trap a member of the "Dead-lurk" gang, and hand him over to the tender mercies of the law.

CHAPTER XIV.

Begging "Dodges".

The "dodges" to which an individual resolved on a vagrant life will resort are almost past reckoning; and, as a natural consequence, the quality of the imposture in modern practice is superior to that which served to delude our grandfathers.

It can be no other. As civilisation advances, and our machinery for the suppression and detection of fraud improves, so, if he would live at all, must the professional impostor exert all the skill and cunning he is endowed with to adjust the balance at his end of the beam. It is with vagrancy as with thieving. If our present system of police had no more formidable adversaries to deal with than lived and robbed in the days of those famous fellows, Richard Turpin and Master Blueskin, Newgate might, in the course of a few years, be converted into a temperance hotel, and our various convict establishments into vast industrial homes for the helplessly indigent. So, if the well-trained staff under the captaincy of that shrewd scenter of make-believe and humbug—Mr. Horsford—was called on to rout an old-fashioned army of sham blindness, and cripples whose stumps were fictitious; and of clumsy whining cadgers, who made filthy rags do duty for poverty, who painted horrid sores on their arms and legs, and employed a mild sort of whitewash to represent on their impudent faces the bloodless pallor of consumption,—we might reasonably hope to be rid of the whole community in a month.

It is scarcely too much to say, that the active and intelligent opposition brought to bear of late years against beggars has caused the trade to be taken up by a class of persons of quite superior accomplishments. I well recollect, on the memorable occasion of my passing a night in the society of tramps and beggars, hearing the matter discussed seriously and at length, and that by persons who, from their position in life, undoubtedly were those to whose opinion considerable weight attached. The conversation began by one young fellow, as he reclined on his hay-bed and puffed complacently at his short pipe, relating how he had "kidded" the workhouse authorities into the belief that he had not applied for relief at that casual-ward for at least a month previously, whereas he had been there for three successive nights. Of course this was a joke mightily enjoyed by his audience; and a friend, wagging his head in high admiration, expressed his wonder as to how the feat could be successfully accomplished. "How!" replied the audacious one; "why, with cheek, to be sure. Anything can be done if you've only got cheek enough. It's no use puttin' on a spurt of it, and knocking under soon as you're tackled. Go in for it up to the heads of your — soul bolts. Put it on your face so gallus thick that the devil himself won't see through it. Put it into your eyes and set the tears a-rollin'. Swear God's truth; stop at nothing. They're bound to believe you. There ain't nothing else left for 'em. They think that there's an end somewhere to lyin' and cheekin', and they're — fools enough to think that they can tell when that end shows itself. Don't let your cheek have any end to it. *That's* where you're right, my lads."

I have, at the risk of shocking the reader of delicate sensibilities, quoted at full the terms in which my ruffianly "casual" chamberfellow delivered himself of his opinion as to the power of "cheek" illimitable, because from the same experienced source presently proceeded as handsome a tribute to the efficiency of the officers of the Mendicity Society as they could desire.

"What shall you do with yerself to-morrow?" one asked of another, who, weary of song and anecdote and blasphemy, preparatory to curling down for the night was yawning curses on the parochial authorities for supplying him with no warmer rug. "It ain't much you can do anyhows atween the time when you finish at the crank and go out, till when you wants to come in agin. It feels like frost; if it is, I shall do a bit of chanting, I think." ("Chanting" is vagrant phraseology for street singing.)

"I'm with you," replied his friend; "unless it's cold enough to work the shaller; that's the best game. 'Taint no use, though, without its perishin' cold; that's the wust on it."

(It may be here mentioned that the "shaller," or more properly "shallow" dodge, is for a beggar to make capital of his rags and a disgusting condition of semi-nudity; to expose his shoulders and his knees and his shirtless chest, pinched and blue with cold. A pouncing of the exposed parts with common powder-blue is found to heighten the frost-bitten effect, and to excite the compassion of the charitable.)

"There you are wrong," broke in the advocate of "cheek;" "that isn't the wust of it. The wust of it is, that there's no *best* of it. It don't matter what you try; all games is a-growing stale as last week's tommy" (bread).

"It's 'cos people get so gallus 'ard-'arted, that's wot it is," remarked with a grin a young gentleman who shared the bed of the 'cheeky' one.

"No, that ain't it, either; people are as soft-'arted and as green as ever they was; and so they would shell-out like they used to do, only for them ——" (something too dreadful for printing) "lurchers of the S'ciety. It's all them. It ain't the reg'lar p'lice. They're above beggars, 'cept when they're set on. It's them Mendikent coves, wot gets their livin' by pokin' and pryin' arter every cove like us whenever they sees him in the street. They gives the public the 'office'" (information), "and the public believes 'em, bust 'em!"

These observations evidently set the "cheeky" one thinking on times past; for he presently took up the subject again.

"Things ain't wot they was one time. Talkin' about the shallow lay; Lor' bless yer, you should have knowed what it was no longer ago than when I was a kid, and used to go out with my old woman. Ah, it was summat to have winter then! I've heerd my old woman say often that she'd warrant to make enough to live on all the rest of the year, if she only had three months' good stiff frost. I recollect the time when you couldn't go a dozen yards without hearing the flying up of a window or the opening of a door, and there was somebody a-beckoning of you to give you grub or coppers. It was the grub that beat us."

"How d'ye mean? Didn't you get enough of it?"

"Hark at him! enough of it! We got a thunderin' sight too much of it. A little of it was all very well, 'specially if it was a handy-sized meaty bone, wot you could relish with a pint of beer when you felt peckish; but, bust 'em, they used to overdo it. It don't look well, don't you know, to carry a bag or anythink, when you are on the shallow lay. It looks as though you was a 'reg'lar,' and that don't 'act.' The old gal used to stow a whacking lot in a big pocket she had in her petticut, and I used to put away a 'dollop' in the busum of my shirt, which it was tied round the waist-bag hid underneath my trousers for the purpose. But, Lor' bless yer, sometimes the blessed trade would go that aggravatin' that we would both find ourselves loaded-up in no time. Lor, how my old woman would swear about the grub sometimes! It used to make me larf; it was a reg'lar pantermime. She'd be reg'lar weighed down, and me stuffed so jolly full that I daren't so much as shiver even, lest a lump of tommy or meat should tumble out in front, and all the while we'd be pattering about us not having eat a mouthful since the day afore yesterday. Then somebody 'ud beckon us; and p'r'aps it was a servant-gal, with enough in a dish for a man and his dawg. And the old woman 'bliged to curtchy and look pleased! They ought to have heard her! 'D— and b— 'em!' my old gal used to say between her teeth, 'I wish they had them broken wittles stuffed down their busted throats; why the —— can't they give us it in coppers!' But she couldn't say that to them, don't yer know; she had to put on a grateful mug, and say, 'Gord bless yer, my dear!' to the gal, as though, if it hadn't been for that lot of grub turning up that blessed minute, she must have dropped down dead of starvation."

"But scran fetched its price in them times, didn't it, Billy? There was drums where you might sell it long afore your time, don't you know, Billy?"

"Course I know. It fetched its price, cert'inly, when you could get away to sell it; but what I'm speaking of is the inconwenience of it. We didn't want no grub, don't you see; it was the sp'iling of us. S'pose now we was served like what I just told you; got reg'lar loaded-up when we was a couple of miles away. What was we to do? We couldn't go on a swearin' as how we was starvin' with wittles bustin' out of us all round. We was 'bliged to shoot the load afore we could begin ag'in. Sometimes we had to do the 'long trot'" (go home) "with it, and so sp'iled a whole arternoon. If we got a chance, we shot it down a gully, or in a dunghole in a mews. Anythink to get rid of it, don't you see. I should like to have just now the rattlin' lot of grub we've been 'bliged to get rid of in that there way."

Despite the decline of the trade of "shallowing," however, as the reader must have observed, it is one that is regarded as worth resorting to in "season." A more favourite "dodge" at the present is to appear before the public not in rags and tatters and with patches of naked flesh disgustingly visible, but in sound thorough labour-stained attire, and affect the style either of the ashamed unaccustomed beggar or that of the honest working mechanic, who, desperately driven by stress of poverty, shapes his loud-mouthed appeal in tones of indignant remonstrance that rich and prosperous England should permit a man such as he is to be reduced to the uncomfortable plight in which you now behold him. He is a solitary cadger, and gets himself up in a manner so artful, that it is only when you pay attention to his "speech," and find that he repeats precisely the same words over and over again, that you begin to have a suspicion that he is not exactly what he seems. Like the "shallow cove," he prefers a very cold or a very wet and miserable day. He does not enter a street walking in the middle of the road, as the common "chanting" or "pattering" beggar does; he walks on the pavement with slow and hesitating gait, and at frequent intervals casts hasty and nervous glances behind him, as though fearful that he is watched or followed. Possibly he is so afraid. At all events, should a policeman by rare chance steal round the corner, his steps will increase in length, and he will pass out of the street just as an ordinary pedestrian might; but should he be free to play his "little game," he will set about it as follows.

After looking about him several times, he proceeds to make himself remarkable to any person or persons who may happen to be gazing streetward from the window. He will stand suddenly still, and button-up his coat as though determined on some desperate action. With a loud-sounding "hem!" he clears his throat and advances towards the roadway; but, alas, before his feet touch the pavement's boundary his courage falters, and he dashes his hand across his eyes and shakes his head, in a manner that at once conveys to beholders the impression that, much as he desires it, he is unequal to the performance of what a moment ago he contemplated and thought himself strong enough to perform. At least, if this is not made manifest to the beholder, the actor has missed his object. On he goes again just a few faltering steps—a very few—and then he cries "hem!" again, louder and fiercer than before, and dashes into the middle of the road.

If you had pushed him there, or set your dog at him and he had bounded there to escape its fangs, the injured look he casts up at you could not be surpassed. He says not a word for a full minute; he simply folds his arms sternly and glares at you up at the window, as though he would say not so much "What do you think of me standing here?" as "What do you think of yourself, after having driven me to do a thing so ignominious and shameful?" These necessary preliminaries accomplished, in a loud impassioned voice he opens:

"WHAT!"—(a pause for some seconds' duration)—"WHAT! will a man not do to drive away from his door the WOLF that assails the wife of his bosom and his innocent horfspring?"

He appears to await an answer to this, as though it were a solemn conundrum; though from the moody contraction of his eyebrows and the momentary scorn that wrinkles the corners of his mouth as he still gazes all round at the windows, he seems to be aware that it is one which on account of your complete ignorance of such matters you will never guess.

"Doubtless, my friends, you are astonished to see me in this humiliating attitude, addressing you like a common beggar. But what else am I? What is the man who implores you to spare him from your plenty—ay, and your luxury—a *penny* to save from starving those that are dearer to him than his HEART'S blood, but a beggar? But, my friends, a man may be a beggar, and still be not ashamed. *I* am not ashamed. I might be, if it was for myself that I asked your charity; but I would not do so. I would die sooner than I would stoop to do it; but what is a HUSBAND to do, when he has a wife weak and ill from her confinement; who is dying by HINCHES for that nourishment that I have not to give her?" (Here a violent blowing of his nose on a clean cotton pocket-handkerchief.) "What, my dear friends, is a FATHER to do, when his little ones cry to him for BREAD? Should he feel ashamed to beg for them? Ask yourselves that question, you who have good warm fires and all that the heart can desire. I am *not* ashamed. It is a desperate man's last resource; and I ask you again, as my fellow-creatures, will you turn away from me and deny me the small assistance I beg of you?"

Generally he is successful. Women—young mothers and old mothers alike—find it hard to resist the artless allusion to the wife, "weak and ill from her confinement," and the amazingly well-acted sudden outburst of emotion that the actor is so anxious to conceal under cover of blowing his nose. To be sure he is not a prepossessing person, and his style of appeal is somewhat coarse and violent; but that stamps it, in the eyes of the unwary, as genuine. If he "knew the trade," he would know that he should be meek and insinuating, not loud-mouthed and peremptory. In short, his behaviour is exactly that of a man—a hard-working fellow when he has it to do—driven to desperation, and with a determination to raise enough to buy a loaf somehow. It would be a monstrous thing to refuse such a poor fellow because of his blunt inapt way of asking; and so the halfpence come showering down. It is several months ago since I last saw this worthy; but I have no doubt that his wife has not yet recovered from her confinement, that his children are yet crying for bread, and that he is still not ashamed to solicit public charity to save them from starving.

There are other types of the shy, blunt-spoken beggar, who affect almost to resent the charity they solicit. These abound, as indeed do all street-beggars, chiefly in the severest months of winter. As long as one can remember, gangs of men have per-ambulated the highways in the frosty months, but until recently they were invariably "chanters," with a legend of coming "all the way from Manchester." But song is eschewed in modern times. It is found better to avoid old-fashioned forms, and appear as men destitute and down-trodden perhaps, but still with self-respect remaining in them. There is no occasion for them to give you a song for your money; they are not called on to give a lengthy and humiliating explanation as to how they came there; *you* know all about it. You must have read in the newspapers, "that, owing to the many stoppages of public and private works, there are at the present time hundreds of able-bodied and deserving labouring men wandering the streets of London, driven to the hard necessity of begging their bread." Well, these are of the number. Observe the unmistakable token of their having laboured on a "public work," to wit, a railway-cutting, in the clay baked on their "ankle-jacks" and fustian trousers. Regard that able-bodied individual, the leader of the gang, with his grimy great fists and the smut still on his face, and for a moment doubt that he is a deserving labouring man. He is an engineer, out of work since last Christmas, and ever since so hard-up that he has been unable to spare a penny to buy soap with. If you don't believe it, ask him. But to this or any other detail himself or his mates will not condescend in a general way. All that they do, is to spread across the street, and saunter along with their hands in their pockets, ejaculating only, "Out of work!" "Willin' to work, and got no work to do!" If you followed them all day, you would find no change in their method of operation, excepting the interval of an hour or so at midday spent in the tap-room of a public-house. If you followed them after that, your steps in all probability would be directed towards Keate-street, Spitalfields, or Mint-street in the Borough, in both of which delightful localities common lodging-houses abound; and if you were bold enough to cross the threshold and descend into the kitchen, there you would discover the jolly crew sitting round a table, and dividing the handsome spoil of the day, while they drank "long lasting to the frost" in glasses of neat rum.

At the same time, I should be very sorry for the reader to mis-understand me, as wishing to convey to him the impression that in every instance the gangs of men to be met with in the streets in winter-time are vagrants and impostors. It is not difficult to imagine a company of hard-up poor fellows genuinely destitute; mates, perhaps, on the same kind of work, resorting to this method of raising a shilling rather than apply at the workhouse for it. An out-o'-work navvy or a bricklayer would never think of going out to beg alone, whereas he would see no great amount of degradation in joining a "gang." He thus sinks his individuality, and becomes merely a representative item of a depressed branch of industry. There can be no doubt that a sixpence given to such a man is well bestowed for the time being; but it would be much better, even though it cost many sixpences, if the labourer were never permitted to adopt this method of supplying his needs. In the majority of cases, it may be, the out-o'-work men who resorted to the streets to beg for money would, when trade improved, hurry back to work, and be heartily glad to forget to what misfortune had driven him; but there are a very large number of labourers who, at the best of times, can live but from hand to mouth as the saying is, and from whom it is desirable to keep secret how much easier money may be got by begging than working. To a man who has to drudge at the docks, for instance, for threepence an hour—and there are thousands in London who do so—it is a dangerous experience for him to discover that as much may be made on an average by sauntering the ordinary length of a street, occasionally raising his hand to his cap. Or he may know beforehand, by rumour, what a capital day's work may be done at "cadging," and in bitter sweat of underpaid labour complain that he is worse off than a cadger. It is as well to provide against giving such a man an excuse for breaking the ice.

There are, however, other impostors amongst the begging fraternity besides those who adopt the professional dress of vagrancy, and impudently endeavour publicly to proclaim their sham distress and privation. The terrible condition of want into which thousands of the working population of London were plunged the winter before last developed the "cadger" in question in a very remarkable degree. This personage is not a demonstrative cheat. His existence is due entirely to the growing belief in decent poverty, and in the conviction that in frosty "hard-up" times much more of real destitution is endured by those whose honest pride will not permit them to clamour of their wants, and so make them known. There can be no doubt but that this is perfectly true, and, despite all that horridly blunt philanthropists say to the contrary, it is a quality to be nurtured rather than despised. As everybody knows, of late years it *has* been nurtured to a very large extent. At the East-end of the town, in Poplar and Shadwell, where, owing to the slackness in the trade pertaining to the building of ships, poverty was specially prevalent, quite a small army of benevolently-disposed private individuals were daily employed going from house to house, and by personal inquiry and investigation applying the funds at their disposal quietly and delicately, and to the best of their ability judiciously. There can be no question that by these means a vast amount of good was done, and many a really decent family provided with a meal that otherwise would have gone hungry; but an alarming percentage of evil clung to the skirts of the good. It is a positive fact that in the most squalid regions—those, indeed, that were most notorious for their poverty—the value of house-property increased considerably. The occupants of apartments, who during the previous summer-time were unable to meet the weekly exactions of the collector, now not only met current demands, but by substantial instalments rapidly paid-up arrears of rent. Landlords who for months past had been glad to take what they could get, now became inexorable, and would insist on one week being paid before the next was due. They could afford to indulge in this arbitrary line of behaviour towards their tenants. Rents were "going up;" rooms that at ordinary times would realise not more than 2s. or 2s. 3d. each, now were worth 3s. 6d. Ragman's-alley and Squalor's-court and Great and Little Grime's-street were at a premium. They were localities famous in the newspapers. Everybody had read about them; everybody had heard the story of the appalling heart-rending misery that pervaded these celebrated places. Day after day gentle-folks flocked thereto, and speedily following these visitations came tradesmen's porters bearing meat and bread and groceries. To be a Squalor's-alleyite was to be a person with undoubted and indisputable claims on the public purse, and to be comfortably provided for. To be a denizen of Great Grime's-street was to reside in an almshouse more fatly endowed than the Printers' or the Drapers' or the Fishmongers'.

It was impossible for such a paradise to exist without its fame being blown to the most distant and out-of-the-way nooks of the town. North, west, and south the cadgers and impostors heard of it, and enviously itched to participate in the good things. And no wonder! Here was bread and meat and coals being furnished to all who asked for them, at the rate of twenty shillingsworth a-week at the least; nay, they were provided without even the asking for. It was unnecessary to cross the threshold of your door to look after them, for those whose happy task it was to distribute the prizes came knocking, and in the tenderest terms made offer of their assistance. All that was needful was to secure a lodging in Rag-man's-court or Little Grime's-street, and pay your rent regularly, and sit down and await the result. And lodgings were so secured. It is positively true that at the height of the "famine season" at the East-end of London, when day after day saw the columns of the daily newspapers heavily laden with the announced subscriptions of the charitable, hundreds of questionable characters, "working men" in appearance, quitted other parts of the metropolis, and cheerfully paid much more rent than they had been accustomed to pay, for the privilege of squatting down in the midst of what was loudly and incessantly proclaimed to be "a colony of helpless out-o'-works, famine-stricken, and kept from downright starvation only by the daily and hourly efforts of the charitable."

This much might of course be expected of the professed beggar and the cadger by education and breeding; but it would be inter-esting to learn how many shiftless ones—those semi-vagabonds who labour under the delusion that they are idle men only because work is denied them, and who are continually engaged in the vague occupation of "looking for a job"—gave way before the great temptation, and became downright cadgers from that time. With such folk the barrier to be broken down is of the flimsiest texture, and once overcome, it is difficult indeed to erect it again. Not sweeter to the industrious is the bread of their labour than to the idle and dissolute the loaf unearned, and the free gift of tobacco to be smoked at ease in working hours. It is terribly hard to struggle out of a slough of laziness in which a man has lain for a length of time, with nothing to do but open his mouth and permit other people to feed him. It is extremely unlikely that such a man would make the struggle while there remained but half a chance of his maintaining his comfortable position. Having grown so far used to the contamination of mire, he would be more likely to struggle a little deeper into it, if he saw what he deemed his advantage in doing so, and by swift degrees he would speedily be engulfed in that hopeless bog of confirmed beggary from which there is no return save those of the prison statician.

CHAPTER XV

Genteel Advertising Beggars.

*The Newspaper Plan and the delicate Process—Forms of Petition—Novel
Applications of Photography—Personal Attractions of the Distressed—
Help, or I perish!*

Besides those I have enumerated, there are at least two other specimens of the beggar tribe that deserve mention. They are genteel
impostors both. One avails himself of the advertising columns of
the newspaper to apprise the benevolent of his modest desires,
while the other prefers the more private and delicate process insured by our modern postal system. Both affect the "reduced
gentleman," and display in their appeals an amount of artlessness
and simple confidence in the charity of their fellow-creatures that
tells unmistakably of their ample possession of that Christian
virtue, while at the same time it conveys to the reader an idea of
the select and highly-exclusive position they should properly
occupy, and from which they have so disastrously descended. It is
evident at a glance that they know nothing of the rough-and-ready
ways of the world, or of its close-fistedness or proneness to
suspicion. We know this, and pity them; otherwise we might be
inclined to class them with those "cheeky" ones in whose praise
the young gentleman before mentioned, of "shallow" extraction,
was so hearty, and to treat their impudent attempts as they
deserve. But the touching simplicity of the unfortunate creatures
at once disarms us of suspicion. For instance, who could refrain
from immediately responding to the subjoined "petition," which
is copied strictly from the original? It was delivered through the
post, and was attached as a fly-leaf to a card on which was affixed
the portraits of six young children, each of whom had evidently
been "got up" with extreme care, as regards hair-curling and
arrangements of dress and ribbons, for the photographic process.

"*Children to save.*—Advertisement sent to a few taken from the
London Directory. The father of these British-born Protestant
children is an elderly gentleman, ruined by competition in business,

and past beginning life again; and the mother is in a very precarious state of health. To seek for adopters is against parental instinct; and besides it might ultimately come to that, as by the time their schooling is over, in ten or fifteen years, they would most likely be orphans, and their willing adopters would be quite welcome to it (*sic*). At present the father, in his alarm for the fate of these creatures, seeks for some that would pay, not to the father, but to good boarding-schools, for their clothing, keeping, and tuition, and after school-time to see that they should not want. Willing benefactors are therefore requested to state what they would feel inclined to do for each child, by one of the numbers given at foot, to 'Alphabet, till called for, at the Post-office, No. 1 Liverpool-street, Moorfields, E.C.,' enclosing card or addressed envelope to insure correct address, if a reply should be wished."

Another method of applying the photographic art to the bolstering-up of a spurious begging petition takes a form even more outrageous than that which was adopted to exhibit the personal attractions of the distressed six British-born Protestant children. In the second case it is the portrait of a handsome young lady, aged about twenty, with a profusion of lovely hair, and an expression of countenance strikingly artless and captivating. Accompanying the portrait was a note, as follows:

"Dear Sir,—I am sure, when you learn the cause, that you will pardon the liberty I take in addressing myself to you. I am impelled to do so, not only on account of your known humanity, but because I have seen you and read in your face that you will not turn a deaf ear to an appeal frankly and trustingly made to you. The fact is, my dear sir, I am absolutely in want of a sixpence to procure a meal. I am the only child of a father whom *misfortune* has reduced to a condition of abject beggary. Mother I have none. One day I may have an opportunity of narrating to you the peculiar causes of our present embarrassment. I should feel it incumbent on me to do so, were I so fortunate as to make you our creditor for a small sum. Pray spare me the pain of detailing more minutely the purport of this letter. I am aware of the boldness of the step I am taking, but the misery of my wretched father must plead for me in excuse. I enclose my likeness (taken, alas, in happier times, though scarcely six months since), so that you may see that I am not a *common beggar*. Should my appeal move your compassion towards me, will you kindly send a note addressed, Adelaide F. T., Post-office, —?"

The gentleman to whom the above artful concoction was addressed is well known for his philanthropy, and his name appears frequently in the newspapers. He is an elderly gentleman, and has grown-up sons and daughters, consequently he was not a likely person to be trapped by the lovely Adelaide, who would "feel it incumbent on her to seek out and personally thank her benefactor," in the event of his forwarding to her a pound or so. But it might have been different, if, instead of a plain-sailing shrewd man of the world, he had been a person afflicted with vanity. Here was this poor young handsome creature, who had seen him and read in his face that which induced her to make to him such a pitiful avowal of her poverty—her *peculiar* poverty! Why, the story of the "peculiar cause" that led to the sudden downfall of such a family must be worth a pound to listen to! Was it justifiable to dishonour the promise his face had assured to the poor young woman? These or similar reflections might have betrayed the better judgment of a less experienced person than Mr. L—. As it was, the artful note served but to ponder over as one of the latest curiosities in the begging-letter line; while as for the portrait, it furnished ample food for moralising on how marvellously deceptive appearances were—especially female appearances.

And if this were the end of the story, the good reader, with all his honest British inclination for giving the accused the benefit of a doubt, might be tempted to exclaim, "And, after all, who knows but that the appeal to this known philanthropist might have been genuine? To be sure, the shape it assumed was one that might well excite the suspicion of an individual alive to the surpassing cleverness and cunning of begging impostors; but at the same time there was sufficient of probability in the application to protect it from the stigma of impudent fraud." Such readers will be glad to hear that all doubts on the matter were set at rest, and in the following singular, and for one party concerned somewhat unpleasant, manner. The portrait in question fell into the hands of a relative of Mr. L—, a gentleman with a hard heart for begging impostors, and sturdy resolution to put them down and punish them whenever he encountered them. He was particularly set against mendicants of the genteel class, and was very severe in his strictures on the abominable cheat attempted by "Adelaide F. T." One afternoon, while walking along Oxford-street, lo, the original of the pictured culprit appeared before him, artlessly and innocently gazing into a linendraper's window, and accompanied by another lady. The resemblance between the first lady and the photograph was so striking as to place her identity beyond a doubt; yet in order to make *quite* sure, our friend withdrew the latter from his pocket-book, and covertly compared it with the original. It was as certain as that he had eyes in his head. There was the hair of golden hue massed behind and raised from the temples; there was the straight nose, the small winning mouth, and the delicately-rounded chin. The stern exposer of imposture, however, was not to be moved to mercy by a pretty face; his course of duty was plain before him, and stepping up to the lady, he addressed with undisguised severity, "Miss Adelaide T., I believe?" "You are mistaken, sir." "Not at all, madam; a friend of mine was lately favoured with a letter from you enclosing your likeness." It was scarcely to be wondered at, that an expression of terror took possession of the lady's face, though it was misinterpreted by the gentleman. Thinking that she was addressed by a drunken man or a maniac, the lady prudently retreated into the shop the window of which she had been regarding. More than ever convinced that he was not mistaken, L—'s friend followed her; and goodness knows what serious consequences might have ensued, had not the lady been a known customer of the draper as the daughter of a gentleman of wealth and station. This, of course, led to an explanation, and to the most earnest and humble apologies on the part of the pursuer of imposture. The photograph was produced, and undoubtedly it was a likeness of the lady. How it had got into the hands of the designing "Adelaide F. T." no one could tell, but doubtless it was selected on account of its beauty and prepossessing artlessness. An endeavour was made to secure the cheats; but from some cause or another they took alarm, and the decoy letter, addressed "Postoffice ——," remained there until it was returned through the Dead-letter Office.

By the bye, the idea of begging "not for myself, but for another," is a dodge not confined to the epistolary impostor. In the neighbourhood in which I reside, some little time since there made her appearance a very fine specimen of disinterested generosity of the kind in question: a little old lady dressed in black, with kid-gloves on her hands, and a cloak soberly trimmed with black crape. She knocked the knock of a person used to the genteel fingering of a knocker, and might she be permitted to speak with the lady of the house? It happened that, at that moment, the gentleman of the house was going out, and he, hearing the application, suggested that possibly he might do as well. Undoubtedly, though it was a trivial matter with which to occupy the attention of a gentleman. The simple fact was, that the little old lady was bound on a mission of charity for a poor soul recently left destitute with nine small children: her aim being the purchase of a mangle and a few washing-tubs, that the widow might earn an honourable livelihood for her numerous brood. "I am too poor to supply her with *all* the money out of my own slender little purse," said the old lady, "but I have plenty of leisure, and I think that you will agree with me, sir, it cannot be employed more worthily. I do not ask for any large sum on the poor creature's behalf; I only ask one single penny. I will not take more than a penny. I put the pence in this little bag, you see, and by perseverance I trust that I shall soon accomplish my aim." As the little old lady spoke, she cheerfully produced from the folds of her cloak a stout linen bag heavy with copper money, and containing, I should say, at least twelve shillings. The little old lady's manner was plausible and smooth, and well calculated to impose on the "lady of the house" nine times out of ten. But unfortunately for her it had been my lot to make the acquaintance of many strange little old ladies as well as of gentlemen, and I had my suspicions. I closed the outer door and confronted her on the mat. "I beg your pardeon, but have we not met before?" I asked her. She looked up suddenly and sharply, with no little alarm on her wizened old face. "I—I think not, sir," she faltered. "Do you happen to know a gentleman named Horsford?" was my next inquiry. The little old lady looked still more embarrassed. "I did not come here to discuss my own affairs, sir," said she with a sorry affectation of indignation, "nor to answer questions that bear no relation to my charitable object. I wish you a good-morning, sir!" And with that she opened the door, and let herself out; and descending the steps quickly, trotted up the street with guilty speed, and turned the corner, and was out of sight before I could make up my mind what to do with her.

Of advertising beggars there is a large variety. A great many of them breathe a pious spirit, or rather gasp;—for it is seldom that these distressed ones muster courage to cry out until they have endured their distress even to death's-door. Not unfrequently the headings or "catch-lines" of these printed appeals are culled from the Bible. Here is one, for example:

"'HELP, OR I PERISH!'—The advertiser (in his sixty-seventh birthday) was once blessed with a handsome fortune. Drink—he confesses it—has been the cause of his ruin. He still drinks; not now for pleasure and in luxury, but to benumb the gnawing of an aroused conscience. Unless this horrid propensity is checked, the advertiser feels that he must perish body and soul! Who will save him? He has two sons in Canada, who are striving men and total abstainers, and who would receive him with open arms, could he but raise money enough to purchase some poor outfit, and to pay for the voyage.—Address, X., Prescott-street, Whitechapel."

One cannot help reflecting, that, before contributing towards a fund to assist the emigration of the aged toper—who appears only to have awoke to a sense of his abasement now that he is stinted of his gin—he would like to have the opinion of those striving men, his sons, the total abstainers in Canada. Possibly they would prefer to honour him at a distance. According to the ingenious old gentleman's own showing, he only regards his sons as possible props to keep him out of a drunkard's grave; and if, fettered under the weight imposed on them, they sank with their father into the same dishonourable sepulchre, it would turn out to be money decidedly ill invested. All this, supposing the appeal to be genuine, which in all probability it is not. Were it investigated, the only truthful bit in the appeal would very likely be found to consist in the three words, "he still drinks."

Here is another of more recent date, in the emigration line:

"A lady has an opportunity of going to America, where she could obtain a good situation as governess, but has not the means of procuring an outfit. She would be very thankful to anyone who would lend her 10*l.*, which she would promise to return with interest at the end of the year."

This is cool, but almost feverish compared with the annexed:

"'MONEY WITHOUT SECURITY!'—Doubtless these mocking words have struck many readers besides the advertiser. In his desperate situation he has often put to himself the question, Is there to be found in this cruel world a good Samaritan who would confer on a fellow-creature a boon so precious? Is there one who, blessed with means, can find delight in raising from the slough of despond a poor wretch stranded on the bank of the black river of despair? Is there one who will account it cheap by *lending* ten pounds, for three months, at twenty-five per cent interest, to elevate to manly altitude a human creature who, for want of such a sum, is groaning in the dust? If so, let him send a Beam of Sunshine to G. S. R., No. 17 Model Lodging Houses, ——."

One cannot but ask the question, is G. S. R. a madman, or simply an idiot, who can regard it as a "joke" to waste five shillings for the privilege of seeing so many lines of empty rubbish in print? Or, again, are there really any grounds of five shillingsworth for supposing that amongst the fifty thousand readers of a daily newspaper one may be met with silly or eccentric or whimsical enough to entertain G. S. R.'s proposition? It is hard to believe in such a possibility. Still, there *are* strange people in the world; every day furnishes evidence of this fact. Not more than a month ago it came to light that an old lady residing at Clapham has for

years past been in the habit of paying an organ-grinder thirty
shillings a-week—a half-sovereign on the evening of every Tuesday,
Thursday, and Saturday—to come and play for half-an-hour under
her window. Supposing a rupture between the lady and her musi-
cian, and she had put an advertisement in the *Times*—"A lady, a
resident in a quiet suburb, is desirous of engaging with an organ-
grinder. Terms of service, three half-hours per week, 75*l*. a-year"—
who would have regarded it but as a silly joke?

There is another begging advertisement of the simple and affecting type:

"A WIDOW'S ONLY COMFORT.—The advertiser begs the kind
assistance of the kind-hearted and benevolent to rescue her piano-
forte from the hands of the broker. It is but a poor old affair
(valued only at 12*l*.), but it has been her only consolation and
solace since the death of a darling only daughter, whose instrument it was, and it would break her heart to part with it. Its music
and her prayers should combine to thank anyone who was generous enough to restore it to her. Address —— Colebrook-row."

One more instance, and we will have done with the advertising
beggar:

"TO THE AGED AND UNPROTECTED.—A young man, aged
twenty-two, well-built, good-looking, and of a frank and affectionate disposition, is desirous of acting the part of a son towards
any aged person or persons who would regard his companionship
and constant devotion as an equivalent for his maintenance and
clothes and support generally. The parents of the advertiser are
both dead, and he has not a relative in the wide world. Affluence
is not aimed at, no more than that degree of comfort that moderate means insure. Address, O. D., ——."

Although it is difficult without a struggle to feel an interest in
this young gentleman's welfare, we cannot help feeling curious to
know what success his advertisement brought him. Is he still a forlorn orphan, wasting his many virtues and manly attributes on a
world that to him is a wilderness; or has he happily succeeded in
captivating "some aged person or persons," and is he at the
present time acting the part of a son towards them, and growing
sleek and fat "on that degree of comfort that moderate means
insure"? Were his initials J. D. instead of O. D., we might imagine
that it was our ancient friend Jeremiah Diddler turned up once
more. O. D. stand for Old Diddler, but Jeremiah the ancient must
be aged considerably more than twenty-two. We may rest assured,
however, that the advertiser is an offshoot of that venerable
family.

IV.

FALLEN WOMEN.

This Curse.

The only explanation that can be offered to the supersensitive reader, who will doubtless experience a shock of alarm at discovering this Part's heading, is, that it would be simply impossible to treat with any pretension to completeness of the curses of London without including it.

Doubtless it is a curse, the mere mention of which, let alone its investigation, the delicate-minded naturally shrinks from. But it is a matter for congratulation, perhaps, that we are not all so delicate-minded. Cowardice is not unfrequently mistaken for daintiness of nature. It is so with the subject in question. It is not a pleasant subject—very far from it; but that is not a sufficient excuse for letting it alone. We should never forget that it is our distaste for meddling with unsavoury business that does not immediately and personally concern us, that is the evil-doers' armour of impunity. The monstrous evil in question has grown to its present dimensions chiefly because we have silently borne with it and let it grow up in all its lusty rankness under our noses; and rather than pluck it up by the roots, rather than acknowledge its existence even, have turned away our heads and inclined our eyes skyward, and thanked God for the many mercies conferred on us.

And here the writer hastens to confess, not without a tingling sense of cowardice too, perhaps, that it is not his intention to expose this terrible canker that preys on the heart and vitals of society in all its plain and bare repulsiveness. Undoubtedly it is better at all times to conceal from the public gaze as much as may be safely hid of the blotches and plague-spots that afflict the social body; but if to hide them, and cast white cloths over them, and sprinkle them with rose-water answers no other purpose (beyond conciliating the squeamish) than to encourage festering and decay, why then it becomes a pity that the whole foul matter may not be brought fairly to board, to be dealt with according to the best of our sanitary knowledge.

The saving, as well as the chastening, hand of the law should be held out to the countless host that constitute what is acknowledged as emphatically *the* social evil. It has been urged, that "to take this species of vice under legal regulation is to give it, in the public eye, a species of legal sanction." Ministers from the pulpit have preached that "it can never be right to regulate what it is wrong to do and wrong to tolerate. To license immorality is to protect and encourage it. Individuals and houses which have a place on the public registers naturally regard themselves, and are regarded by others, as being under the law's guardianship and authority,—not, as they ought to be, under its ban and repression."

Against this grim and essentially unchristian doctrine, let us set the argument of a learned and brilliant writer, who some years since was courageous enough to shed a little wholesome light on this ugly subject, from the pages of a popular magazine.

"It is urged that the 'tacit sanction' given to vice, by such a *recognition* of prostitution as would be involved in a system of supervision, registration, or license, would be a greater evil than all the maladies (moral and physical) which now flow from its unchecked prevalence. But let it be considered that by ignoring we do not abolish it, we do not even conceal it; it speaks aloud; it walks abroad; it is a vice as patent and as well-known as drunkenness; it is already 'tacitly sanctioned' by the mere fact of its permitted, or connived-at, existence; by the very circumstance which stares us in the face, that the legislative and executive authorities, seeing it, deploring it, yet confess by their inaction their inability to check it, and their unwillingness to prohibit it, and virtually say to the unfortunate prostitutes and their frequenters, 'As long as you create no public scandal, but throw a decent veil over your proceedings, we shall not interfere with you, but shall regard you as an inevitable evil.' By an attempt to regulate and control them, the authorities would confess nothing more than they already in act acknowledge, viz. their desire to mitigate an evil which they have discovered their incompetency to suppress. By prohibiting the practice of prostitution *under certain conditions,* they do not legalise or authorise it under all other conditions; they simply announce that, *under these certain conditions,* they feel called upon promptly to interfere. The legislature does not forbid drunkenness, knowing that it would be futile to do so: but if a man, when drunk, is disorderly, pugnacious, or indecent, or in other mode compromises public comfort or public morals, it steps forward to arrest and punish him; yet surely by no fair use of words can it be represented as thereby sanctioning drunkenness when unaccompanied by indecorous or riotous behaviour, for it merely declares that in the one case interference falls within its functions, and that in the other case it does not."

No living writer, however, *dare* bring the subject before the public as it should be brought. A penman bolder than his brethren has but to raise the curtain that conceals the thousand-and-one abominations that find growth in this magnificent city of ours, but an inch higher than "decorum" permits, than the eyes of outraged modesty immediately take refuge behind her pocket-handkerchief, and society at large is aghast at the man's audacity, not to say "indecency." Warned by the fate of such daring ones, therefore, it shall be the writer's care to avoid all startling revelations, and the painting of pictures in their real colours, and to confine himself to plain black-and-white inoffensive enumerations and descriptions, placing the plain facts and figures before the reader, that he may deal with them according to his conscience.

It should incline us to a merciful consideration of the fallen-woman when we reflect on the monotony of misery her existence is. She is to herself vile, and she has no other resource but to flee to the gin-measure, and therein hide herself from herself. She has no pleasure even. Never was there made a grimmer joke than that which designates her life a short and *merry* one. True, she is found at places where amusement and wild reckless gaiety is sought; but does she ever appear amused, or, while she remains sober, reckless-ly gay? I am not now alluding to the low prostitute, the con-scienceless wretch who wallows in vice and mire and strong liquor in a back street of Shadwell, but to the woman of some breeding and delicacy, the "well-dressed" creature, in fact, who does not habitually "walk the streets," but betakes herself to places of popular resort for persons of a "fast" turn, and who have money, and are desirous of expending some of it in "seeing life." Such a woman would be a frequent visitant at the Argyll Rooms, for instance; let us turn to Mr. Acton, and see how vastly she enjoys herself there.

"The most striking thing to me about the place was an upper gallery fringed with this sort of company. A sprinkling of each class seemed to be there by assignation, and with no idea of seek-ing acquaintances. A number of both sexes, again, were evidently visitors for distraction's sake alone; the rest were to all intents and purposes in quest of intrigues.

"The utter indifference of the stylish loungers in these shambles contrasted painfully with the anxious countenances of the many unnoticed women whom the improved manners of the time by no means permit to make advances. I noticed some very sad eyes, that gave the lie to laughing lips, as they wandered round in search of some familiar face in hope of friendly greeting. There was the sly triumph of here and there a vixenish hoyden with her leash of patrons about her, and the same envy, hatred, and malice of the neglected 'has-been' that some have thought they saw in everyday society. The glory of the ascendant harlot was no plainer than the discomfiture of her sister out of luck, whom want of elbow-room and excitement threw back upon her vacant self. The affectation of reserve and gentility that pervaded the pens of that upper region seemed to me but to lay more bare the skeleton; and I thought, as I circulated among the promiscuous herd to ground-lings, that the sixpenny balcony would better serve to point a moral than the somewhat more natural, and at all events far more hilarious, throng about me. As far as regarded public order, it seemed an admirable arrangement; to the proprietor of the rooms, profitable; of most of its cribbed and cabined occupants, a voluntary martyrdom; in all of them, in making more plain their folly and misfortunes, a mistake.

"The great mass of the general company were on that occasion males—young, middle-aged, and old, married and single, of every shade of rank and respectability; and of these again the majority seemed to have no other aim than to kill an hour or two in philosophising, staring at one another and the women about them, and listening to good music, without a thought of dancing or intention of ultimate dissipation. A few had come with companions of our sex to dance, and many had paid their shillings on speculation only. Some pretty grisettes had been brought by their lovers to be seen and to see; and once or twice I thought I saw 'a sunbeam that had lost its way,' where a modest young girl was being paraded by a foolish swain, or indoctrinated into the charms of town by a designing scamp. There were plenty of dancers, and the casual polka was often enough, by mutual consent, the beginning and end of the acquaintance. There was little appearance of refreshment or solicitation, and none whatever of ill-behaviour or drunkenness. It was clear that two rills of population had met in Windmill-street—one idle and vicious by profession or inclination, the other idle for a few hours on compulsion. Between them there was little amalgamation. A few dozen couples of the former, had there been no casino, would have concocted their amours in the thoroughfares; the crowd who formed the other seemed to seek the place with no definite views beyond light music and shelter. Many, whose thorough British gravity was proof against more than all the meretriciousness of the assembly, would, I fancy, have been there had it been confined to males only. I am convinced they were open to neither flirtation nor temptation, and I know enough of my countryman's general taste to affirm that they ran little hazard of the latter."

Again, Cremorne Gardens "in the season" would seem a likely place to seek the siren devoted to a life mirthful though brief. Let us again accompany Mr. Acton.

"As calico and merry respectability tailed off eastward by penny steamers, the setting sun brought westward hansoms freighted with demure immorality in silk and fine linen. By about ten o'clock age and innocence—of whom there had been much in the place that day—had retired, weary of amusement, leaving the massive elms, the grass-plots, and the geranium-beds, the kiosks, temples, 'monster platforms,' and 'crystal circle' of Cremorne to flicker in the thousand gaslights there for the gratification of the dancing public only. On and around that platform waltzed, strolled, and fed some thousand souls, perhaps seven hundred of them men of the upper and middle class, the remainder prostitutes more or less *pronouncées*. I suppose that a hundred couples—partly old acquaintances, part improvised—were engaged in dancing and other amusements, and the rest of the society, myself included, circulated listlessly about the garden, and enjoyed in a grim kind of way the 'selection' from some favourite opera and the cool night breeze from the river.

"The extent of disillusion he has purchased in this world comes forcibly home to the middle-aged man who in such a scene attempts to fathom former faith and ancient joys, and perhaps even vainly to fancy he might by some possibility begin again. I saw scores, nay hundreds, about me in the same position as myself. We were there, and some of us, I feel sure, hardly knew why; but being there, and it being obviously impossible to enjoy the place after the manner of youth, it was necessary, I suppose, to chew the cud of sweet and bitter fancies; and then so little pleasure came, that the Britannic solidity waxed solider than ever even in a garden full of music and dancing, and so an almost mute procession, not of joyous revellers, but thoughtful careworn men and women, paced round and round the platform as on a horizontal treadmill. There was now and then a bare recognition between passers-by: they seemed to touch and go like ants in the hurry of business. I do not imagine for a moment they could have been aware that a self-appointed inspector was among them; but, had they known it never so well, the intercourse of the sexes could hardly have been more reserved—*as a general rule,* be it always understood. For my part I was occupied, when the first chill of change was shaken off, in quest of noise, disorder, debauchery, and bad manners. Hopeless task! The picnic at Burnham Beeches, that showed no more life and merriment than Cremorne on the night and time above mentioned, would be a failure indeed, unless the company were antiquarians or undertakers. A jolly burst of laughter now and then came bounding through the crowd that fringed the dancing-floor and roved about the adjacent sheds in search of company; but that gone by, you heard very plain the sigh of the poplar, the surging gossip of the tulip-tree, and the plash of the little embowered fountain that served two plaster children for an endless shower-bath. The function of the very band appeared to be to drown not noise, but stillness."

CHAPTER XVII.

The Plain Facts and Figures of Prostitution.

Statistics of Westminster, Brompton, and Pimlico—Methods of conducting the nefarious Business—Aristocratic Dens—The High Tariff—The Horrors of he Social Evil—The Broken Bridge behind the Sinner—"Dress Lodgers" —There's always a "Watcher"—Soldiers and Sailors—The "Wrens of the Curragh."

Let us in the first place consider the extent to which the terrible malady in question afflicts us. I am not aware if more recent returns have been made than those I have at hand. Were it possible to obtain exact statistics of this as of almost every other branch of social economy, I should have been at the trouble of inquiring for them further than I have; but I find that the calculations made differ so widely one from the other, and are, as a whole, so irreconcilable with probability, that it will be better to take an authentic return, albeit ten years old, and make allowance for time since. The Metropolitan-Police authorities are responsible for the accompanying figures.

It appears that at the date above indicated there were within the Metropolitan-Police district the enormous number of 8600 prostitutes, and they were distributed as follows:

	Brothels.		Prostitutes.
Within the districts of Westminster, Brompton, and Pimlico, there are	153	..	524
St. James, Regent-street, Soho, Leicester-square	152	..	318
Marylebone, Paddington, St. John's-wood ..	139	..	526
Oxford-street, Portland-place, New-road, Gray's-inn-lane	194	..	546
Covent-garden, Drury-lane, St. Giles's	45	..	480
Clerkenwell, Pentonville, City-road, Shoreditch	152	..	349
Spitalfields, Houndsditch, Whitechapel, Ratcliff	471	..	1803

179

Bethnal-green, Mile-end, Shadwell to Blackwall	419 ..	965
Lambeth, Blackfriars, Waterloo-road	377 ..	802
Southwark, Bermondsey, Rotherhithe	178 ..	667
Islington, Hackney, Homerton	185 ..	445
Camberwell, Walworth, Peckham	65 ..	228
Deptford and Greenwich	148 ..	401
Kilburn, Portland, Kentish, and Camden Towns	88 ..	231
Kensington, Hammersmith, Fulham	12 ..	106
Walham-green, Chelsea, Cremorne	47 ..	209

Without entering into repulsive detail, I will endeavour to give the reader some idea of the different methods under which the nefarious business is conducted. The "houses of ill-fame" differ as widely in the extent and quality of their dealings as the houses of honesty and fair commerce. There are houses of "ill-fame" in the most fashionable quarters of the town, just as there are in Wapping —houses that are let and sub-let until they reach a rental as high as three and four hundred pounds a-year. It is not in those aristocratic dens of infamy, however, that women suffer most; none but the most costly wares are on sale at such establishments, and it is to the interest of the hucksters who traffic in them to deal with them delicately as circumstances will permit, to humour and coax and caress them as pet animals are coaxed and humoured. Nor would the creatures themselves tolerate anything in the shape of brutal treatment at the hands of those who harbour them. They "know their value," and as a rule are exacting, imperious, and insolent towards their "landlords." Unlike their sister unfortunates lower sunk in iniquity, they would experience no difficulty in procuring new "lodgings." The doors of a hundred establishments such as that she now honours with residence are open to her. With a handsome face and a full purse, the whole of the devilish crew of brothel-keepers are her slaves, her fawning, cringing slaves, ready to lick the dust from her shoes, so that she pays regularly her rent of ten guineas a-week, and fails not to induce her "friends" to drink champagne at a guinea a bottle.

Possibly the gay lady may come to the "bitter end" some day, but at present, except from the moral point of view, she is not an object for commiseration. She at least has all that she deliberately bargains for—fine clothes, rich food, plenty of money, a carriage to ride in, the slave-like obedience of her "inferiors," and the fulsome adulation of those who deal with her for her worth. Very often (though under the circumstances it is doubtful if from any aspect this is an advantage) she finds a fool with money who is willing to marry her; but whether she is content to accept the decent change, and to abide by it, of course depends on her nature. Whether her husband adheres to his rash bargain is a question that time only can solve. He at least, if he be a vicious man as well as a fool, may argue that she will be little the worse than when he found her if he leaves her; while possibly she may gather consolation from the same method of argument.

Anyway, she has a long way to descend before she may be branded as "common." At present she is not even included in the police-returns. Any blue-coated guardian of the peace, in humble hope of earning a sixpence, would be only too eager to touch his hat to her and open her carriage-door to-morrow, and that even at the door of her genteel residence, which is in a neighbourhood much too respectable to permit it to be stigmatised as a "brothel."

The police-report just quoted specifies that the 8600 prostitutes infesting the metropolis include 921 well-dressed and living in houses of ill-fame. This on the face of it, however, is significant of how very little the police really know of the matter they venture to report on. The women here alluded to are of the unobtrusive and orderly sort, the mainstay of whose occupation is to pass as respectable persons. They would be the last to resort for permanent lodging at houses whose fame was so ill that the greenest police-man on beat could point them out. It is altogether too hard to fasten the imputation of infamous on the holders of the houses in which this class of unfortunate seeks lodging. In very many cases the women are actuated by a twofold reason in gaining admission to the house of a householder who does not suspect her real character. In the first place, and as already stated, she wishes to pass in the immediate neighbourhood as respectable; and in the next place she not unnaturally seeks to evade payment of the monstrously high rate of rent that the common brothel-keeper would impose on her. Moreover, the peculiar branch of the terrible business she essays prospers under such management, where it would not if it were otherwise conducted. As a body, the women in question must be regarded as human creatures who have not gone *altogether* to the bad; and though in grim truth it may be in the highest degree absurd for anyone to cast herself deliberately into a sea of abomination, and then to affect a mincing manner of seriousness, much allowance should be made for the possibility that the fatal leap was not taken with cool forethought, or that the urging to it was due to some devilish genius whom there was no resisting. Anyhow, it would be hard on them, poor wretches, to compel them to give up their endeavours to conceal their degradation if, apart from mercenary motives, they are heartily desirous of concealing it.

"A vast proportion of those who, after passing through the career of kept mistresses, ultimately come upon the town, fall in the first instance from a mere exaggeration and perversion of one of the best qualities of a woman's heart. They yield to desires in which they do not share, from a weak generosity which cannot refuse anything to the passionate entreaties of the man they love. There is in the warm fond heart of woman a strange and sublime unselfishness, which men too commonly discover only to profit by,—a positive love of self-sacrifice, an active, so to speak, an *aggressive* desire to show their affection by giving up to those who have won it something they hold very dear. It is an unreasoning and dangerous yearning of the spirit, precisely analogous to that which prompts the surrenders and self-tortures of the religious devotee. Both seek to prove their devotion to the idol they have enshrined, by casting down before his altar their richest and most cherished treasures. This is no romantic or over-coloured picture; those who deem it so have not known the better portion of the sex, or do not deserve to have known them."

It would soften the hearts of many, and hold the hands of those who would break down the bridge behind the sinner, could they know the awful misery that frequently attends the life of a fallen woman. The 921 questionably quoted as "well dressed, and living in houses of ill-fame," do not at all represent the horrors of the social evil in all its ghastly integrity. Such women are at least free to a certain extent to act as they please. No restriction is set on their movements; they may remain at home or go abroad, dress as they please, and expend their miserable gains according to their fancy. But they have sisters in misfortune to whom the smallest of these privileges is denied. They are to be found amongst the unhappy 2216 who are described as "well dressed, and walking the streets." Unlike the gay lady, who makes her downy nest in the top-most branches of the deadly upas-tree, and is altogether above suspicion or vulgar reproach, this poor wretch is without a single possession in the wide world. She is but one of a thousand walking the streets of London, the most cruelly used and oppressed of all the great family to which they own relationship. They are bound hand and foot to the harpies who are their keepers. They are infinitely worse off than the female slaves on a nigger-plantation, for they at least may claim as their own the rags they wear, as well as a share of the miserable hut common to the gang after working-hours. But these slaves of the London pavement may boast of neither soul nor body, nor the gaudy skirts and laces and ribbons with which they are festooned. They belong utterly and entirely to the devil in human shape who owns the den that the wretched harlot learns to call her "home." You would never dream of the deplorable depth of her destitution, if you met her in her gay attire. Splendid from her tasselled boots to the full-blown and flowery hat or bonnet that crowns her guilty head, she is absolutely poorer than the meanest beggar that ever whined for a crust.

These women are known as "dress lodgers." They are poor wretches who somehow or another are reduced to the lowest depths of destitution. Sometimes illness is the cause. Sometimes, if a girl gets into a bad house, and is as yet too new to the horrible business to conform without remonstrance to the scandalous extortions practised by the brothel-keeper, she is "broken down and brought to it" by design and scheming. A girl not long since confided to a clergyman friend of mine the following shocking story. Rendered desperate by the threats of the wretch who owned her, she applied to him for advice. "I was bad enough before, I don't deny it; but I wasn't a thief. I hadn't been used to their ways for more than a month, and had a good box of clothes and a silver watch and gold chain, when I went to lodge there, and it was all very well while I spent my money like a fool, bought gin, and treated 'em all round; but when I wouldn't stand it any longer, and told her (the brothel-keeper) plain that I would pay her the rent and no more (nine shillings a-week for a small back room), she swore that she'd break me down, and 'bring me to her weight.' I didn't know that at the time; I didn't hear of it till afterwards. She was fair enough to my face, and begged me not to leave her, flattering me, and telling me she would be ruined when her customers found out that the prettiest woman had left her. That's how she quieted me, till one day, when I came home, she accused me of robbing a gentleman the night before of a diamond shirt-pin, and there was a fellow there who said he was a 'detective,' and though my box was locked he had opened it before I came home, and swore that he had found the pin, which he showed me. It was all a lie. I had been with a gentleman the night before, but he wore a scarf with a ring to it; that I could swear to. But it was no use saying anything; I was the thief, they said, and I was to be taken into custody. What was I to do? I begged of the detective not to take me; I implored Mother H— to intercede for me, and she pretended to. She went into another room with the detective, and then she came back and told me that the man would take ten pounds down to hush it up. I've seen that man since; he is a 'bully' at a bad house in the Waterloo-road, but I truly believed that he was a private-clothes policeman, as he said he was. Of course I didn't have ten pounds, nor ten shillings hardly; but Mother H— said that she would lend the money 'on security;' and I made over to her—sold to her, in fact—in writing, every scrap of clothes that I had in my box and on my back. 'Let's have them too, Meg,' Mother H— said, 'and then you're safe not to run away.' I made over to her the box as well, and my watch, and gave her an IOU besides for five pounds, and then she 'squared' it with the detective, and he went off.

"That's how I came to be a 'dress lodger.' She didn't wait long before she opened her mind to me. She up and told me that very night: 'You've got a new landlady now, my fine madam,' said she; 'you've got to *work* for your living now; to work for *me*, d'ye understand? You can't work—can't earn a penny without you dress spicy, and every rag you've got on is *mine*; and if you say one wry word, I'll have 'em off and bundle you out.' So what could I do or say?" continued the poor wretch, tears streaming down her really handsome face; "all the girls there were 'dress lodgers,' and I believe that they were glad to see me brought to their level. They only laughed to hear Mother H— go on so. I've been a 'dress lodger' ever since, not being able to get a shilling for myself, for she takes away all I get, and besides is always threatening to strip me and turn me out, and to sue me for the five pounds I owe her."

My informant asked her, "How does she exercise this amount of control over you? She is not always with you; you leave her house to walk the streets, I suppose?"

"So I do, but not alone. Dress lodgers are never allowed to do that, sir. I haven't been one long, but long enough to find that out. There's always a 'watcher.' Sometimes it's a woman—an old woman, who isn't fit for anything else—but in general it's a man. He watches you always, walking behind you, or on the opposite side of the way. He never loses sight of you, never fear. You daren't so much as go into a public for a drain of gin but he is in after you in a minute, and must have his glass too, though he isn't allowed to do it—to have the gin, I mean; and *you* ain't allowed it either, not a drop, if the old woman knows it. You're supposed to walk about and look for your living, and the watcher is supposed to see that you do do it—to take care that you look sharp, and above all that you don't take customers anywhere but *home*. And what do you get for it all? You're half fed, and bullied day and night, and threatened to be stripped and turned out; and when you're at home, the watcher is generally hanging about, and he'll 'down' you with a 'one'r' in the back or side (he won't hit you in the face, for fear of spoiling it) if Mother H— only gives him the wink, though perhaps you've risked getting into trouble, and stood many a glass of gin to him the night before."

It is difficult, indeed, to imagine a human creature more deplorably circumstanced than the one whose sad story is above narrated, and who is only "one of a thousand." There are those of the sisterhood who appear in a more hideous shape, as, for instance, the horde of human tigresses who swarm in the pestilent dens by the riverside at Ratcliff and Shadwell. These may have fallen lower in depravity, indeed they are herded in the very mud and ooze of it, but they do not *suffer* as the gaily-bedizened "dress lodger" does. They are almost past human feeling. Except when they are ill and in hospital, they are never sober. As soon as her eyes are open in the morning, the she-creature of "Tiger Bay" seeks to cool her parched mouth out of the gin-bottle; and " — your eyes, let us have some more gin!" is the prayer she nightly utters before she staggers to her straw, to snore like the worse than pig she is.

Soldiers' women are different from sailors' women. As a rule, they are much more decent in appearance, and they are insured against habits of bestial intoxication by the slender resources of the men on whose bounty they depend. It is not possible to dip very deeply into the wine-cup or even the porter-pot on an income of about fourpence-halfpenny per diem, and it painfully illustrates what a wretched trade prostitution may become that it is driven even to the barracks.

Beyond the barracks; out on to the wild bleak common, where, winter and summer, the military tents are pitched.

A year or so since there appeared in the pages of the *Pall Mall Gazette* three graphic and astounding letters concerning the dreadful condition of a colony of women who "squatted" amongst the furze of Curragh Common, and subsisted on such miserable wage as the soldiers there quartered could afford to pay them. These creatures are known in and about the great military camp and its neighbourhood as "wrens." They do not live in houses, or even huts, but build for themselves "nests" in the bush. To quote the words of the writer in question, these nests "have an interior space of about nine feet long by seven feet broad; and the roof is not more than four and a half feet from the ground. You crouch into them as beasts crouch into cover, and there is no standing upright till you crawl out again. They are rough misshapen domes of furze, like big rude birds'-nests, compacted of harsh branches, and turned topsy-turvy upon the ground. The walls are some twenty inches thick, and they do get pretty well compacted—much more than would be imagined. There is no chimney—not even a hole in the roof, which generally slopes forward. The smoke of the turf-fire which burns on the floor of the hut has to pass out at the door when the wind is favourable, and to reek slowly through the crannied walls when it is not. The door is a narrow opening, nearly the height of the structure—a slit in it, kept open by two rude posts, which also serve to support the roof. To keep it down and secure from the winds that drive over the Curragh so furiously, sods of earth are placed on top, here and there, with a piece of corrugated iron (much used in the camp, apparently—I saw many old and waste pieces lying about) as an additional protection from rain. Sometimes a piece of this iron is placed in the longitudinal slit aforesaid, and then you have a door as well as a doorway. Flooring there is none of any kind whatever, nor any attempt to make the den snugger by burrowing down into the bosom of the earth. The process of construction seems to be to clear the turf from the surface of the plain to the required space, to cut down some bushes for building material, and to call in a friendly soldier or two to rear the walls by the simple process of piling and tramp-ling. When the nest is newly made, as that one was which I first examined, and if you happen to view it on a hot day, no doubt it seems tolerably snug shelter. A sportsman might lie there for a night or two without detriment to his health or his moral nature. But all the nests are not newly made; and if the sun shines on the Curragh, bitter winds drive across it, with swamping rains for days and weeks together, and miles of snow-covered plain sometimes lie between this wretched colony of abandoned women and the nearest town. Wind and rain are their worst enemies (unless we reckon-in mankind) and play 'old gooseberry' with the bush-dwellings. The beating of the one and the pelting of the other soon destroy their bowery summery aspect. They get crazy, they fall toward this side and that, they shrink in and down upon the out-cast wretches that huddle in them, and the doorposts don't keep the roof up, and the clods don't keep it down. The nest is nothing but a furzy hole, such as, for comfort, any wild-beast may match anywhere, leaving cleanliness out of the question."

In each of these wretched lairs, the writer—who, be it borne in mind, was an eye-witness of what he describes—goes on to inform us, companies of these awful "birds," varying in number from three to six, eat, drink, sleep, cook, and receive company. As regards the furniture and domestic utensils with which each hut is provided, "the most important piece of furniture was a wooden shelf running along the back of the nest, and propped on sticks driven into the earthen floor. Some mugs, some plates, some cups and saucers, a candlestick; two or three old knives and forks, battered and rusty; a few dull and dinted spoons; a teapot (this being rather a rich establishment), and several other articles of a like character, were displayed upon the shelf; and a grateful sight it was. I declare I was most thankful for the cups and saucers; and as for the teapot, it looked like an ark of redemption in crockery-ware. If they were not—as I told myself when my eyes first rested on them—the only human-looking things in the place, they did give one a comfortable assurance that these wretched and desperate outcasts had not absolutely broken with the common forms and habits of civilised life.

"Beneath it was heaped an armful of musty straw, originally smuggled in from the camp stables: this, drawn out and shaken upon the earth, was the common bed. A rough wooden box, such as candles are packed in, stood in a corner; one or two saucepans, and a horrid old tea-kettle, which had all the look of a beldame punished by drink, were disposed in various nooks in the furzy walls; a frying-pan was stuck into them by the handle, in company with a crooked stick of iron used as a poker; and—undoubtedly *that* was there—a cheap little looking-glass was stuck near the roof. These things formed the whole furniture and appointments of the nest, if we exclude a petticoat or so hung up at intervals. There was not a stool in the place; and as for anything in the shape of a table, there was not room even for the idea of such a thing. Except for the cups and saucers, I doubt whether any Australian native habitation is more savage or more destitute: *he* can get an old saucepan or two, and knows how to spread a little straw on the ground. Nor were any of the other nests (and I believe I looked into them all) better or differently furnished. The only difference was in the quantity of crockery. In every one the candle-box was to be found. I discovered that it was the receptacle of those little personal ornaments and cherished trifles which women, in every grade of life, hoard with a sort of animal instinct. In every one an upturned saucepan was used for a seat, when squatting on the earth became too tiresome. In all, the practice is to sleep with your head under the shelf (thus gaining some additional protection from the wind) and your feet to the turf-fire, which is kept burning all night near the doorway. Here the use of the perforated saucepan becomes apparent. It is placed over the burning turf when the wrens dispose themselves to rest, and as there is no want of air in these dwellings, the turf burns well and brightly under the protecting pot. Another remembrance of a decent life is seen in the fact, that the women always undress themselves to sleep upon their handful of straw, their day-clothes serving to cover them."

The "wrens" themselves are described as being almost all young, and all, without an exception, Irish. They range from seventeen to twenty-five years old, and almost all come out of cabins in country places. Occasionally a delicate-looking "wren" may be met, but as a rule they are sturdy, fine-limbed women, full of health and strength; many are good-looking. In their style of dress, no less than undress, they are peculiar. "All day they lounge in a half-naked state, clothed simply in one frieze petticoat, and another, equally foul, cast loosely over their shoulders; though, towards evening, they put on the decent attire of the first girl I met there. These bettermost clothes are kept bright and clean enough; the frequency with which they are seen displayed on the bushes to dry, shows how often they are washed, and how well. These observations apply to the cotton gown, the stockings, the white petticoat alone; frieze and flannel never know anything of soap-and-water at all, apparently. The 'Curragh-petticoat' is familiarly known for miles and miles round; its peculiarity seems to be that it is starched, but not ironed. The difference in the appearance of these poor wretches when the gown and petticoat are donned, and when they are taken off again (that is to say, the moment they come back from the 'hunting-grounds'), answers precisely to their language and demeanour when sober and when tipsy." The communistic principle governs each "nest;" and share-and-share alike is the rule observed. "None of the women have any money of their own; what each company get is thrown into a common purse, and the nest is provisioned out of it. What they get is little indeed: a few halfpence turned out of one pocket and another when the clean starched frocks are thrown off at night, make up a daily income just enough to keep body and soul together."

Inquiry careful and judicious disclosed to the daring literary investigator that the "wrens" take it in turns to do the marketing and keep house while their sisters are abroad "on business." As need not be mentioned, it is the youngest and best-looking women who engage in the money-getting branch. Considering how severe are their privations, and the unceasing life of wretchedness they lead, it is not without surprise that we hear that many of the "wrens" have occupied the ground they still squat on during the past eight or nine years. "I asked one of these older birds how they contrived their sleeping-accommodation before 'nests' were invented. Said she, 'We'd pick the biggest little bush we could find, and lay under it, turnin' wid the wind.' 'Shifting round the bush as the wind shifted?' 'Thrue for ye. And sometimes we'd wake wid the snow covering us, and maybe soaked wid rain.' 'And how did you dry your clothes?' 'We jist waited for a fine day.' "

The above and much more information concerning the habits and customs of these bushwomen of the Curragh was obtained in the daytime; but this was not enough for the plucky *Pall-Mall* adventurer. He was well aware that the wren was a night-bird, and could only be seen in her true colours by candle-glimmer within her nest, or by the light of the stars or moon while abroad hunting for prey. Setting out after dark, our friend made his way across the common towards the nests he had visited the day before, and particularly to one known as No. 2 nest, the inmates of which had shown themselves very civil and obliging.

"As I approached it," says the writer, "I saw but one wretched figure alone. Crouched near the glowing turf, with her head resting upon her hands, was a woman whose age I could scarcely guess at, though I think, by the masses of black hair that fell forward upon her hands and backward over her bare shoulders, that she must have been young. She was apparently dozing, and taking no heed of the pranks of the frisky little curly-headed boy whom I have made mention of before; he was playing on the floor. When I announced myself by rapping on the bit of corrugated iron which stood across the bottom of the doorway, the woman started in something like fright; but she knew me at a second glance, and in I went. 'Put back the iron, if ye plaze,' said the wren as I entered; 'the wind's blowing this way to-night, bad luck to it!' . . . I wanted to know how my wretched companion in this lonely, windy, comfortless hovel, came from being a woman to be turned into a wren. The story began with 'no father nor mother,' an aunt who kept a whisky-store in Cork, an artilleryman who came to the whisky-store and saw and seduced the girl. By and by his regiment was ordered to the Curragh. The girl followed him, being then with child. 'He blamed me for following him,' said she. 'He'd have nothing to do with me. He told me to come here, and do like other women did. And what could I do? My child was born here, in this very place; and glad I was of the shelter, and glad I was when the child died—thank the blessed Mary! What could I do with a child? His father was sent away from here, and a good riddance. He used me very bad.' After a minute's silence the woman continued, a good deal to my surprise, 'I'll show you the likeness of a betther man, far away, one that never said a cross word to me—blessed's the ground he treads upon!' And fumbling in the pocket of her too scanty and dingy petticoat, she produced a photographic portrait of a soldier, enclosed in half-a-dozen greasy letters. 'He's a bandsman, sir, and a handsome man he is; and I believe he likes me too. But they have sent him to Malta for six years; I'll never see my darlint again.' And then this poor wretch, who was half crying as she spoke, told me how she had walked to Dublin to see him just before he sailed, 'because the poor craythur wanted to see me onst more.'

"From this woman, so strangely compounded, I learned that she had suffered so much privation last winter, that she had made up her mind not to stay in the bush another such a season. 'At the first fall of snow I'll go to the workhouse, that I will!' she said in the tone of one who says that in such an event he is determined to cut his throat. 'Why, would you belave it, sir?—last winter the snow would be up as high as our little house, and we had to cut a path through it to the min, or we'd been ruined intirely.'

". . . Presently the report of a gun was heard. 'Gun-fire!' cried my companion. 'They'll be back soon now, and I hope it's not drunk they are.' I went out to listen. All was dead quiet, and nothing was to be seen but the lights in the various bushes, till suddenly a blaze broke out at a distance. Some dry furze had been fired by some of the soldiers wandering on the common, and in search of whom the picket presently came round, peeping into every bush. Presently the sound of distant voices was heard; it came nearer and nearer, and its shrillness and confusion made it known to me that it was indeed a party of returning wrens, far from sober. They were in fact, mad drunk; and the sound of their voices as they came on through the dense darkness, screaming obscene sounds broken by bursts of horrible laughter, with now and then a rattling volley of oaths which told that fighting was going on, was staggering. I confess I now felt uncomfortable. I had only seen the wren sober, or getting sober; what she might be in that raging state of drunkenness I had yet to find out, and the dis-covery threatened to be very unpleasant. The noise came nearer, and was more shocking because you could disentangle the voices and track each through its own course of swearing, or of obscene singing and shouting, or of dreadful threats, which dealt in detail with every part of the human frame. 'Is this your lot?' I asked my companion with some apprehension, as at length the shameful crew burst out of the darkness. 'Some of 'em, I think.' But no, they passed on; such a spectacle as made me tremble. I felt like a man respited when the last woman went staggering by. Again voices were heard, this time proceeding from the women belonging to the bush where I was spending such an uncomfortable evening. Five in all,—two tipsy and three comparatively sober,—they soon presented themselves at the door; one of them was Billy's mother. At the sound of her voice the child woke up and cried for her. She was the most forbidding-looking creature in the whole place; but she hastened to divest herself outside of her crinoline and the rest of her walking attire (nearly all she had on), and came in and nursed the boy very tenderly. The other wrens also took off gown and petticoat, and folding them up, made seats of them within the nest. Then came the important inquiry from the watching wren, 'What luck have you had?' to which the answer was, 'Middling.' Without the least scruple they counted up what they had got amongst them—a poor account. It was enough to make a man's heart bleed to hear the details, and to see the actual money.

"In order to continue my observations a little later in a way agreeable to those wretched outcasts, I proposed to 'stand supper,' a proposition which was joyfully received, of course. Late as it was, away went one of the wrens to get supper, presently returning with a loaf, some bacon, some tea, some sugar, a little milk, and a can of water. The women brought all these things in such modest quantities that my treat cost no more (I got my change, and I remember the precise sum) than two shillings and eightpence-halfpenny. The frying-pan was put in requisition, and there seemed some prospect of a 'jolly night' for my more sober nest of wrens. One of them began to sing—not a pretty song; but presently she stopped to listen to the ravings of a strong-voiced vixen in an adjoining bush. 'It's Kate,' said one, 'and she's got the drink in her —the devil that she is.' I then heard that this was a woman of such ferocity when drunk that the whole colony was in terror of her. One of the women near me showed me her face, torn that very night by the virago's nails, and a finger almost bitten through. As long as the voice of the formidable creature was heard, everyone was silent in No. 2 nest—silent out of fear that she would presently appear amongst them. Her voice ceased: again a song was commenced; then the frying-pan began to hiss; and that sound it was, perhaps, that brought the dreaded virago down upon us. She was heard coming from her own bush, raging as she came. 'My God, there she is!' one of the women exclaimed. 'She's coming here; and if she sees you she'll tear every rag from your back!' The next moment the fierce creature burst into our bush, a stalwart woman full five feet ten inches high, absolutely mad with drink. Her hair was streaming down her back; she had scarcely a rag of clothing on; and the fearful figure made at me with a large jug, intended to be smashed upon my skull. I declare her dreadful figure appalled me. I was so wonder-stricken, that I believe she might have knocked me on the head without resistance; but, quick as lightning, one of the women got before me, spreading out her petticoat. 'Get out of it!' she shouted in terror; 'run!' And so I did. Covered by this friendly and grateful wren, I passed out of the nest, and made my way homeward in the darkness. One of the girls stepped out to show me the way. I parted from her a few yards from the nest, and presently 'lost myself' on the common. It was nearly two o'clock when I got to Kildare from my last visit to that shameful bush-village."

CHAPTER XVIII

The Present Condition of the Question.

The Laws applying to Street-walkers—The Keepers of the Haymarket Night-houses—Present Position of the Police-magistrates—Music-hall Frequenters — Refreshment-bars — Midnight Profligacy — "Snuggeries" — Over-zealous Blockheads.

Six or seven years since, such alterations were made in the laws applying to nocturnal street-walkers and disorderly persons generally, as enabled the London magistrates, with the assistance of the police, to reduce the great Haymarket disgrace to manageable dimensions. To completely abolish so renowned and prodigious a nuisance at a blow was more than could be expected; but the public generally were quite satisfied with the gradual and successful working of the plans adopted for the final extinction of the infamous "oyster-shops," and cafes, and wine-shops, that in the olden time made night hideous from St. James's-street to Piccadilly. Suddenly, however, the good work has received a serious check. According to the usual custom, the keeper of a refreshment-house, on being summoned before the magistrate (Mr. Knox) for an infringement of the Act, was fined for the offence; and nothing else was expected but that the fine would be paid, and, except for its salutary effect, there an end of it. But it would seem that the fined "night-house" keeper had cunning advisers, who assured him that the conviction was bad, and that he had only to appeal to a superior court to insure its being set aside. The course suggested was adopted, and crowned with success. Mr. Knox's decision was reversed, it not being clearly shown that the loose women discovered on the premises were really assembled for an immoral purpose.

The *Times,* commenting on this, says: "It is matter for general regret, since its probable result will be that in future the keepers of the Haymarket 'night-houses' will do pretty much what they please, without let or hindrance. It was decided by Sir William Bodkin and his brother magistrates sitting at the Middlesex Sessions, on an appeal brought from Marlborough-street, that no case is made out against the keeper of a 'night-house,' unless the police can prove that the women found in the house were assembled there for an immoral purpose; it was possible they might be there merely for the legitimate purpose of refreshment, and not in prosecution of their wretched trade. It is perfectly obvious that this interpretation of the law, whether or not true to the letter, utterly violates the spirit. The character of the women who frequent these 'night-houses' is perfectly well known. They have, moreover, but one possible object in frequenting them. It is clear, therefore, that they come within the spirit of the law against harbouring improper characters quite as much as if they visited these houses actually in company of men; and hence it follows that no new principle of legislation, requiring long consideration and repeated discussion, would be introduced if the law were made to reach them. We should, in fact, be not making a new law, but giving an old law its proper effect—an effect actually given it, as Mr. Knox points out, for seven years, and latterly with admirable results. Under these circumstances, we can see no objection to replacing the law on its former satisfactory footing by the simple expedient of a short clause in the Habitual Criminals' Bill. The Bill already deals with the low beer-houses, which are the favourite resorts of certain dangerous classes of the community; and the addition of a few words would enable it to deal with such 'night-houses' as those we have been discussing. This would not interfere with subsequent more mature and more comprehensive legislation on the subject, while it would obviate the delay which has driven the police authorities to desperation, and which threatens to give a fresh lease to a grave national scandal, just as it was in the way of being repressed."

The old law alluded to by the *Times* is the Act of Parliament of the 2d and 3d Vict. cap. 47, and is entitled "An Act for further empowering the Police in and near the Metropolis;" being an amendment of Sir Robert Peel's original statute, the 10th Geo. IV. Clauses 44, 52, 54, 58, and 63, bear especially on the penalties incurred by disorderly fallen women.

The 44th clause runs as follows:

"And whereas it is expedient that the provisions made by law for preventing disorderly conduct in the houses of licensed victuallers be extended to other houses of public resort; be it enacted that every person who shall have or keep any house, shop, room, or place of public resort within the Metropolitan-Police district, wherein provisions, liquors, or refreshments of any kind shall be sold or consumed (whether the same shall be kept or retailed therein, or procured elsewhere), and who shall wilfully or knowingly permit drunkenness or other disorderly conduct in such house, shop, room, or place, or knowingly suffer any unlawful games or any gaming whatsoever therein, or knowingly suffer or permit *prostitutes,* or persons of notoriously bad character, to meet together and remain therein, shall for every such offence be liable to a penalty of not more than five pounds."

The 52d clause of the same statute provides:

"That it shall be lawful for the Commissioners of Police from time to time, and as occasion may require, to make regulation for the route to be observed by all carts, carriages, horses, and persons, and for preventing obstructions of the streets or thoroughfares within the Metropolitan-Police district, in all times of public processions, public rejoicings, or illuminations; and also to give directions to the constables for keeping order and for preventing any obstruction of the thoroughfares in the immediate neighbourhood of her Majesty's palaces and public offices, the High Court of Parliament, the courts of law and equity, the police-courts, the theatres, and other places of public resort, and in any case when the streets or thoroughfares may be thronged or may be liable to be obstructed."

The 54th clause provides, in continuation:

"That every person who, after being made acquainted with the regulations or directions which the Commissioner of Police shall have made for regulating the route of horses, carts, carriages, and persons during the time of divine service, and for preventing obstructions during public processions, and on other occasions hereinbefore specified, shall wilfully disregard, or not conform himself thereto, shall be liable to a penalty of not more than forty shillings. And it shall be lawful for any constable belonging to the Metropolitan-Police force to take into custody, *without warrant,* any person who shall commit any such offence within view of any such constable."

The same 54th clause also provides:

"That every common prostitute or night-walker, loitering, or being in any thoroughfare or public place, for the purpose of prostitution or solicitation, to the annoyance of the inhabitants or passengers, shall be liable to a penalty of not more than forty shillings, and to be dealt with in the same manner."

And again, that "every person who shall use any profane, indecent, or obscene language to the annoyance of the inhabitants or passengers;" and also "every person who shall use any threaten-

ing, abusive, or insulting words or behaviour with intent to provoke a breach of the peace, or whereby a breach of the peace may
be occasioned," may be also so dealt with.

The 58th clause enacts:

"That every person who shall be found drunk in any street or
public thoroughfare within the said district, and who while drunk
shall be guilty of any riotous or indecent behaviour, and also every
person who shall be guilty of any violent or indecent behaviour in
any police station-house, shall be liable to a penalty of not more
than forty shillings for every such offence, or may be committed,
if the magistrate by whom he is convicted shall think fit, instead
of inflicting upon him any pecuniary fine, to the House of Cor-
rection for any time not more than seven days."

The 63rd clause enacts:

"That it shall be lawful for any constable belonging to the
Metropolitan-Police district, and for all persons whom he shall call
to his assistance, to take into custody, without a warrant, any
person who within view of such constable, shall offend in any
manner against this Act, and whose name and residence shall be
unknown to such constable, and cannot be ascertained by such
constable."

The police are, under the same Act, empowered to deal with
disorder, drunkenness, disorderly conduct, brawling, loitering and
obstruction, whether coming by prostitutes or others. Habitual
loitering upon certain fixed spots they already keep in check,
generally speaking, without tyranny; and next comes to be considered what can be done in case of what is called "solicitation" or
importunity, a prominent feature in the general bill of indictment
against prostitution.

To a person uninitiated in the law's subtleties, it would seem
that the clauses of the Act of Parliament above quoted armed the
police with all necessary authority, and that all that was requisite
was to compel the observance of the said clauses, strictly and without favour, to insure a considerable mitigation of the great evil.
Indeed, as has been shown, believing themselves justified in the
course they have been for years pursuing, the police have undoubtedly effected a vast and important change in the aspect of the
Haymarket and its neighbourhood after midnight. The result, however, of the Assistant-Judge's decision appears to have put the
worthy and indefatigable Mr. Knox quite out of heart, as may be
gathered from the subjoined newspaper account of the last case
that was brought before him:

"Rose Burton, keeper of a refreshment-house in Jermyn-street, lately known as Kate Franks, appeared to answer two summonses for harbouring prostitutes. The police gave the usual evidence. They visited the house at night. They found men and women there; the women known prostitutes, some taking refreshment. There was no disorder, and the usual signal by ringing a bell had been given when the police presented themselves at the house. For the defence it was urged, that the evidence was similar to that given before the Middlesex magistrates on appeal, after hearing which they quashed the conviction, and that the magistrate should dismiss the summonses. Mr. Knox said he must send the case to the Sessions in order to get a clear declaration of what was meant. If the judgment of the Court was against him, he must wash his hands of the matter. He should inflict the reduced fine of 10s. in order that the conviction should be taken to the Sessions. Mr. Froggatt asked for a decision in the second case. Mr. Knox would act in it the same as in the last case. It was, so to say, a last desperate effort. If he failed, his honest determination was to take no further trouble in the matter; but to report to the Home Office that the efforts to reform the condition of the Haymarket had entirely broken down. Mr. Edward Lewis, after some consultation with Mr. Allen jun. and Mr. Froggatt, said that, owing to technical difficulties, it would be impossible to get an appeal to Quarter Sessions before the 24th July. Mr. Knox said that would be too late for Parliament to deal with the matter, as the session would most probably close early in August. There was no help for it; the nighthouse-keepers must go on in their own way; the police might give up their supervision and refrain from taking out summonses, as he certainly should decline to convict. He should cancel the three convictions that day, and dismiss the summonses; he was powerless, and therefore disinclined to enforce what for seven years had been considered as law, but what had been suddenly upset by Quarter Sessions. Mr. Knox then requested Mr. Superintendent Dunlop to communicate what had occurred to the Commissioners of Police."

At the same time, it is no more than fair to lay before the reader the explanation given by the Assistant-Judge on the last occasion of the matter coming before him. It should be understood that the case in question was not that of "Rose Burton," but of another of the fraternity who had been fined by Mr. Knox. The party in question gave notice of appeal, and the police authorities intimated their intention of supporting the magistrate in his conviction. From some unexplained cause, however, at the last moment the Commissioners of Police withdrew altogether from the case, leaving it all undefended to be dealt with by Mr. Bodkin. The judgment of the learned Assistant-Judge was as follows:

"There are two cases in the paper of appeals against convictions by Mr. Knox for causing or allowing prostitutes to assemble; and upon these two cases being called, counsel intimated that the solicitors of the Commissioners of Police had written a letter to say that they should not support these convictions. Under those circumstances no other course was open to us but to quash them. But I mention the fact now because these convictions have been the subject of considerable comment and of interrogation in the House of Commons. I can only say that there is no law in these cases at all. It is entirely a question of fact, and each case must stand upon its own merits. On one occasion we quashed a conviction on the hearing, and upon that decision a great deal has been said. The sole evidence there was, that a policeman went into the house between twelve and one and found men and women having refreshment, some of the women being prostitutes. No question was asked; and there was nothing to show that the person who kept the house knew they were prostitutes. There was nothing to show that any warning had been previously given against harbouring or encouraging them to come. There was no ringing of any bell to give notice of the approach of the police. In fact, there was nothing but the mere incident that the police, before the hour of one, when these houses should be closed, found persons in them taking refreshments—some of those persons being prostitutes. Although I do not shrink from taking on myself the chief responsibility, there were many magistrates present who formed their own opinion upon the question, which was a question of fact; and it seemed so clearly not to be a case which satisfied the requirements of the law, that we did not call upon the counsel for the appellants, but at once quashed the conviction. Indeed, after all that has been said, I have no hesitation in stating that if another case came here, and was presented to us in such a bald and unsatisfactory manner, we should again quash the conviction. We are as desirous as Mr. Knox to put an end to any nuisance, whether in the Haymarket or elsewhere; but we cannot forget that we are in a court of law, bound to act upon such testimony as is sworn before us, and not to embark upon inquiries of another kind. There was not a tittle of evidence as to ringing a bell, or of anything more than persons taking refreshment within the hours allowed by law, some of those persons being 'unfortunates.' I do not think that any bench of magistrates in the kingdom could, under the circumstances, have arrived at a different conclusion. If other cases come before us, we shall treat them as we treated the last, according to the effect of the sworn evidence in court, and in no other way. I am very sorry if our decision should have induced Mr. Knox, for whom I entertain a great respect, to abstain from convicting in other cases, unless those were cases of the same bald and unsatisfactory character as that which we decided."

From one point of view maybe it is difficult to overrate the importance of this judgment, especially if, as the *Times* predicts, it will have the effect of giving the keepers of the Haymarket haunts of infamy liberty to do pretty much as they please. Laying too much stress on this Haymarket business, however, may be harmful in another direction. It may lead the public to the decidedly wrong conclusion that the well-known thoroughfare indicated, and the taverns and refreshment-houses it contains, are the head-quarters, the one main source, from which flows the prodigious stream of immorality that floods the town with contamination.

Now this is very far from being the fact. The extent to which the Haymarket haunts are criminal is equalled, and in many cases far excelled, in a dozen different parts of London every night between the hours of ten and one—and that without remonstrance or hindrance on the part of the police authorities or anyone else. I allude to the London music-halls. One of the most disreputable was burnt down the other day; and it would be a matter for rejoicing—for public thanksgiving almost—if the score or so of similar places of popular amusement, polluting every quarter of the metropolis, shared a similar fate. To be sure, the music-halls keep within the letter of the law in the matter of closing their doors before one o'clock; but in every other respect their operation is as mischievous as any of the prosecuted dens at the Westend. And I beg of the reader to distinctly understand that I am not quoting from hearsay. There is not a single music-hall—from the vast "Alhambra" in Leicester-square, to the unaristocratic establishment in the neighbourhood of Leather-lane, originally christened the "Raglan," but more popularly known as the "Rag" —that I have not visited. And I am bound to confess that the same damning elements are discoverable in one and all.

At the same time it must be admitted—shameful and disgraceful as the admission is—that it is not the music-hall of the vulgar East-end or "over the water" that presents in special prominence the peculiar features here spoken of, and which, in plain language, are licentiousness and prostitution. He who would witness the perfection to which these twin curses may be wrought under the foster-

ing influences of "music," &c., must visit the west, and not the
east or south, of the metropolis. He must make a journey to
Leicester-square, and to the gorgeous and palatial Alhambra there
to be found. What he will there discover will open his eyes to what
a farcical thing the law is, and how within the hour it will strain at
gnats, and bolt entire camels without so much as a wry face or a
wince, or a wink even.

I speak fearlessly, because all that I describe may be witnessed
to-night, to-morrow, any time, by the individual adventurous and
curious enough to go and see for himself. There is no fear of his
missing it; no chance of his fixing on a wrong night. It is *always*
the same at the music-hall. Its meat is other men's poison; and it
can fatten and prosper while honesty starves. The bane and curse
of society is its main support; and to introduce the purging besom
would be to ruin the business.

At the same time, I would wish it to be distinctly understood,
that I do not desire to convey to the reader the impression that
the numerical majority of music-hall frequenters are persons of
immoral tendencies. On the contrary, I am well convinced that
such places are the resort of a vast number of the most respectable
portion of the working-class. This, I believe, is a fact carefully
treasured by music-hall proprietors, and elaborately displayed by
them whenever their morality is attacked. They point to the well-
filled body of the hall, the sixpenny part, where artisans and
working-men congregate, and not unfrequently bring with them
their wives and daughters; and triumphantly inquire, "Is it likely
that the music-hall can be what slanderers represent, when it is so
patronised?" And it is quite true that a very large number of
honest and intelligent folk are attracted thither in search of harmless amusement. Let them bless God for their ignorance of the
world's wicked ways if they succeed in finding it. It is not impossible. Provided they look neither to the right nor left of them, but
pay their sixpence at the door, and march to the seats apportioned
them; and, still at eyes right, direct their gaze and their organs of
hearing towards the stage, from which the modern "comic voca-
list" doles out to a stolen tune feeble jingling idiotcies of "his own
composing,"—if they are steadfast to this, they may come away
not much the worse for the evening's entertainment. But let him
not look about him, especially if he have his wife or daughters
with him, or he may find himself tingling with a feeling it was
never his misfortune to experience before.

The honest believer in the harmlessness of music-halls would,
if he looked about him as he sat in the sixpenny "pit," discover

in more quarters than one that which would open his innocent eyes. If his vision were directed upwards towards the boxes and balconies, there he would discover it. Brazen-faced women, blazoned in tawdry finery, and curled and painted, openly and without disguise bestowing their blandishments on "spoony" young swells of the "commercial" and shopman type, for the sake of the shilling's-worth of brandy-and-water that steams before them, and in prospect of future advantages. There is no mistaking these women. They do not go there to be mistaken. They make no more disguise of their profession than do cattle-drovers in the public markets. They are there in pursuit of their ordinary calling, and, splendid creatures though they appear, it is curious to witness the supreme indifference to them of the door-keepers as they flaunt past them. It makes good the old proverb about the familiarity that breeds contempt; besides, as a customer in simple, the painted free-drinking lady is not desirable. I should not for a moment wish to impute without substantial proof so dastardly a feature of "business" to any spirited music-hall proprietor in particular; but I am positively assured by those who should know, that on certain recognised nights loose women are admitted to these places *without payment*. I know as a fact, too, that it is no uncommon thing for these female music-hall frequenters to enlist the services of cabmen on "spec," the latter conveying their "fare" to the Alhambra or the Philharmonic without present payment, on the chance that she will in the course of the evening "pick up a flat," who will with the lady require his services to drive them to the Haymarket or elsewhere. How much of extortion and robbery may be committed under such a convenient cloak it is not difficult to guess. The evidence not being quite so unobjectionable as it might be, I will not mention names; but I was recently informed with apparent sincerity by one of those poor bedizened unfortunates—a "dress lodger" possibly—that a certain music-hall proprietor issued to women of her class "weekly tickets" at half-price, the main condition attaching to the advantage being that the holder did not "ply" in the low-priced parts of the hall; that is to say, amongst those who could afford to pay for nothing more expensive than pints of beer.

But it is at the refreshment-bars of these palatial shams and impostures, as midnight and closing time approaches, that profligacy may be seen reigning rampant. Generally at one end of the hall is a long strip of metal counter, behind which superbly-attired barmaids vend strong liquors. Besides these there are "snuggeries," or small private apartments, to which bashful gentlemen desirous of sharing a bottle of wine with a recent acquaintance may retire. But the unblushing immodesty of the place concentrates at this long bar. Any night may here be found *dozens* of prostitutes enticing simpletons to drink, while the men who are *not* simpletons hang about, smoking pipes and cigars, and merely sipping, not drinking deeply, and with watchful wary eyes on the pretty game of fox-and-goose that is being played all round about them. No one molests them, or hints that their behaviour is at variance with "the second and third of Victoria, cap. 47." Here they are in dozens, in scores, prostitutes every one, doing exactly as they do at the infamous and prosecuted Haymarket dens, and no one interferes. I say, doing all that the Haymarket woman does; and it must be so, since the gay patroness of the music-halls does simply all she can to lure the dupe she may at the moment have in tow. She entices him to drink; she drinks with him; she ogles, and winks, and whispers, and encourages like behaviour on his part, her main undisguised object being to induce him to prolong the companionship after the glaring gaslight of the liquor-bar is lowered, and its customers are shown to the outer door. If that is not "knowingly suffering prostitutes to meet together" for the more convenient prosecution of their horrible trade, what else is it? And yet the cunning schemes and contrivances for misleading and throwing dust in the eyes of the police are not practised here. There are no scouts and "bells," the former causing the latter to chime a warning on the approach of the enemy. The enemy, the police, that is to say, are on the spot. In almost every case there will be found in the music-hall lobby an intelligent liveried guardian of the public peace, here stationed that he may take cognisance of suspicious-looking persons, and eject improper characters. Should he happen, as is most likely, to be a policeman whose "beat" is in the neighbourhood, he will by sight be quite familiar with every loose woman who for a mile round in the streets plies her lawless trade. He recognises them, as with a nod of old acquaintance they pass the money-taker; he saunters to the bar, where the women gather to prime their prey, and he witnesses their doings, but he takes no notice, and never complains.

To be sure, the man is not to blame; were he ordered to disperse congregations of prostitutes wherever he found them, and to warn the persons who dispense liquors to them—just as is expected of him in the case of the ordinary public-house—that they are harbouring bad characters, and must cease to do so, undoubtedly the policeman would perform his duty. Until he receives express orders on the subject, however, he is helpless, and very properly

so. Although one would desire to see ample powers for the suppression of prostitution placed in the hands of the police, it is
highly necessary that the said power, in the hands of ordinary
constable X, should be scrupulously watched by those who are set
in authority over him. Policemen make sad mistakes at times, as
witness the following monstrous instance, furnished by the police-
reports not more than a month since:

At Southwark, Mrs. Catherine C——, aged twenty-eight, the wife
of a respectable man in the employ of the South-Eastern Railway
Company, but who was described on the charge-sheet as a prostitute, was charged by Jas. Benstead, police-constable 17 M Reserve,
with soliciting prostitution near the London-bridge railway terminus. The constable said that about ten o'clock on the previous
night he was on duty near the railway terminus, when he saw the
prisoner accost a gentleman. Believing her to be a prostitute, he
went up to the gentleman, and from what he said he took her into
custody for soliciting him. The prisoner here said she had been
most cruelly used. She was a respectable married woman, and
lived with her husband in the Drummond-road, Bermondsey. She
had been to see her sister at Peckham, and had a return-ticket for
the Spa-road; but when she arrived at the London-bridge terminus,
she was too late for the train; consequently she determined to
walk home, and as soon as she turned into Duke-street, a gentleman stopped her and asked her whether there was an omnibus left
there for Whitechapel. She told him she did not know, and as soon
as he left, the constable came up and took her into custody. She
had been locked up all night. The prisoner here produced the half
of a return-ticket for the magistrate's inspection. The husband of
the prisoner said he was in the employ of the South-Eastern Railway Company, and resided at No. 190 Drummond-road, Bermondsey. His wife left home on the previous afternoon to visit her sister
at Peckham, and he expected her home at ten o'clock. He was
surprised at her absence, and as soon as he ascertained she was
locked up, he went to the police-station, but was not permitted to
see her. He could produce several witnesses to prove the respectability of his wife. Mr. Burcham ordered the prisoner to be discharged immediately.

And so terminated the case as far as the magistrate was concerned; but one cannot help feeling curious to know whether no
more was done in the matter. The outraged and cruelly-used
woman was discharged, but was Reserve-constable James Benstead
permitted to retain his situation in the police-force? How did the
monstrous "mistake" arise? It is evident that the poor young

woman spoke the truth; Mr. Burcham settled that point by ordering her immediate discharge. From any point of view, James Benstead showed himself utterly unworthy to remain a constable. In interfering with a decently-dressed woman, who must have been a stranger to him, simply because he saw her "accost a gentleman," he exhibited himself in the light of an over-zealous blockhead. If the woman's statement is to be believed, he told a wicked and malicious lie when he said that he took her into custody "on account of what the gentleman told him." Where one is left in the dark, to solve a mystery as one best may, it is not impossible that one may guess wide of the mark; but it will under such conditions occur to the recollection that before now "unfortunates," new to the life, have given deadly offence to policemen by not "paying their footing," as black-mail of a certain abominable kind is called; and blundering James Benstead may have sustained a pecuniary disappointment. It is to be sincerely hoped that that secret tribunal before which erring policemen are arraigned (where is it?) will not let so flagrant a case pass without notice; and if, after close investigation, policeman James Benstead is proved to be the dangerous person he appears, that he may be promptly stripped of his official uniform. Even supposing that James Benstead is nothing worse than a blundering Jack-in-office, he is just of the sort to bring the law into contempt and ridicule, and the sooner he is cashiered the better.

CHAPTER XIX.

Suggestions.

Ignoring the Evil—Punishment fit for the "Deserter" and the Seducer—The "Know-nothing" and "Do-nothing" Principle—The Emigration of Women of Bad Character.

It is easy enough to understand, if one finds the courage to face this worst of all social evils, and inquire calmly into the many shapes its origin takes, how very possible it is that there may be living in a state of depravity scores and hundreds of women who are what they are out of no real *fault* of their own. "Then why do they not turn, and reform their infamous lives?" the indignant reader may ask. "They may if they will. Is there not this, that, and the other asylum open to them?" Perhaps so. Only perhaps. But for reasons hinted at in the commencement of this chapter, it might be clearly enough shown that, "this, that, and t'other," to a very large extent, really and truly represent the substantiality of the asylums to which the curse is admitted for purgation. We have foolishly and blindly ignored the evil, and consequently we have not been free to provide adequately for the reception of those who have lived in it, and are now desirous of returning, if they may, to decent life. We have some asylums of the kind; but in capacity they are about as well adapted to perform the prodigious amount of work ready for them as a ten-gallon filter would be to purify the muddy waters of the Thames.

Undoubtedly there are thousands of debased and wanton wretches for whom the doors of such houses of reform and refuge, did they exist in plenty, might in vain stand open. But let the reader for a moment consider how many there are at this moment whose fall was mainly due to misplaced trust and foolish confidence, and who are kept in their degradation out of a sort of mad and bitter spite against themselves. As everyone can vouch who has taken an interest in these fallen ones, and kindly questioned them on their condition and their willingness to turn from it, nothing is more common in their mouths than the answer, "I don't care. It's a life good enough for me. A pretty image I should appear in well-bred company, shouldn't I? It's no use your preaching to me. I've made my bed, and I must lie on it." And it would be found in countless cases that these poor wretches did not in the original "make their bed," as they call it, and that it reveals a wonderful amount of forgiving and generosity in them to profess that they did. If we could discover the truth, we might get at the real bed-makers—the villanous conjurers of couches of roses that were so speedily to turn to thorns and briars—in the seducer and the base deserter. If ever the Legislature finds courage enough to take up this great question in earnest, it is to be hoped that ample provision will be made for the proper treatment of the heartless scoundrel. As says a writer in an old number of the *Westminster Review*:

"The *deserter,* not the seducer, should be branded with the same kind and degree of reprobation with which society now visits the coward and the cheat. The man who submits to insult rather than fight; the gambler who packs the cards, or loads the dice, or refuses to pay his debts of honour, is hunted from among even his unscrupulous associates as a stained and tarnished character. *Let the same measure of retributive justice be dealt to the seducer who deserts the woman who has trusted him, and allows her to come upon the town.* We say the deserter—not the seducer; for there is as wide a distinction between them as there is between the gamester and the sharper. Mere seduction will never be visited with extreme severity among men of the world, however correct and refined may be their general tone of morals; for they will always make large allowances on the score of youthful passions, favouring circumstances, and excited feeling. Moreover, they well know that there is a wide distinction—that there are all degrees of distinction —between a man who commits a fault of this kind, under the influence of warm affections and a fiery temperament, and the cold-hearted, systematic assailer of female virtue, whom all reprobate and shun. It is universally felt that you cannot, with any justice, class these men in the same category, nor mete out to them the same measure of condemnation. But the man who, when his caprice is satisfied, casts off his victim as a worn-out garment or a damaged toy; who allows the woman who trusted his protestations to sink from the position of his companion to the loathsome life of prostitution, because his seduction and desertion has left no other course open to her; who is not ready to make any sacrifice of place, of fortune, of reputation even, in order to save one whom he has once loved from such an abyss of wretched infamy—

must surely be more stained, soiled, and hardened in soul, more utterly unfitted for the company or sympathy of gentlemen or men of honour, than any coward, any gambler, any cheat!"

I may not lay claim to being the discoverer of this well-written outburst of manly indignation. It is quoted by a gentleman—a medical gentleman—who has inquired deeper and written more to the real purpose on this painful subject than any other writer with whom I am acquainted. I allude to Dr. Acton. The volume that contains it is of necessity not one that might be introduced to the drawing-room, but it is one that all thinking men would do well to procure and peruse. Dr. Acton handles a tremendously difficult matter masterly and courageously; and while really he is of as delicate a mind as a lady, he does not scruple to enunciate his honest convictions respecting the prevalent evil of prostitution, as though it were an evil as commonly recognised and as freely discussed as begging or thieving. In his introductory pages he says:

"To those who profess a real or fictitious ignorance of prostitution, its miseries and its ill-effects, and those again who plead conscience for inaction, I have this one reply. Pointing to the outward signs of prostitution in our streets and hospitals, I inquire whether we can flatter ourselves that the subject has drifted into a satisfactory state on the 'know-nothing' and 'do-nothing' principle. I hint at the perilous self-sufficiency of the Pharisee, and the wilful blindness of the Levite who 'passed by on the other side,' and I press upon them that, after reading this work and testing its author's veracity, they should either refute its arguments or be themselves converted. . . . I have little to say in the way of apology for my plain-speaking. The nature of the subject has forced this upon me. To have called things here treated of by another than their right name would have been in any writer an absurdity, in me a gross one. The experiences I have collected may to optimists and recluses appear exaggerated. The visions I have indulged in may be hard to grasp. But this more complicated knot demands a swordsman, not an infant. The inhabitants of a provincial city demanded of Lord Palmerston that the angel of pestilence should be stayed by a day of national prayer and fasting. 'I will fast with you and pray with you,' was the statesman's answer; 'but let us also drain, scrub, wash, and be clean.'"

If by this taste of the preface to Dr. Acton's book I induce my male readers to dip into it for themselves, I shall feel that I have done the cause the worthy writer has at heart good service. It will be something if the brief quotation bespeaks attention to the other extracts from the same genuine source that herein appear.

On the subject of seduction and desertion, Mr. Acton writes:

"If I could not get imprisonment of the male party to a seduction substituted for the paltry fine of half-a-crown a-week, I would
at least give to the commonwealth, now liable to a pecuniary
damage by bastardy, some interest in its detection and punishment. The union-house is now often enough the home of the
deserted mother and the infant bastard; and the guardians of the
poor ought, I think, to have the right, in the interest of the com-
mune, to act as bastardy police, and to be recouped their charges.
I would not allow the maintenance of an illegitimate child to be at
the expense of any but the father. I would make it the incubus on
him, not on its mother; and I would not leave his detection, exposure, and money loss at the option of the latter. A young man
who has a second and third illegitimate child, by different women,
has not lived without adding some low cunning to his nature. It
often happens that a fellow of this sort will, for a time, by
specious promises and presents to a girl he fully intends ultimately to desert, defer making any payments for or on account of
her child. If he can for twelve months, and without entering into
any shadow of an agreement (and we may all guess how far the
craft of an injured woman will help her to one that would hold
water), stave-off any application on her part to the authorities, her
claim at law is barred; and she herself, defied at leisure, becomes
in due course chargeable to her parish or union. But not thus
should a virtuous state connive at the obligations of paternity
being shuffled on to its public shoulders, when, by a very trifling
modification of the existing machinery, they might be adjusted on
the proper back, permanently or temporarily, as might be considered publicly expedient. I would enact, I say, by the help of
society, that, in the first place, the seduction of a female, properly
proved, should involve the male in a heavy pecuniary fine, according to his position—not at all by way of punishment, but to
strengthen, by the very firm abutment of the breeches-pocket,
both him and his good resolutions against the temptations and
force of designing woman. I would not offer the latter, as I foresee
will be instantaneously objected, this bounty upon sinfulness—this
incentive to be a seducer; but, on the contrary, the money should
be due to the community, and recoverable in the county-court or
superior court at the suit of its engine, the union; and should be
invested by the treasurer of such court, or by the county, or by
some public trustee in bastardy, for the benefit of the mother and
child. The child's portion of this deodand should be retained by
such public officer until the risk of its becoming chargeable to the

community quasi-bastard should be removed by the mother's marraige or otherwise; and the mother's share should be for her benefit as an emigration-fund or marriage-portion."

"We cannot imagine," says another authority, "that anyone can seriously suppose that prostitution would be made either more generally attractive or respectable by the greater decency and decorum which administrative supervision would compel it to throw over its exterior. We know that the absence of these does not deter one of irregular passions from the low pursuit; and we know, moreover, wherever these are needed for the behoof of a more scrupulous and refined class of fornicators, they are to be found. We are convinced also that much of the permanent ruin to the feelings and character which results from the habit of visiting the haunts of prostitution is to be attributed to the coarse language and the brutal manners which prevail there; and that this vice, like many others, would lose much of its evil by losing all of grossness that is separable from it. Nor do we fear that the improvement in the *tone* of prostitution which would thus result would render its unhappy victims less anxious to escape from it. Soften its horrors and gild its loathsomeness as you may, there will always remain enough to revolt all who are not wholly lost. Much too—everything almost—is gained, if you can retain *any* degree of self-respect among the fallen. The more of this that remains, the greater chance is there of ultimate redemption; it is always a mistaken and a cruel policy to allow vice to grow desperate and reckless." It is for the interest of society at large, as well as for that of the guilty individual, that we should never break down the bridge behind such a sinner as the miserable "unfortunate" even.

V.

THE CURSE OF DRUNKENNESS.

CHAPTER XX

Its Power.

The crowning Curse—No form of sin or sorrow in which it does not play a part—The "Slippery Stone" of Life—Statistics—Matters not growing worse —The Army Returns—The System of Adulteration.

Whatever differences of opinion may arise as to the extent and evil operation of the other curses that, in common with all other cities, afflict the city of London, no sane man will contest the fact that drunkenness has wrought more mischief than all other social evils put together. There is not a form of human sin and sorrow in which it does not constantly play a part. It is the "slippery stone" that in countless instances has betrayed the foot careless or over-confident, and the downhill-path is trod never to be retraced. As Dr. Guthrie writes: "Believe me, it is impossible to exaggerate, impossible even truthfully to paint, the effect of this evil, either on those who are addicted to it or on those who suffer from it; crushed husbands, broken-hearted wives, and, most of all, those poor innocent children that are dying under cruelty and starvation, that shiver in their rags upon our streets, that walk unshod the winter snows, and, with their matted hair and hollow cheeks, and sunken eyes, glare out on us wild and savage-like from patched and filthy windows. Nor is the curse confined to the lowest stratum of society. Much improved as are the habits of the upper and middle classes, the vice may still be met in all classes of society. It has cost many a servant her place, and yet greater loss —ruined her virtue; it has broken the bread of many a tradesman; it has spoiled the coronet of its lustre, and sunk the highest rank into contempt."

It is satisfactory, however, to discover that matters are not growing worse.

In the number of persons "summarily proceeded against" for divers offences, we find a steady decrease during the last three years in the numbers charged with "drunkenness" and being "drunk and disorderly," the respective figures being 105,310,

104,368, and 100,357, showing a diminution in the three years of nearly 5,000 cases per annum. In the total number of inquests for 1867, viz. 24,648, there is a decrease of 278, as compared with the number in the preceding year. In the verdicts of murder there is a decrease of 17, and of manslaughter 44, or 19.7 per cent, following a decrease of 59, or 20.9 per cent, as compared with the number in 1865. Under "natural death," as compared with the numbers for 1866, there is a decrease of 51, or 13.6 per cent, in the verdicts "from excessive drinking," following a decrease of 12 in 1866, as compared with the number in 1865. The number of persons committed or bailed for trial for indictable offences during the year, as shown in the police-returns, was 19,416, and of these it may be calculated that about 14,562 (75 per cent being about the usual proportion) would be convicted. To this number is to be added (in order to show the total number of convictions during the year) 335,359 summary convictions before the magistrates (280,196 males and 55,163 females). A large proportion of these cases were, it is true, for offences of a trifling character. They include, however, 74,288 cases of "drunkenness" and being "drunk and disorderly" (59,071 males and 15,217 females), and 10,085 offences against the Licensed Victuallers' and Beer Acts, viz. 6,506 by beer-shop-keepers (5,792 males and 714 females); 3,258 by licensed victuallers (2,944 males and 314 females); the remaining 321 (293 males and 28 females) consisting of other offences under the above Acts. The total number of convictions for offences against the Refreshment Houses' Act was 3,032, viz. 2,871 males and 161 females.

This as regards civilians and those over whom the police have control. The army-returns, however, are not so favourable.

The last annual report of Lieutenant-Colonel Henderson, R.E., the Inspector-General of Military Prisons, reveals the startling fact that, "during four years the committals for drunkenness have steadily increased as follows: 1863, 882; 1864, 1,132; 1865, 1,801; 1866, 1,926.

The Inspector-General observes that the explanation of this increase "is to be found in the fact that soldiers who formerly were summarily convicted and sentenced to short periods of imprisonment in regimental cells by their commanding officers for drunkenness are now tried by court-martial and sentenced to imprisonment in a military prison." But precisely the same explanation was given, in the report for the preceding year, of the increase of the committals in 1865 over those in 1864. Therefore, however applicable this consideration might have been to a comparison with former periods when drunkenness was not dealt with by court-martial, it totally fails to account for the further increase which has occurred since the change was made.

It must not be supposed that the 1,926 cases in the year 1866 were cases of simple drunkenness, such as we see disposed of in the police-courts by a fine of five shillings. The offence was "habitual drunkenness," of which there are several definitions in the military code; but much the largest portion of the committals are for having been drunk "for the fourth time within 365 days." In order, therefore, to form a just idea of the prevalence of this vice in the army, we must add to the cases brought before a court-martial the far more numerous instances in which the offenders are discovered less than four times a year, and are punished by their commanding officers, or in which they are not discovered at all. Drunkenness is *the* vice of the army. The state of feeling which pervaded society two generations ago still survives in the army. That species of "good fellowship," which is only another name for mutual indulgence in intoxicating drink, is still in the ascendant in the most popular of English professions, and from this vantage-ground it exercises an injurious influence over the moral condition of the entire community.

The following order, relative to the punishment of drunkenness in the army, as directed by the Horse Guards, has just been published:

"First and second acts, admonition or confinement to barracks at the discretion of the commanding officer. For every subsequent act of drunkenness within three months of former act, 7s. 6d.; if over three and within six months, 5s.; if over six and within nine months, 2s 6d.; if over nine and within twelve months, company entry; if over twelve months, to be treated as the first act. When the four preceding acts have been committed in twelve months, 2s 6d. to be added to the foregoing amounts, and the *maximum* daily stoppage is to be 2d."

Drink, strong drink, is responsible for very much of the misery that afflicts our social state; but it is scarcely fair to much-abused Alcohol—a harmless spirit enough except when abused—to attribute to it all the ruin that flows from the bottle and the public-house gin-tap. Alcohol has enough to answer for; but there can be no doubt that for one victim to its intoxicating qualities, two might be reckoned who have "come to their death-bed" through the various deadly poisons it is the publican's custom to mix with his diluted liquors to give them a fictitious strength and fire. Let us here enumerate a few of the ingredients with which the beer-shop-keeper re-brews his beer, and the publican "doctors" his gin and rum and whisky.

As is well known, the most common way of adulterating beer is by means of *cocculus indicus.* This is known "in the trade" as "Indian berry," and is the fruit of a plant that grows on the coast of Malabar. It is a small kidney-shaped, rough, and black-looking berry, of a bitter taste, and of an intoxicating or poisonous quality. It is extensively used to increase the intoxicating properties of the liquor.

Fox-glove is a plant with large purple flowers, possessing an intensely bitter nauseous taste. It is a violent purgative and vomit; produces languor, giddiness, and even death. It is a poison, and is used on account of the bitter and intoxicating qualities it imparts to the liquor among which it is mixed.

Green copperas, a mineral substance obtained from iron, is much used to give the porter a frothy top. The green copperas is supposed to give to porter in the pewter-pot that peculiar flavour which drinkers say is not to be tasted when the liquor is served in glass.

Hartshorn shavings are the horns of the common male deer rasped or scraped down. They are then boiled in the worts of ale, and give out a substance of a thickish nature like jelly, which is said to prevent intoxicating liquor from becoming sour.

Henbane, a plant of a poisonous nature, bearing a close resemblance to the narcotic poison, opium. It produces intoxication, delirium, nausea, vomiting, feverishness, and death, and appears chiefly to be used to increase the intoxicating properties of intoxicating liquors; or, in other words, to render them more likely to produce these effects in those who use these liquors.

Jalap, the root of a sort of convolvulus, brought from the neighbourhood of Xalapa, in Mexico, and so called Jalap. It is used as a powerful purgative in medicine. Its taste is exceedingly nauseous; and is of a sweetish bitterness. It is used to prevent the intoxicating liquor from turning sour; and probably to counteract the binding tendency of some of the other ingredients.

Multum is a mixture of opium and other ingredients, used to increase the intoxicating qualities of the liquor.

Nut-galls are excrescences produced by the attacks of a small insect on the tender shoots of a tree which grows in Asia, Syria, and Persia. They are of a bitter taste, and are much used in dyeing. They are also used to colour or fine the liquor.

Nux vomica is the seed of a plant all parts of which are of a bitter and poisonous nature. The seeds of this plant are found in the fruit, which is about the size of an orange. The seeds are about an inch round and about a quarter of an inch thick. They have no smell. It is a violent narcotic acrid poison, and has been used very extensively in the manufacture of intoxicating ale, beer, and porter.

Opium is the thickened juice of the white poppy, which grows most abundantly in India, though it also grows in Britain. It is the most destructive of narcotic poisons, and it is the most intoxicating. It has been most freely used in the manufacture of intoxicating liquors, because its very nature is to yield a larger quantity of intoxicating matter than any other vegetable.

Oil of vitriol, or sulphuric acid, is a mineral poison of a burning nature. In appearance it is oily and colourless, and has no smell. It is used to increase the heating qualities of liquor.

Potash is made from vegetables mixed with quick-lime, boiled down in pots and burnt—the ashes remaining after the burning being the potash. It is used to prevent the beer souring, or to change it, if it has become sour.

Quassia is the name of a tree which grows in America and the West Indies. Both the wood and the fruit are of an intensely bitter taste. It is used instead of hops to increase the bitter in the liquor.

Wormwood is a plant or flower with downy leaves, and small round-headed flowers. The seed of this plant has bitter and stimulating qualities, and is used to increase the exciting and intoxicating qualities of liquors.

Yew tops, the produce of the yew-tree. The leaves are of an extremely poisonous nature, and so are the tops, or berries and seeds. It is used to increase the intoxicating properties of the liquors.

The quantities of cocculus-indicus berries, as well as of black extract, brought into this country for adulterating malt liquors, are enormous. The berries in question are ostensibly destined for the use of tanners and dyers. Most of the articles are transmitted to the consumer in their disguised state, or in such a form that their real nature cannot possibly be detected by the unwary. An extract, said to be innocent, sold in casks containing from half a cwt. to five cwt. by the brewers' druggists, under the name of "bittern," is composed of calcined sulphate of iron (copperas), extract of cocculus-indicus berries, extract of quassia and Spanish liquorice. This fraud constitutes by far the most censurable offence committed by unprincipled brewers.

To both ale and porter an infusion of hops is added, and in general porter is more highly hopped than ale. New ale and porter, which are free from acid, are named mild; those which have been kept for some time, and in which acid is developed, are called hard. Some prefer hard beer; and to suit this taste, the publicans are accustomed, when necessary, to convert mild beer into hard by a summary and simple process, to wit, the addition of sulphuric acid. Again, others prefer mild beer; and the publicans, when their supply of this is low, and they have an abundance of old or hard beer, convert the latter into mild, by adding to it soda, potash, carbonate of lime, &c. Various other adulterations are practised. The narcotic quality of hop is replaced by cocculus inducus; sweetness and colour by liquorice (an innocent fraud); thickness by lint-seed; a biting pungency by caraway-seed and cayenne-pepper. Quassia is also said to be used, with the latter view. Treacle is likewise employed to give sweetness and consistency; while to give beer a frothy surface, sulphate of iron and alum are had recourse to. Such is the wholesome beverage of which nine-tenths of the English people daily partake!

Nor is the more aristocratic and expensive liquid that assumes the name of wine exempt from the "doctor's" manipulations. Mr. Cyrus Redding, in his evidence before a select committee, describes the mode by which wines are made by manufacturers in London. He stated that brandy cowl—that is, washings of brandy-casks—colouring, probably made of elder-berries, log-wood, salt-of-tartar, gum-dragon, tincture of red sanders or cudbear, were extensively used in preparing an article which sells as port. The entire export of port-wine is 20,000 pipes, and yet 60,000, as given in evidence, are annually consumed in this country. As regards champagne, the same authority says, "In England, champagne has been made from white and raw sugar, crystallised lemon or tartaric acid, water, home-made grape-wine, or perry, and French brandy. Cochineal or strawberries have been added to imitate the pinks. Such a mixture at country balls or dinners passes off very well; but no one in the habit of drinking the genuine wine can be deceived by the imposition. The bouquet of real champagne, which is so peculair, it is repeated, cannot be imitated—it is a thing impossible. Acidity in wine was formerly corrected in this country by the addition of quicklime, which soon falls to the bottom of the cask. This furnished a clue to Falstaff's observation, that there was 'lime in the sack,' which was a hit at the landlord, as much as to say his wine was little worth, having its acidity thus disguised. As to the substances used by various wine-doctors for flavouring wine, there seems to be no end of them. Vegetation has been exhausted, and the bowels of the earth ransacked, to supply trash for this quackery. Wines under the names of British madeira, port, and sherry are also made, the basis of which is pale salt, sugar-candy; French brandy and port-wine are added to favour the deception. So impudently and notoriously are the frauds avowed, that there are books published called *Publicans' Guides,* and *Licensed Victuallers' Directors,* in which the most infamous receipts imaginable are laid down to swindle their customers. The various docks on the Thames do not secure purchasers from the malpractices of dishonest dealers; in this many are deceived. It has been naturally, yet erroneously, imagined that wine purchased in the docks must be a pure article. Malaga sherry is constantly shipped to England for the real sherry of Xeres, Figueras for port, and so on. Port-wine being sent from the place of its growth to Guernsey and Jersey, and there reshipped, with the original quantity tripled for the English market, the docks are no security."

Professor C. A. Lee, of New York, informs us that "a cheap Madeira is made by extracting the oils from common whisky, and passing it through carbon. There are immense establishments in this city where the whisky is thus turned into wine. In some of those devoted to this branch of business, the whisky is rolled-in in the evening, but the wine goes out in the broad daylight, ready to defy the closest inspection. A grocer, after he had abandoned the nefarious traffic in adulterations, assured me that he had often purchased whisky one day of a country merchant, and before he left town sold the same whisky back to him turned into wine, at a profit of from 400 to 500 per cent. The trade in empty wine-casks in this city with the Custom-house mark and certificate is immense; the same casks being replenished again and again, and always accompanied by that infallible test of genuineness, the Custom-house certificate. I have heard of a pipe being sold for twelve dollars. There is in the neighbourhood of New York an extensive manufactory of wine-casks, which are made so closely to imitate the foreign as to deceive experienced dealers. The Custom-house marks are easily counterfeited, and certificates are never wanting. I have heard," said Dr. Lee, "dealers relate instances in which extensive stores were filled by these artificial wines; and when merchants from the country asked for genuine wines, these have been sold them as such, assuring them there could be no doubt of their purity. It is believed," he observes, "that the annual importation of what is called port-wine into the United States far exceeds the whole annual produce of the Alto-Douro."

Mr. James Forrester, an extensive grower of wines in the Alto-Douro and other districts of the north of Portugal, and another witness, stated that there was a mixture called jeropiga, composed of two-thirds 'must,' or grape-juice, and one-third brandy, and which brandy is about twenty per cent above British brandy-proof, used for bringing up character in ports. He further declared that sweetening-matter, in every variety, and elder-berry dye, is administered for the purpose of colouring it and giving it a body. Moreover, Mr. Forrester testified that, by the present Portuguese law, *no unsophisticated port-wine is allowed to reach this country.* "If any further colouring-matter be absolutely requisite by the speculator—I would not suppose by the merchants (for the merchants generally do not like, unless they are obliged, to sell very common wines, and do not like to have recourse to these practices)—then the elder-berry is, I believe, the only dye made use of in this country, and *costs an enormous lot of money.*"

Dr. Munroe of Hull, the author of *The Physiological Action of Alcohol,* and other scientific works, gives evidence as follows of the danger attending the use of alcoholic drinks as medicine:

"I will relate a circumstance which occurred to me some years ago, the result of which made a deep impression on my mind. I was not then a teetotaler—would that I had been!—but I conscientiously, though erroneously, believed in the health-restoring properties of stout. A hard-working, industrious, God-fearing man, a teetotaler of some years' standing, suffering from an abscess in his hand, which had reduced him very much, applied to me for advice. I told him the only medicine he required was rest; and to remedy the waste going on in his system, and to repair the damage done to his hand, he was to support himself with a bottle of stout daily. He replied, 'I cannot take it, for I have been some years a teetotaler.' 'Well,' I said, 'if you know better than the doctor, it is no use applying to me.' Believing, as I did then, that the drink would really be of service to him, I urged him to take the stout as a medicine, which would not interfere with his pledge. He looked anxiously in my face, evidently weighing the matter over in his mind, and sorrowfully replied, 'Doctor, I was a drunken man once; I should not like to be one again.'

"He was, much against his will, prevailed on to take the stout, and in time he recovered from his sickness. When he got well, I of course praised up the virtues of stout as a means of saving his life, for which he ought ever to be thankful; and rather lectured him on being such a fanatic (that's the word) as to refuse taking a bottle of stout daily to restore him to his former health. I lost sight of my patient for some months; but I am sorry to say that on one fine summer's day, when driving through one of our public thoroughfares, I saw a poor, miserable, ragged-looking man leaning against the door of a common public-house drunk, and incapable of keeping an erect position. Even in his poverty, drunkenness, and misery, I discovered it was my teetotal patient whom I had, not so long ago, persuaded to break his pledge. I could not be mistaken. I had reason to know him well, for he had been a member of a Methodist church; an indefatigable Sunday-school teacher; a prayer-leader whose earnest appeals for the salvation of others I had often listened to with pleasure and edification. I immediately went to the man, and was astonished to find the change which drink in so short a time had worked in his appearance. With manifest surprise, and looking earnestly at the poor wretch, I said, 'S—, is that you?' With a staggering reel, and clipping his words, he answered, 'Yes, it's me. Look at me again. Don't you know me?' 'Yes, I know you,' I said, 'and am grieved to see you in this drunken condition. I thought you were a teetotaler?'

"With a peculiar grin upon his countenance, he answered, 'I was before I took your medicine.' 'I am sorry to see you disgracing yourself by such conduct. I am ashamed of you.' Rousing himself, as drunken people will at times, to extraordinary effort, he scoffingly replied, 'Didn't you send me here for my medicine?' and with a delirious kind of chuckle he hiccupped out words I shall never forget. 'Doctor, your medicine cured my body, but it damned my soul!'

"Two or three of his boozing companions, hearing our conversation, took him under their protection, and I left him. As I drove away, my heart was full of bitter reflections, that I had been the cause of ruining this man's prospects, not only of this world, but of that which is to come.

"You may rest assured I did not sleep much that night. The drunken aspect of that man haunted me, and I found myself weeping over the injury I had done him. I rose up early the next morning and went to his cottage, with its little garden in front, on the outskirts of the town, where I had often seen him with his wife and happy children playing about, but found, to my sorrow, that he had removed some time ago. At last, with some difficulty, I found him located in a low neighbourhood, not far distant from the public-house he had patronised the day before. Here, in such a home as none but the drunkard could inhabit, I found him laid upon a bed of straw, feverish and prostrate from the previous day's debauch, abusing his wife because she could not get him some more drink. She, standing aloof with tears in her eyes, broken down with care and grief, her children dirty and clothed in rags, all friendless and steeped in poverty! What a wreck was there!

"Turned out of the church in which he was once an ornament, his religion sacrificed, his usefulness marred, his hopes of eternity blasted, now a poor dejected slave to his passion for drink, without mercy and without hope!

"I talked to him kindly, reasoned with him, succoured him till he was well, and never lost sight of him or let him have any peace until he had signed the *pledge* again.

"It took him some time to recover his place in the church; but I have had the happiness of seeing him restored. He is now more than ever a devoted worker in the church; and the cause of temperance is pleaded on all occasions.

"Can you wonder, then, that I never order strong drink for a patient now?"

One of the most terrible results of hard drinking is that kind of insanity that takes the name of "delirium tremens;" and its characteristic symptoms may be described as follows: Muscular tremors—more especially of the hands and of the tongue when protruded—along with complete sleeplessness, and delirium of a muttering, sight-seeing, bustling, abrupt, anxious, apprehensive kind. The afflicted patient has not the ability to follow out a train of thought, to explain fully an illusion or perverted sensation, or to perform any act correctly; for he may be one moment rational and the next incoherent, now conscious of his real condition and of surrounding realities, and then again suddenly excited by the most ridiculous fancies—principally of a spectral kind—such as strange visitors in the shape of human beings, devils, cats, rats, snakes, &c.; or by alarming occurrences, such as robberies, fires, pursuits for crimes, and the like. He is easily pleased and satisfied by gentleness and indulgence, and much fretted and agitated by restraint and opposition. The face is generally of a pale dirty colour and wearing an anxious expression; eyes startled but lustreless, sometimes considerably suffused, and the pupils not contracted unless considerable doses of opium have been administered, or very decided arachnitic symptoms have supervened; skin warm and moist, often perspiring copiously; tongue sometimes loaded, but generally pale and moist, occasionally remarkably clean; appetite small, but the patient will often take whatever is presented to him; thirst by no means urgent, and seldom or never any craving for spirituous liquors; urine scanty and high-coloured, and, in some cases which Dr. Munroe (from whose volume this description is derived) tested, containing a large quantity of albumen, which, however, disappears immediately after the paroxysm is over; alvine evacuations bilious and offensive; and the pulse generally ranges from 98 to 120, generally soft, but of various degrees of fulness and smallness, according to the strength of the patient and the stage of the affection. The precursory symptoms are by no means peculiar or pathognomonic, but common to many febrile affections, implicating the sensorium in the way of repeatedly-disturbed and sleepless nights, with perhaps more of a hurried and agitated manner than usual for some days previously. The paroxysm which is distinguished by the phenomena above described—occurring with remarkable uniformity, independently of age and constitution—usually runs its course, if uncomplicated and properly treated, on the second or third day, though sometimes earlier, and it seldom extends beyond the fifth day. It then terminates in a profound natural sleep, which may continue for many hours, and from which, if it even lasts for six hours, the patient awakes weak and languid, but quite coherent. The casualties of the disease are convulsions or coma, which, if not immediately fatal, are apt to leave the sufferer a wreck for the remainder of life.

CHAPTER XXI

Attempts to Arrest It.

*The Permissive Liquors Bill—Its Advocates and their Arguments—The Drunk-
enness of the Nation—Temperance Facts and Anecdotes—Why the Advocates of Total Abstinence do not make more headway—Moderate Drinking
—Hard Drinking—The Mistake about childish Petitioners.*

There has recently appeared on the temperance stage a set of well-
meaning gentlemen, who, could they have their way, though they
would sweep every public-house and beershop from the face of the
land, are yet good-natured enough to meet objectors to their extreme views a "third" if not "half-way." Sir Wilfred Lawson is the
acknowledged head and champion of the party, and its views on
the all-important subject are summed up in a Permissive Prohibitory Liquor Bill. It may be mentioned that the said Bill was rejec-
ted in the House of Commons by a very large majority, and is
therefore, for the present, shelved. It stands, however, as an
expression of opinion on the part of eighty-seven members of
parliament, backed by 3,337 petitions, more or less numerously
signed, from various parts of the kingdom, as to what should be
done to check the advancing curse of drunkenness, and, as such,
its merits may be here discussed.

The Permissive Prohibitory Liquors Bill, as Sir Wilfred Lawson
describes it, provides that no public-houses shall be permitted in
any district, provided that two-thirds of its population agree that
they should be dispensed with. If there are thirty thousand inhabitants of a parish, and twenty thousand of them should be of
opinion that public-houses are a nuisance that should be abolished,
the remaining ten thousand may grumble, but they must submit,
and either go athirst or betake themselves to an adjoining and
more generous parish.

Sir W. Lawson, in moving the second reading of his Bill, said
"that no statistics were needed to convince the House of Commons of the amount of drunkenness, and consequent poverty and
crime, existing in this country; and even if here and there drunk-

enness might be diminishing, that did not affect his argument, which rested upon the fact that drunkenness in itself was a fertile and admitted source of evil. The Bill was called a 'Permissive Bill;' but had the rules of the House permitted, it might with truth be called a Bill for the Repression of Pauperism and of Crime. The measure was no doubt unpopular in the House, but it was a consolation to him that, although honourable members differed in opinion as to the efficacy of the remedy proposed, they all sympathised with the object its promoters had in view. The trouble to which he feared honourable members had been put during the last few days in presenting petitions and answering letters showed the depth and intensity of the interest taken in the question out of doors. No less than 3,337 petitions had been presented in favour of the Bill. It would be remembered that in the parliament before last a bill similar in its character had been defeated by an overwhelming majority, all the prominent speakers in opposition to it at that time declaring that they based their hopes as to the diminution of drunkenness upon the spread of education. He agreed in that opinion, but the education, to be successful, must be of the right sort; and while an army of schoolmasters and clergymen were engaged in teaching the people what was good, their efforts, he feared, were greatly counteracted by that other army of 150,000 publicans and beersellers encouraging the people to drinking habits. All these dealers in drink had been licensed and commissioned by the Government, and were paid by results; they had, consequently, a direct pecuniary interest in promoting the consumption of as large an amount of drink as possible. Naturally, if a man entered into a trade, he wished to do as large a trade as possible; and he had always felt that the advocates of temperance did more harm than good in using hard language against the beersellers, when it was the law which enabled them to engage in the trade, which was primarily responsible for the result."

The honourable member explained that the Bill did not in any way interfere with or touch the licensing system as at present existing; where it was the wish of the inhabitants that licenses should be granted, licenses would continue to be granted as at present. But what the measure sought to do was, to empower the inhabitants of a neighbourhood, or the great majority of them, to vote within that neighbourhood the granting of any licenses at all —to crystallise public opinion, as it were, into law. The first objection that had been taken to the measure was, that it would be impossible to carry out prohibition in England; but why should that be impossible in this country which had been successfully carried out in America, in Canada, and in Nova Scotia? All he had to say upon the revenue question was, that no amount of revenue to be derived from the sale of intoxicating drinks should be allowed for a moment to weigh against the general welfare of the people; and that, if the present Bill were passed, such a mass of wealth would accumulate in the pockets of the people, that the Chancellor of the Exchequer would meet with no difficulty in obtaining ample funds for carrying on the government of the country. It was further objected that great inconvenience would be inflicted upon the minority by the operation of the Bill; but there, again, the balance of advantage and disadvantage must be looked at, and the convenience of the few should not be allowed to counterbalance the benefit that would be conferred upon the great mass of the people. Then it was said that every year there would be a great fight upon the question; but was not an annual moral contest better than nightly physical conflicts at the doors of the public-houses? The movement in favour of prohibiting the sale of liquor had proceeded from the poor, and it had been supported by what he might call the aristocracy of the working-classes. He asked the House whether it would not be wise, when the future of this country must be in the hands of the working-classes, to pay some attention to their demand for a straight-forward measure of this sort, which was intended to put an end to an acknowledged evil of great magnitude.

"What," says the *Times,* when commenting on Sir Wilfred Lawson's argument, "would it matter to Sir Wilfred Lawson, or to any of the gentlemen who figure on the temperance platform, if all the public-houses of their districts were closed to-morrow? Their own personal comfort would be in no way affected; not one of them probably enters a public-house, except at canvassing times, from one year's end to another. But it would matter a great deal to those humbler and poorer classes of the population who make daily use of the public-house. If it were closed, their comfort would be most materially affected. A large proportion of them use strong liquor without abusing it, and have therefore as much right to it, both legal and moral, as they have to their meat or clothes. Many of them could not get through the work by which they gain their own and their children's bread without it; and their only means of procuring it is provided by the present public-house system. They have not usually capital enough to lay in for themselves a stock of liquor; and even if they had, this plan would be not only wasteful and inconvenient, but would tempt them to commit the very crime which it was employed to avoid. They find it both cheaper and more comfortable to get their liquor in small quantities as they want it, and they can only do this at a public-house. Besides, it should not be forgotten—though well-to-do reformers are very apt, from their inexperience, to forget it—that to many of these poor people living in overcrowded, ill-ventilated, ill-lighted rooms, the public-house is the only place in which they can enjoy a quiet evening in pleasant, and perhaps instructive, intercourse with their neighbours after a hard day's work. To drive them from this genial place of resort would be in some cases almost as great a hardship as it would be to the rich man to turn him out of both private house and club. We shall perhaps be told that all this may be true, but that the question reduces itself to a choice of evils, and that, on the whole, much more misery results to the poorer classes from the use of the public-house than would result if they were deprived of it. But, even if we grant this for the sake of argument, it seems to us strangely unjust to debar one man forcibly from a privilege at once pleasant and profitable to him, simply because another abuses it. The injustice, too, is greatly heightened by the fact that those who take the most prominent and influential part in debarring him feel nothing of the suffering they inflict."

Following Sir Wilfred Lawson in the House of Commons came Mr. Besley, who declared that something like one hundred millions sterling was annually expended in this country in intoxicating drinks; and in our prisons, our lunatic asylums, and our work-houses, large numbers of the victims of intemperate indulgence in those drinks were always to be found. Mr. Besley believed that the present mode of restricting the sale of liquors was anything but a satisfactory one. In this respect the people would be the best judges of their own wants—of what their own families and their own neighbourhoods required; and he believed that if the decision was placed in their hands, as it would be by this Bill, the evils of intoxication would be very much mitigated. He did not entertain the hope that we should ever make people sober by Act of Parliament, but he did believe that it was in the power of the Legislature to diminish the evil to a very great extent. Supposing the expenditure on intoxicating drinks were reduced one-half, how usefully might not the fifty millions thus saved be employed in the interests of the poor themselves! He believed that dwellings for the poor would be among the first works undertaken with that money. For fifty millions they might erect 250,000 dwellings, costing 200*l.* each, and this was an expenditure which would cause an increased demand for labour in a variety of trades.

I cannot do better than wind up these brief extracts by repro-
ducing the loudly-applauded objections of the Home Secretary,
Mr. Bruce, to the Permissive Prohibitory Liquor Bill.

"The most complete remedy for drunkenness was to be found
in the cultivation among the people of a better appreciation of
their own interests, rather than in legislation. This had undoubtedly been the cause of the almost complete disappearance of
drunkenness among the upper classes, coupled with an increased
desire for and consequent supply of intellectual amusement among
them. But, although education in its largest sense was the true
remedy for drunkenness, there was no reason against the introduction of repressive or preventive measures in behalf of those in our
manufacturing districts, especially that large class irregularly employed and often oscillating between starvation and occasional
well-doing, to whom drunkenness was a refuge from despair. The
question was, in whom should the power of restriction be reposed? Some thought in the resident ratepayers, others in the
magistrates, and others in a body elected for the purpose. He
could not say which proposal should be adopted, but confessed
that there was some reason in the demand, that the number of
public-houses should be uniformly regulated according to the
population. He had been asked whether he would undertake to
deal with the matter. To deal with the matter in the manner
proposed by the honourable baronet would at once deprive some
portion of the people of means of enjoyment, and the owners of
public-houses of their property. That would be a proceeding unnecessary and unjust, because, although the admitted evils of
drunkenness were very grievous, there was no doubt that public-
houses, especially when well managed, really did furnish to a large
portion of the people a means of social comfort and enjoyment.
His objection to the Bill was, that it would not only cause a great
deal if disturbance in many parts of the country, but would almost
inevitably cause riot. Certainly the rigorous treatment proposed by
the Bill was unsuited to people whose only pleasures were sensu-
ous. The honourable member proposed that a majority of two-
thirds of the ratepayers of a borough should be able to put the Bill
in operation; but in this proposal he ignored a large proportion of
those most interested. Two-thirds of the ratepayers left much
more than one-third of the population on the other side, and the
more important portion of the population as regards this matter,
because it was made up in a great measure by those who lived in
all the discomfort of lodgings. Again, it was suggested that the
settlement of the question might in each case be left to a majority

of the population; but here, again, it might be said that the question would probably be decided by a majority of persons least interested in the question—interested, that was, only as regards peace and order, and careless how far the humbler classes of society were deprived of their pleasure. What the Legislature had to do was, not to deprive the people of means of innocent enjoyment, but to prevent that means being used to foster crime and gross self-indulgence."

However much one might feel disposed, in the main, to agree with Sir Wilfred Lawson and his colleagues, it is not easy to grant him the position he assumes at the commencement of his argument, that "statistics are unnecessary." It is a singular fact, and one that everyone taking an interest in the great and important question of the drunkenness of the nation must have noticed, that amongst the advocates of total-abstinence principles "statistics" invariably are regarded as "unnecessary." This undoubtedly is a grave mistake, and one more likely than any other to cast a deeper shade of distrust over the minds of doubters. It would seem either that the great evil in question is so difficult of access in its various ramifications as to defy the efforts of the statistician, or else that total abstainers, as a body, are imbued with the conviction that the disasters arising from the consumption of intoxicating drinks are so enormous, and widespread, and universally acknowledged, that it would be a mere waste of time to bring forward figures in proof. Perhaps, again, the drunkard is such a very unsavoury subject, that the upright water-drinker, pure alike in mind and body, has a repugnance to so close a handling of him. If this last forms any part of the reason why the question of beer-drinking *v.* water-drinking should not be laid before us as fairly and fully as two and two can make it, the objectors may be referred to social subjects of a much more repulsive kind, concerning which many noble and large-hearted gentlemen courageously busy themselves, and studiously inquire into, with a view to representing them exactly as they are discovered. In proof of this, the reader is referred to the sections of this book that are devoted to the consideration of Professional Thieves and of Fallen Women.

There can no question that, in a matter that so nearly affects the domestic economy of a people, statistics are not only necessary but indispensable. No man's word should be taken for granted, where so much that is important is involved. The man may be mistaken; but there is no getting away from figures. A man, in his righteous enthusiasm, may exaggerate even, but a square old-fashioned 4 can never be exaggerated into a 5, or a positive 1 be so twisted by plausible argument as to falsely represent 2. Yet, somehow, those who urge even so complete a revolution in the ancient and sociable habit of drinking as to make it dependent on the will of Brown and Robinson whether their neighbour Jones shall partake of a pint of beer out of the publican's bright pewter, afford us no figures in support of their extreme views.

Nor is this deficiency observable only in those unaccustomed persons who mount the platform to make verbal statements, and with whom the handling of large and complicated numbers might be found inconvenient. Practised writers on teetotalism exhibit the same carelessness. I have before me at the present moment a goodly number of total-abstinence volumes, but not one furnishes the desired information. Among my books I find, first, John Gough's *Orations*; but that able and fervent man, although he quotes by the score instances and examples that are enough to freeze the blood and make the hair stand on end of the horrors that arise from indulgence in alcoholic drinks, deals not in statistics. Dr. James Miller writes an excellent treatise on alcohol and its power; but he deals in generalities, and not in facts that figures authenticate. Here is a volume containing a *Thousand Temperance Facts and Anecdotes*; but in the whole thousand, not one of either tells us of how many customers, on a certain evening, visited a single and well-used public-house, went in sober, and came out palpably drunk. It would be coming to the point, if such information—quite easy to obtain—was set before us. Lastly, I have the *Temperance Cyclopaedia*. Now, I thought, I am sure, in some shape or another, to find here what I seek; but I searched in vain. The volume in question is a bulky volume, and contains about seven hundred pages, in small close type. In it you may read all about the physical nature of intemperance, and the intellectual nature of intemperance, and of the diseases produced by the use of alcohol, and of the progress of intemperance amongst the ancient Greeks and Romans, together with the history and origin of the teetotal cause in America; but as to the number of drunkards brought before the magistrates and fined, or of the number of crimes shown at the time of trial to have been committed through drunkenness, the *Cyclopaedia* is dumb. This last is an oversight the more to be deplored because we very well know that if the said numbers were exhibited, they would make a very startling display. It may be urged that, since we already have the testimony of magistrates, and jail-governors, and judges, of the enormous amount of crime that is attributable to strong drinks, it is unreasonable to ask for more; but this objection may be fairly met by the answer, that magistrates themselves, even when discussing the temperance question, occasionally make unreasonable remarks; as did a metropolitan magistrate the other day, who in open court declared, that "if publicans were compelled to shut up their shops, there would be no further use for his." He must have known better. If it were as the worthy magistrate stated, it was equivalent to saying that teetotalers never appeared at his bar; but I think that he would hardly have ventured to that length.

In my belief, it is the tremendous steam and effervescence of language indulged in by the advocates of total abstinence that keeps them from making more headway. The facts they give us, like the drunkard's grog, are generally "hot and strong," though with very, *very* little of the sugar of forbearance. I find, for instance, in the temperance records before me, frequent allusion to the great number of drunkards who nightly are thrown out at the doors of public-houses where they have been passing the evening, and left to wallow in the kennel. Not only do we read of this in books, we have it from the mouths of preachers in the pulpit, and speakers on public platforms and in temperance lecture-halls. But I venture to declare that whoever believes anything of the kind, believes what is not true. Every man has a right to speak according to his experience; and I speak from mine. I think that I may lay claim to as extensive a knowledge of the ways of London—especially the bye and ugly ways—as almost any man; and I can positively say that it has never once been my lot to witness the throwing ("throwing" is the expression) of a man from a public-house-door, followed by his helpless wallowing in the kennel. What is more, it was by no means necessary for me to witness such a hideous and disgusting spectacle to convince me of the evils of intemperance, and of how necessary it was to reform the existing laws as applying to the reckless granting of licenses in certain neighbourhoods. It is quite enough, more than enough, to satisfy me of what a terrible curse a bestial indulgence in gin and beer is, when I see a human creature turned helpless from the public-house, and left to stagger home as he best may. To my eyes, he is then no better than a pig; and if he took to wallowing in the gutter, it would be no more than one might expect; but he does *not* "wallow in the gutter;" and it is not necessary to picture him in that wretched predicament in order to bring home to the decent mind how terrible a bane strong drink is, or to shock the man already inclined to inebriation into at once rushing off to a teetotal club and signing the pledge.

And now I must be permitted to remark that no man more than myself can have a higher appreciation of the efforts of those who make it the duty of their lives to mitigate the curse of drunkenness. What vexes me is, the wrong-headed, and not unfrequently the weak and ineffectual, way in which they set about it. As I view the matter, the object of the preacher of total abstinence is not so much the reclamation of the drunkard already steeped and sodden, as the deterring from reckless indulgence those who are not averse to stimulative liquors, but are by no means drunkards. Therefore they appeal as a rule to men who are in the enjoyment of their sober senses, and in a condition to weigh with a steady mind the arguments that are brought forward to induce them to abandon alcoholic stimulants altogether. Now, it must be plain to these latter—sound-headed men, who drink beer, not because they are anxious to experience the peculiar sensations of intoxication, but because they conscientiously believe that they are the better for drinking it—it must be evident to these that teetotal triumphs, exhibited in the shape of converted drunkards, are at best but shallow affairs. "Any port in a storm," is the wrecked mariner's motto; and no doubt the wretched drunkard, with his poor gin-rotted liver, and his palsied limbs, and his failing brain, with perhaps a touch of *delirium tremens* to spur him on, might be glad, indeed, to escape to a teetotal harbour of refuge; and it is not to be wondered at, if, reclaimed from the life of a beast and restored to humanity, he rejoices, and is anxious to publish aloud the glad story of his redemption. As a means of convincing the working man of the wrong he commits in drinking a pint of fourpenny, the upholder of total-abstinence principles delights to bring forth his "brand from the burning"—the reclaimed drunkard—and get him, with a glibness that repetition insures, to detail the particulars of his previous horrible existence—how he drank, how he swore, how he blasphemed, how he broke up his home, and brutally ill-treated his wife and children. All this, that he may presently arrive at the climax, and say, "This I have been, and *now* look at me! I have a black coat instead of a ragged fustian jacket; my shirt-collar is whiter and more rigid in its purity even than your own. See what teetotalism has done for me, and adopt the course I adopted, and sign the pledge."

To which the indulger in moderate and honest fourpenny replies, "I see exactly what teetotalism has done for you, and you can't be too grateful for it; but there is no demand for it to do so much for me. If I was afire, as you say that you once were, and blazing in the consuming flames of drunkenness,—to use your own powerful language—no doubt I should be as glad as you were to leap into the first water-tank that presented itself. But I am not blazing and consuming. I am no more than comfortably warm under the influence of the pint of beer I have just partaken of; and though I am glad indeed to see *you* in the tank, if you have no objection, I will for the present keep outside of it."

Again, from the tone adopted by certain total-abstinence professors, people who are compelled to take such matters on hearsay —the very people, by the way, who would be most likely, "for his good," to join the majority of two-thirds that is to shut up taverns —would be made to believe that those who frequent the public-house are drunkards as a rule; that though occasionally a few, who have not at present dipped very deep in the hideous vice, may be discovered in the parlour and the taproom bemusing themselves over their beer, the tavern is essentially the resort of the man whose deliberate aim and intention is to drink until he is tipsy, and who does do so. The moderate man—the individual who is in the habit of adjourning to the decent tavern-parlour, which is his "club," to pass away an hour before supper-time with a pipe and a pint of ale and harmless chat with his friends—is well aware of this exaggerated view of his doings; and it is hardly calculated to soften his heart towards those who would "reform" him, or incline him to listen with any amount of patience to their arguments. He feels indignant, knowing the imputation to be untrue. He is not a drunkard, and he has no sympathy with drunkards. Nay, he would be as forward as his teetotal detractor, and quite as earnest, in persuading the wretched reckless swiller of beer and gin to renounce his bestial habit. It is a pity that so much misunderstanding and misrepresentation should exist on so important a feature of the matter in debate, when, with so little trouble, it might be set at rest. If public-houses are an evil, it must be mainly because the indolent and the sensual resort thither habitually for convenience of drinking until they are drunk. Is this so? I have no hesitation in saying that in the vast majority of cases it is not. The question might easily be brought to the test; and why has it not been done? Let a hundred public-houses in the metropolis be selected at random, and as many impartial and trustworthy men be deputed to keep watch on the said public-houses every night for a week. Let them make note particularly of those who are not dram-drinkers, but who go to the public-house for the purpose of passing an hour or so there; let them mark their demeanour when they enter and again when they emerge; and I have no doubt that, by a large majority, the working man in search simply of an hour's

evening amusement and sociable society will be acquitted of anything approaching sottishness, or such an inclination towards mere
tipsiness even, as calls for the intervention of the Legislature.

And now, while we are on the subject of statistics, and the
peculiar influences it is the custom of the total abstainer to bring
to bear against his erring brother the moderate drinker, I may
mention what appears to me the highly objectionable practice of
enlisting the cooperation of boys and girls—mere little children—
in the interest of their cause. In the parliamentary discussion on
the Permissive Prohibitory Liquor Bill, Colonel Jervis remarked,
on the subject of the 3,337 petitions that were presented in its
support: "I do not know whether the petitions that have been
presented in its favour are properly signed; but certainly I have
seen attached to one of those petitions which come from my
neighbourhood names that I do not recognise. The signatures
might, perhaps, be those of Sunday-school children; but I do not
think that petitions from children should carry a Bill of this kind."
Were it any other business but teetotal business, one might feel
disposed to pass by as meaningless the hint conveyed in Colonel
Jervis's words. None but those, however, who are conversant with
the strange methods total abstainers will adopt to gain their ends
will be inclined to attach some weight to them. The children are a
weapon of great strength in the hands of the teetotal. Almost as
soon as they begin to lisp, they are taught sentences condemna-
tory of the evils that arise from an indulgence in strong drink;
soon as they are able to write, their names appear on the volumi-
nous roll of total abstainers. At their feasts and picnics they carry
banners, on which is inscribed their determination to refrain from
what they have never tasted; and over their sandwiches Tommy
Tucker, in his first breeches, pledges Goody Twoshoes in a glass
from the crystal spring, and expresses his intention of dying as he
has lived—a total abstainer. I am not a bachelor, but a man long
married, and with a "troop of little children at my knee," as
numerous, perhaps, as that which gathered about that of "John
Brown," immortalised in song. But I must confess that I do chafe
against children of a teetotal tendency one occasionally is introduced to. I have before made allusion to a recently-published
volume entitled *A Thousand Temperance Facts and Anecdotes.*
This is the title given on the cover; the title-page, however, more
liberally reveals the nature of its contents. Thereon is inscribed,
"One Thousand Temperance Anecdotes, Facts, Jokes, Riddles,
Puns, and Smart Sayings; suitable for Speakers, Penny Readings,
Recitations, &c." And, to be sure, it is not in the least objection-

able that the teetotaler should have his "comic reciter;" nor can there be a question as to the possibility of being as funny, as hilarious even, over a cup of wholesome, harmless tea as over the grog-glass. But I very much doubt if any but total abstainers could appreciate some of the witticisms that, according to the book in question, occasionally issue from the mouths of babes and sucklings. Here is a sample:

"A CHILD'S ACUMEN.—'Pa, does wine make a beast of a man?'

'Pshaw, child, only once in a while!'

'Is that the reason why Mr. Goggins has on his sign—Entertainment for man and beast?'

'Nonsense, child, what makes you ask?'

'Because ma says that last night you went to Goggins's *a man*, and came back *a beast*! and that he entertained you.'

'That's mother's nonsense, dear! Run out and play; papa's head aches!'"

I may have a preposterous aversion to a development of cuteness of a certain sort in children, but I must confess that it would not have pained me much had the above brilliant little anecdote concluded with a reference to something else being made to ache besides papa's head.

Again: "Two little boys attended a temperance meeting at Otley in Yorkshire, and signed a pledge that they should not touch nor give strong drink to anyone. On going home, their father ordered them to fetch some ale, and gave them a can for the purpose. They obeyed; but after getting the ale neither of them felt inclined to carry it; so they puzzled themselves as to what they could do. At last they hit upon an expedient. A long broomhandle was procured, and slinging the can on this, each took one end of the broom-handle, and so conveyed the liquor home without spilling it."

One really cannot see what moral lesson is to be deduced from these two "funny" teetotal stories, unless it is intended to show that, from the lofty eminence of total abstinence, a child may with impunity look down upon and "chaff" and despise his beer-drinking parent. It would rather seem that too early an indulgence in teetotal principles is apt to have an effect on the childish mind quite the reverse of humanising. Here is still another instance quoted from the "smart-saying" pages:

"Two poor little children attending a school in America, at some distance from their home, were shunned by the others because their father was a drunkard. The remainder at dinner-time went into the playground and ate their dinner; but the poor twins could only look on. If they approached near those who were eating, the latter would say, 'You go away; your father is a drunkard.' But they were soon taught to behave otherwise; and then it was gratifying to see how delicate they were in their attention to the two little unfortunates."

If such contemptible twaddle enters very largely into the educational nourishment provided for the young abstainer, we may tremble for the next generation of our beer-imbibing species. It appears, moreover, that those doughty juveniles, when they are well trained, will fearlessly tackle the enemy, alcohol, even when he is found fortified within an adult being; and very often with an amount of success that seems *almost* incredible. However, the veracious little book of temperance anecdotes vouches for it, and no more can be said. Here following is an affecting instance of how, "once upon a time," a band of small teetotal female infants were the means of converting from the error of his ways a full-blown drunkard:

"We used to furnish little boys and girls with pledge-books and pencils, and thus equipped, they got us numerous signatures. A man was leaning, much intoxicated, against a tree. Some little girls coming from school saw him there, and at once said to each other, 'What shall we do for him?' Presently one said, 'O, I'll tell you: let's sing him a temperance song.' And so they did. They collected round him, and struck up, 'Away, away with the bowl!' And so on, in beautiful tones. The poor drunkard liked it, and so would you. 'Sing again, my little girls,' said he. 'We will,' said they, 'if you will sign the temperance pledge.' 'No, no,' said he, 'we are not at a temperance meeting; besides, you've no pledges with you.' 'Yes, we have, and pencils too;' and they held them up to him. 'No, no, I won't sign now; but do sing to me!' So they sang again, 'The drink that's in the drunkard's bowl is not the drink for me.' 'O, do sing again!' he said. But they were firm this time, and declared they would go away if he did not sign. 'But,' said the poor fellow, striving to find an excuse, 'you've no table. How can I write without a table?' At this one quiet, modest, pretty little creature came up timidly, with one finger on her lips, and said, 'You can write upon your hat, while we hold it for you.' The man signed; and he narrated these facts before 1,500 children, saying, 'Thank God for those children!—they came to me as messengers of mercy.'"

It is to be hoped this affecting, not to say romantic, episode in the history of "conversions," will not be so lightly read that its chief beauties will be missed. It presents a picture full of the love-liest "bits" that to be thoroughly enjoyed should be lingered over. First of all, let us take the drunkard, too "far gone" for locomo-tion, leaning "against a tree." Leaning against a tree, with an idiotic leer on his flushed and tipsy face, and maybe trying to re-call to his bemuddled memory the burden of the drinking-song that he recently heard and participated in in the parlour of the village alehouse. "What shall we do with him?" "O, I'll tell you: let us sing him a temperance song." There you have a prime bit of the picture complete. The sot with his back to the tree, the sway-ing green boughs of which have tilted his battered hat over his left eye, and the band of little girls gathered in a semi-circle about him, and rousing him to consciousness by the first thrilling note of "Away, away with the bowl!" The words sound as though they would go best with a hunting-tune, a sort of "heigh-ho, tantivy!" and one can imagine the intoxicated one first of all mistaking it for that roistering melody, and gently snapping his thumbs at it, he being for the present somewhat hampered as regards his vocal abilities. One can imagine him chuckling tipsily and snapping his thumbs—feebler and still more feeble as he discovers his error. It is *not* a hunting-song; it is a temperance ditty of the first, the purest water! His heart is touched. His now disengaged thumbs seek the corners of his eyes, and the scalding tears steal shimmering down his red-hot nose! "Sing—sing it again!" he gasps. But no; the artless chanters have gained a step, and they mean to retain it. "Not till you sign the pledge," say they. However, he begs so hard that they concede to the extent of a verse and a half. Still he is obdurate; but he gradually yields, till, driven into a corner, he falters, "But you have no table." Then comes the crowning triumph of the picture—the incident of the hat. "You can write upon your hat—we will hold it for you." And the deed was done!

The same volume reveals another story of so similar a kind that it would almost seem that the children of the first story had con-fided their miraculous experience to the children of the second story.

"A CRYSTAL-PALACE INCIDENT.—The following pleasing incident was related to me by a youthful member of the choir, at the recent Crystal-Palace *fête*. It seems that some of the young choristers were amusing themselves in the grounds, and saw a poor man lying on the grass partially intoxicated. Their medals attrac-ted his attention, and he began to dispute the motto, "Wine is a mocker." This led to conversation, and the children endeavoured to induce him to become an abstainer, and sang several melodies.

One of the conductors was also present. The man seemed much affected during the singing, and cried, my young informant said, until he was quite sober. He confessed that he had once been a teetotaler for three years, during which time he had been much benefited; but had broken his pledge through the influence of his companions. However, he was happily prevailed upon to sign again, and to put down his name in a pledge-book at hand, and before they separated he thanked the young people heartily, saying, 'I did not come here expecting to sign the pledge. I shall now be able to go home to my wife and children and tell them; and to-morrow I shall be able to go to my work, instead of being at the public-house.' What a blessing it may prove to that wife and family should the poor man keep to his resolution! Let no child despair of doing something towards reclaiming the drunkard, but let all endeavour, by loving, gentle persuasion whenever opportunity offers, to help to make the wretched drunkard blessed by living soberly."

I should be sorry indeed to "make fun" of any attempt earnestly and heartily made by anyone for a fellow-creature's good, but really there is so much that is of questionable sincerity in such effusions as those above quoted, that one feels by no means sure it is not intended as a joke. Just, for instance, take that one feature of the drunkard "lying on the grass," and "crying himself sober," while, led by their conductor, the youthful members of the choir sang him all the songs they knew! Such a scene would make the fortune of a farce with Mr. Toole to play the tipsy man.

VI.

BETTING GAMBLERS

CHAPTER XXII

"Advertising Tipsters" and "Betting Commissioners".

The Vice of Gambling on the increase among the Working-classes—Sporting "Specs"—A "Modus"- Turf Discoveries—Welshers—The Vermin of the Betting-field—Their Tactics—The Road to Ruin.

There can be no doubt that the vice of gambling is on the increase amongst the English working-classes. Of this no better proof is afforded than in the modern multiplication of those newspapers specially devoted to matters "sportive." Twenty years ago there were but three or four sporting newspapers published in London; now there are more than a dozen. It would, however, be unfair to regard the rapid growth of these questionable prints as an undoubted symptom of the deepening depravity of the masses. The fact is this: that though the national passion for gambling, for betting, and wagering, and the excitement of seeing this or that "event" decided, has increased of late, it is chiefly because the people have much more leisure now than of yore. They must have amusement for their disengaged hours, and they naturally seek that for which they have the greatest liking.

It is a comforting reflection, however, that in their sports and pastimes Englishmen, and especially Londoners, of the present generation, are less barbarous than those of the last. Setting horse-racing aside, anyone who now takes up for perusal the ordinary penny sporting paper will find therein nothing more repugnant to his sensibilities, as regards human performers, than records of swimming, and cricket, and running, and walking, and leaping; and as regards four-footed creatures, the discourse will be of dogs "coursing" or racing, or killing rats in a pit. In the present enlightened age we do not fight cocks and "shy" at hens tied to a stake at the Shrove-Tuesday fair; neither do we fight dogs, or pit those sagacious creatures to bait bulls. In a newspaper before me, not a quarter of a century old, there is a minute and graphic account of a bull-baiting, at which in the pride of his heart the owner of a bull-dog did a thing that in the present day would insure for him twelve months of hard labour on the treadmill, but which in the "good old time" was merely regarded as the act of a spirited sportsman. A white bull-dog, "Spurt" by name, had performed prodigies of valour against a bear brought before him and before a crowded audience. Finally, however, the exhausted creature bungled in a delicate act of the performance, and those who had bet against the dog exasperated its master by clapping their hands. "D'ye think that he can't do it?" roared the dog's owner; "why, I'll take ten to one in twenties that he does it on three legs—with one foot chopped off." "Done!" somebody cried. Whereon the valiant bull-dog owner called for a cleaver, and setting the left forepaw of his faithful dog on the ledge of the pit, he hacked it off at a blow. Then instantly he urged the creature at the bear again, and, raging with pain, it at once sprang at its shaggy opponent and pinned it.

It cannot be denied that occasionally there still appears in the sporting newspapers some brief account of a "mill" that has recently taken place between those once highly-popular gentlemen —the members of the "P.R." But public interest in this department of "sport" is fast dying out; and not one reader in a hundred would care to wade through column after column of an account of how the Brompton Bison smashed the snout of the Bermondsey Pet; and how the latter finally gained the victory by battering his opponent's eyes until he was blind and "came up groggy," and could not even see his man, let alone avoid the sledge-hammer blows that were still pounding his unhappy ribs. There are left very few indeed of those individuals who, as "sportsmen," admire Raw-Head-and-Bloody-Bones as master of the ceremonies.

All the while, however, it is to be feared that the sporting newspaper of the present day reveals the existence of really more mischief, more substantial immorality and rascality than ever appeared in their pages before. As a quarter of a century since pugilism was the main feature with the sporting press, now it is horse-racing; not for its sake, but for the convenient peg it affords to hang a bet on. It may be safely asserted that among Londoners not one in five hundred could mention the chief qualities a racer should possess; but this goes for nothing; or perhaps it might be said that it goes for everything. It is each man's faith in the ignorance of his neighbour, and his high respect for his own sagacity and his "good luck," wherein resides the secret of the horse-betting mania at the present time afflicting the nation.

As the reader will have remarked, so rapidly has the disease in question spread during the past few years that Government has at last thought fit to interpose the saving arm of the law between the victim and the victimiser. Numerous as are the sporting papers, and to the last degree accommodating in acting as mediums of communication between the ignorant people who stand in need of horsey counsel and the "knowing ones" of the turf who, for a small consideration, are ever ready to give it, it was discovered by certain bold schemers that a yet wider field of operation was as yet uncultivated. To be sure, what these bold adventurers meditated was contrary to law, and of that they were well aware, and at first acted on the careful Scotch maxim of not putting out their hand farther than at a short notice they could draw it back again. Success, however, made them audacious. Either the law slept, or else it indolently saw what they were up to and winked, till at last, growing each week more courageous, the new gambling idea, that took the name of "Spec," became of gigantic dimensions.

Throughout lower London, and the shady portions of its suburbs, the window of almost every public-house and beer-shop was spotted with some notice of these "Specs." There were dozens of them. There were the "Deptford Spec," and the "Lambeth Spec," and the "Great Northern Spec," and the "Derby Spec;" but they all meant one and the same thing—a lottery, conducted on principles more or less honest, the prize to be awarded according to the performances of certain racehorses. All on a sudden, however, the officers of the law swooped down on the gambling band, and carried them, bag and baggage, before a magistrate to answer for their delinquency.

At the examination of the first batch at Bow-street, as well as at their trial, much curious information was elicited. It appeared that the originator of the scheme lived at Deptford, and that he had pursued it for so long as six or seven years.

The drawings were on Saturday nights, when the great majority of the working-people had received their wages, and when, it having been noised abroad that these lotteries were going on, they were likely to attend and to expend their money in the purchase of such of the tickets as had not been sold already.

If all the tickets were not sold, a portion of each prize was deducted, and the holders of prizes were paid in proportion to the number of tickets that were sold; and, as it was impossible to know what number of tickets had actually been sold, it could not be determined whether the distribution had or had not been carried out with fairness, or how much had been deducted to pay for expenses, and to afford a profit to the promoters of the concern. Several cabloads of tickets, result-sheets, &c. were seized at the residences of the managers of the "spec."

There were numerous "partners" in the firm, and they were frequently at the chief's residence, and were instrumental in carrying out the lotteries. One or other was always present at the drawing of the numbers and at the distribution of the prizes. One partner was a stationer in the Strand, and at his shop were sold the tickets for these lotteries, and also what are termed the "result-sheets," which were sold at one penny each, and each of which contained the results of a "draw," setting forth which of the ticket-holders had been fortunate enough to draw the several prizes, and also advertising the next "spec" or lottery. Each of these "specs" related to a particular race, and the tickets were substantially alike. Each had on the top the words "Deptford Spec," with a number and letter, and in the corner the name of a race, as "Newmarket Handicap Sweep," "Liverpool Grand National Steeplechase." In each of these there were 60,000 subscribers, and in that for the Thousand Guineas 75,000. The prizes varied in proportion; but in one they were £500 for the first horse, £300 for the second, and £150 for the third. Among the starters was to be divided £500, and among the non-starters £600. There were also 200 prizes of £1, and 300 prizes of 10s. It was stated on the tickets that the prizes would go with the stakes, and that the result-sheets would be published on the Monday after the draw. There was also a stipulation that, in the event of any dispute arising, it should be referred to the editors of the *Era, Bell's Life,* and the *Sporting Times,* and the decision of the majority to be binding. If the numbers were not filled up, the prizes were to be reduced in proportion; with some other details. There was no printer's name to the tickets or result-sheets.

The detective police-officers, in whose hands the getting-up of evidence for the prosecution had been intrusted, proved that, after they purchased their tickets, they went up the stairs in a public-house about a quarter to seven o'clock. They went into the club-room, where about sixty or seventy persons had assembled, and where the managers of the lotteries were selling tickets. The witness purchased one, and paid a shilling for it. It had the same form as the others, and the draw was to be held that night. Someone got up and said (reading from several sheets of paper in his hand), "4,200 tickets not sold;" this he repeated twice. He then proceeded to read from the papers the numbers of the tickets unsold. The reading occupied about half-an-hour. After the numbers were read out, they commenced to undo a small bundle of tickets, which they placed upon the table. They fetched down some more bundles similar to the first, and continued undoing them until they had undone about a bushel. The tickets were all numbered. They then proceeded to place all the tickets in a large wheel-of-fortune, after mixing them up well with a quantity of sand to prevent their sticking together. The wheel was a kind of barrel revolving on axles, with a hole for the hand. One of the managers asked if any gentleman had got a sporting paper. No one answered, so he produced one himself; he (witness) believed the *Sporting Life*. He said, "Will any gentleman read the names of the horses for the Grand National?" The names of the horses were then read out by those at the table, while tickets were drawn for each till all the horses were called. The tickets were then put down on the table, and the defendants proceeded to undo another packet. They undid a heap, about a quarter the bulk of the first lot. They put these into another wheel-of-fortune. Having done so, two boys about fourteen or fifteen years old came into the room, and after divesting themselves of their jackets and tucking up their sleeves, each went to the wheels, which were turned by some of the persons in the room. One of the managers called out the numbers of the tickets and the name of the horse to each prize.

It need only be mentioned, in proof of the popularity enjoyed by these "specs," that within a fortnight afterwards a similar scene was enacted at the same public-house. A detective went to the Bedford Arms, where he heard that a distribution of prizes was to be made. He went into the club-room. The managers were there, with about forty prizeholders. A person produced a ticket and handed it to one of the directors, who, after examining it, said "All right," and paid the money—405*l.*—which consisted of cheques, notes, and gold. The holder of the prize got 405*l.* for a 500*l.* prize, it being supposed all the tickets were not sold, and a reduction was made in proportion. About forty prizes were given away in this manner during the evening. After the prizes were drawn, each person was asked to put something in the bowl for the two boys.

The prisoners were committed for trial, but were lucky enough to escape punishment. For years they had been defying the law, and feathering their nests on the strength of the silly confidence reposed in them by the thousands of dupes who ran after their precious "specs;" and the sentence of the judge was in effect no more severe than this—it bade them beware how they so committed themselves for the future. Of course the released lottery-agents promised that they *would* beware, and doubtless they will. Without being called on to do so, they even volunteered an act of noble generosity. As before stated, the police had found in their possession and seized a large sum of money—fourteen hundred pounds. This the good gentlemen of the lottery suggested might be distributed amongst the charities of that parish their leader honoured with his residence, and with the Recorder's sanction, and amid the murmured plaudits of a crowded court, the suggestion was adopted. The oddest part of the business was, however, that the benevolent gentlemen gave away what didn't belong to them, the fourteen hundred pounds representing the many thousand shillings the believers in "specs" had intrusted to their keeping. However, everybody appeared to think that the discharged "speculators" had behaved honourably, not to say nobly, and there the case ended.

The "spec" bubble exploded, the police authorities show symptoms of bringing the machinery of the law to bear on a widerspread and more insidious mischief of the same breed. With the betting infatuation there has naturally sprung up a swarm of knowing hungry pike ready to take advantage of it. There are the advertising tipsters, the "turf prophets," and the "betting commissioners." Driven from the streets, where for so long they publicly plied their trade, they have resorted to the cheap sporting press to make known their amiable intentions and desires, and the terms on which they are still willing, even from the sacred privacy of their homes, to aid and counsel all those faint-hearted ones who despair of ruining themselves soon enough without such friendly help.

Were it not for the awful amount of misery and depravity it involves, it would be amusing to peruse the various styles of address from the "prophet" to the benighted, and to mark the many kinds of bait that are used in "flat-catching," as the turf slang has it, as well as the peculiar method each fisherman has in the sort and size of hook he uses, and the length of line.

Entitled to rank foremost in this numerous family is an unassuming but cheerful and confident gentleman, who frequently, and at an expensive length, advertises himself as the happy originator and proprietor of what he styles a "Modus." It is described as an instrument of "beauty, force, and power," and it is, doubtless, only that its owner, if he kept it all to himself, and set it going at full blast, would undoubtedly win all the money in the country, and so put an end to the sport, that he is induced to offer participation in its working at the small equivalent of a few postage-stamps. In his modest description of his wonderful "Modus," Mr. M. says:

"In daily realising incomparably rich winnings with this Modus, another great and distinguished victory was very successfully achieved at Newmarket Spring Meeting. Mr. M.'s distinguished Winning Modus, for beauty, force, and power, has never yet failed in clearly realising treasures of weekly winnings and successes. For this reason, this week's eminent and moneyed success was the result with this Modus at the Newmarket Spring Meeting. For acquiring an ascendency over any other capital-making turf discovery, either secret or public, it is truly marvellous. In fact, this Winning Modus never deteriorates in its character, immense riches, or winnings, for it is strikingly and truthfully infallible and never-failing. At any rate, it will win 18,000*l.* or 20,000*l.* for any investor ere the final close of the season. Do not think this anywise fiction, for it is strict verity. Mr. M. takes this opportunity to respectfully thank his patronisers for their compliments, congratulations, and presents. It is needless to remind his patrons that an illustrious and rich success will easily be achieved at Chester next week, when Mr. M.'s Winning Modus will again realise its infallible success in thousands."

It is to be assumed that Mr. M. has already by means of his own "Modus" fished out of the risky waters of gambling a few of these "18,000*l.* or 20,000*l.*" he speaks so lightly of; and doubtless the reader's first reflection will be, that he should hasten to expend a trifle of his immense winnings in securing for himself at least as fair a knowledge of the English language as is possessed by a "dame-school" scholar of six years old. It is evident that Mr. M. has all the money at his command which he is ever likely to require, or, of course, he would not reveal his precious secret on such ridiculously easy terms. He would patent it, and come down heavily on any rash person who infringed his rights, more valuable than those that rest in Mr. Graves, or even Mr. Betts, the great captain of "capsules." No, he has won all the money he is ever likely to need; indeed, how can a man ever be poor while he retains possession of that wonderful talismanic "Modus," a touch of which converts a betting-book into a solid, substantial gold-mine? Still, he is exacting as regards the gratitude of those whom his invention enriches. It is his pride to record as many instances as possible of the dutiful thankfulness of his fellow-creatures, and as, with pity and regret, he is aware that the only earnest of a man's sincerity is that which takes the shape of the coinage of the realm, he is compelled, though sorely against his own confiding and generous nature, to attach much weight to thankofferings of a pecuniary nature. Every week he appends to his sketch of the working of his "Modus" a list of those "patronisers" from whom he has most recently heard. It may be urged by unbelievers that in this there is no novelty, since from time immemorial the quacks of other professions have done precisely the same thing; but it must be admitted that this should at least be taken as proof of Mr. M.'s indifference to the evil opinion of the censorious. Let us take the testimonials for the week of the Chester Races, which, as he says, "are promiscuously selected from a vast number:"

"SIR,—For distinction, honour, and fame, your marvellous winning Modus is worthy of its renown. I am happy in asserting it has won me 4,220*l.* nett so quickly and readily this season. Accept the 200*l.* enclosed.—I am, &c.   M. ARTHUR PORSON."

"Mr. M. undoubtedly considers his winning Modus an infallible one. Mr. G. Melville certainly considers it is too. At any rate, Mr. Melville is the very fortunate winner of upwards of 6,400*l.* 6,400*l.* at once is a tangible criterion as to its great worth for procuring these heavy winnings. Mr. Melville forwards a sum of money with his congratulations, as a present. Mr. M. will please accept the same."

"SIR,—Do me a favour in accepting the enclosed cheque for 50*l.* Through the instrumentality of your certainly very successful winning Modus, I am, to my infinite pleasure, quickly becoming a certain and never-failing winner of thousands; for already has its golden agency marvellously won me 3,400*l.*

"C. CONYERS GRESHAM."

In conclusion, this benefactor of his species says: "For this successful winning 'Modus,' and its infinite riches, forward a stamped directed envelope, addressed Mr. M., Rugby." That is all. Forward a directed envelope to Rugby, and in return you shall be placed, booted and spurred, on the road to infinite riches. If, starting as a beggar, you allow your head to be turned by the bewildering pelting of a pitiless storm of sovereigns, and ride to the devil, Mr. M. is not to blame.

The astounding impudence of these advertising dodgers is only equalled by the credulity of their dupes. How long Mr. M. has presented his precious "Modus" to the sporting public through the columns of "horsey" newspapers, I cannot say; but this much is certain: that according to his success has been the proportion of vexation and disappointment he has caused amongst the geese who have trusted him. We are assured that impostors of the M. school reap golden harvests; that thousands on thousands weekly nibble at his baits; consequently thousands on thousands weekly have their silly eyes opened to the clumsy fraud to which they have been the victims. But M. of Rugby flourishes still; he still vaunts the amazing virtues, and the beauty, force, and power of his "Modus," and brags of this week's eminent and moneyed success as though it were a matter of course. Mr. M. of Rugby is less modest than some members of his fraternity. Here is an individual who affects the genteel:

"A CARD.—Private Racing Information!!—A gentleman who has been a breeder and owner of racehorses, and now in a good commercial position, attained by judicious betting, enjoying rare opportunities of early intelligence from most successful and dangerous stables, being himself debarred by partnership restrictions from turf speculations on his own account, thinks he might utilise the great advantages at his disposal by leaving himself open to correspondence with the racing public. This is a genuine advertisement, and worth investigating.—Address, ——, Post-office, Stafford. Unquestionable references. Directed envelopes. No 'systems' or other fallacies."

It will be observed that, despite the good position attained by the advertiser by "judicious betting," not only was he glad to escape from the field where his fortune was founded, and to take refuge in the dull jog-trot regions of commerce, but his "partners" prohibit him in future from collecting golden eggs from any racing mare's-nest whatsoever. He has made a fat pocket by the judicious exercise of a peculiar and difficult science he is well versed in; but still he is tolerated by his brother-members of the firm only on the distinct understanding that he never does it again. Perhaps he has grown over-rich, and the rest and seclusion is necessary to the complete restoration of his health. Perhaps he owes to "Modus"— but no, the retired breeder and owner of racehorses distinctly informs us that he has no faith in "systems" or other fallacies: "lying excepted," is the amendment that at once occurs to the individual of common sense.

Education is reckoned as a prime essential to success in most trades; but in that of betting it would appear unnecessary, in order to realise a fortune for himself or his fellow-mortals, that an advertising tipster or betting-man should be master of the English language, let alone of the cardinal virtues. Here is a member of the Manchester Subscription-rooms, in proof:

"George D——y, member of the Manchester Subscription-rooms, attends personally all the principal race-meetings. Some persons having used the above name, G. D. gives notice that he has not anyone betting for him, and anyone doing so are welshers."

Another gentleman eschews prophecy, and would throw "Modus" to the dogs, only that possibly his natural instincts peculiarly qualify him for knowing that to do so would be to cast an undeserved indignity on those respectable creatures. He goes in for "secret information." He does not seek to mystify his readers by adopting a *nom-de-plume,* such as "Stable Mouse," or "Earwig," or "Spy in the Manger." He boldly owns his identity as John ——, of Leicester-square, London, and arrogates to himself an "outsider" that is to beat anything else in the field. "Do not be guided," says this frank and plain-spoken sportsman—"do not be guided by the betting, but back my outsider, whose name has scarcely ever been mentioned in the quotations, because the very clever division to which it belongs have put their money on so quietly that their secret is known to only a few. I am in the swim, and know that the horse did not start for one or two races it could have won easily, but has been expressly saved for this. I have several other absolute certainties, and guarantee to be particularly successful at Chester. Terms: fourteen stamps the full meeting. Many of the minor events will be reduced to certainties; and in order to take advantage of it, I am willing to telegraph the very latest, without charge, to those who will pay me honourably from winnings; or I will invest any amount remitted to me, guaranteeing to telegraph before the race is run the full particulars.—John G., Leicester-square, London."

What a pity it is that those who flatter themselves that they are intellectually qualified to embark in one of the most hazardous and difficult ways of making money should not be at the pains of carefully reading and deliberating on barefaced attempts at imposture, such as are disclosed in the above! John G. is one of the "clever division," he says. So much for his honesty, when he admits that he is in the "swim" with men who have been tampering with the same wonderful "outsider," and so manoeuvering as to throw dust in the eyes of unsuspecting persons. So much for the wealth and position of the "swim," when John G., a confessed member of it, is ready to betray his confederates for the small consideration of fourteenpence, or less, should you fall short of that amount of faith in his integrity. He will "leave it to you, sir," as does the sweeper who clears the snow from your door, or the industrious wretch who brushes the dust from your coat on the racecourse. Or he will invest any sum you may feel disposed to intrust to him. There is not the least doubt of it; and what is more, you may rest assured that he will invest it so as to make sure of a substantial return. How else is he to cut a respectable figure at Epsom or Ascot, and join the bold-faced, leather-lunged gang, who, with a little money-pouch slung at their side, and a little, a *very* little money within the pouch, elbow their way through the press, bawling, "I'll lay" on this, that, or t'other?

J. G. of Leicester-square is not the only advertising tipster who professes to be "in the swim," and on that account to be in a position to act as a traitor to his friends, and the benefactor of the strange public. Here is the announcement of another gentleman.

"GREAT EVENTS!—Enormous odds!!—Two horses have been expressly saved; and one of the best judges on the turf tells me they are the greatest certainties he ever knew. As for another event, it is quite at the mercy of the owner of a certain animal. I do not hesitate to say that there never was, and never will be, a better chance of pulling off a large stake at a trifling risk; for I can obtain the enormous odds of 1,840*l.* to 1*l.*, or 920*l.* to 10*s.*, or 460*l.* to 5*s.*; or I will send the secret for fourteen stamps."

Here is a Munchausen fit to shake hands with and claim as a brother J. G. of Leicester-square. He knows of a forthcoming race, and he likewise knows of a man who intends to run in it a certain horse that will hold the equine contest at his mercy. It is but reasonable to assume that the noble animal in question will obey the dictates of his nature, and not give way to weak forbearance or foolish generosity. Undoubtedly, therefore, it will win the race; and the advertiser, if he puts 5*s.* on it, is *sure* of bagging 460*l.*! And yet he is found competing in the same dirty field with a score of his kindred, clamouring for fourteenpence in postage-stamps.

"Stable secrets! stable secrets!" shrieks the "Sporting Doctor;" secrets so very precious that he cannot possibly betray them for less than fivepence each. Send fifteen stamps, and receive in return the "true and certain winners of the Chester, the Derby, and the Oaks." The "Sporting Doctor" hails from a back-street in the Blackfriars-road. The "Barber-poet" of Paddington, in touching terms, implores his noble patrons to assist him in advising his fellow-creatures of the "good things he has for them." "Show my circulars to your friends," he says; "it will be to my interest for you to do so. I will give 100*l.* to any charitable institution, if the advice I give is not in every instance the best that money can obtain." The next tipster on the list goes farther than this. He boldly avows he will forfeit a large sum of money unless he "spots" the identical winners "first and second." Of course, nothing can be more transparent than bombast of this sort; but here it is in black-and-white:

"Mr. Ben W. will forfeit 500*l.* if he does not send first and second for the Chester Cup. Send four stamps and stamped envelope, and promise a present, and I will send you the Chester Cup, Great Northern, Derby, and Oaks winners.—Address, ——, Waterloo-road, London."

Mr. Benjamin W.'s suggestion of a "promised present" is, however, no novelty with the advertising tipster. Many of the fraternity ask a cash-down payment for the "tip" they send—a sum barely sufficient to buy them a pint of beer—professing to rely contentedly on the generosity of their "patronisers," as Mr. Modus styles them. Occasionally are appended to the advertisements gentle remonstrances and reminders that the confidence the tipster reposed in his patroniser seems to have been misplaced. The latter is requested "not to forget what is due from one gentleman, though in a humble sphere, to another." One gentleman becomes quite pathetic in an appeal of this kind:

"The winners of Great Northern, Derby, and Oaks for thirteen stamps, or one event four stamps, with promise of present from winnings. Send a stamped envelope without delay. Gentlemen are requested to act honourably, and send me the promised percentage on the Two Thousand, for the labourer is worthy of his hire. —Address, —— Cumberland-street, Chelsea, London."

Another gentleman, blessed with an amount of coolness and candour that should insure him a competency if every horse were swept off the face of the earth to-morrow, publishes the following; and the reader will please bear in mind that these various advertisements are clipped out of the sporting papers, and copied to the letter:

"TAKE NOTICE!!—I never advertise unless I am confident of success. I have now a real good thing for Derby at 100 to 1; sure to get a place, for which 25 to 1 can be obtained.—Enclose 1*s.* stamps and stamped addressed envelope, and secure this moral.— Remember Perry Down. Address, H—— Post-office, Reading."

It may be remarked, that everything that is highly promising becomes, in the slang of the advertising tipster, a "moral;" but there are two dictionary definitions of the term—one affecting its relation to good or bad human life, and the other which is described as "the instruction of a fable." It is possibly in this last sense that the tipster uses the word. "Send for my 'moral' on the Great Northern Handicap," writes Mr. Wilson of Hull. "It is said that the golden ball flies past every man once in his lifetime!" cries "Quicksight" of John-street, Brixton. "See it in my moral certainty for the Derby. See it, and fail not to grasp it. Fourteen stamps (uncut) will secure it."

This should indeed be glad news for those unfortunates whose vision has hitherto been gladdened in the matter of golden balls only by seeing them hanging in triplet above the pawnbroker's friendly door. Fancy being enabled to grasp the golden ball—the ball that is to stump out poverty, and send the bails of impecuniosity flying into space never to return, at the small cost of fourteen postage-stamps! They must be uncut, by the way, or their talismanic virtue will be lost. The worst of it is, that you are unable either to see it or grasp it until Quicksight sees and grasps your fourteen stamps; and if you should happen to miss the golden ball after all, it is doubtful if he would return you your poor one-and-twopence as some consolation in your disappointment. He would not do this, but he would be very happy to give you another chance. His stock of "golden balls" is very extensive. He has been supplying them, or rather the chance of grasping them, at fourteenpence each any time during this five years, and he is doubtless in a position to "keep the ball rolling" (the golden ball) until all his customers are supplied.

By the way, it should be mentioned, that the advertiser last quoted, as well as several others here instanced, terminate their appeals by begging the public to beware of welshers!

Does the reader know what is a "welsher"—the creature against whose malpractices the sporting public are so emphatically warned? Probably he does not. It is still more unlikely that he ever witnessed a "welsher" hunt; and as I there have the advantage of him, it may not be out of place here to enlighten him on both points. A "welsher" is a person who contracts a sporting debt without a reasonable prospect of paying it. There is no legal remedy against such a defaulter. Although the law to a large extent countenances the practice of betting, and will even go the length of lending the assistance of its police towards keeping such order that a multitude may indulge in its gambling propensities comfortably, it will not recognise as a just debt money owing between two wagerers. It is merely "a debt of honour," and the law has no machinery that will apply thereto. The consequence is, that amongst the betting fraternity, when a man shows himself dishonourable, he is punished by the mob that at the time of the discovery of his defalcation may happen to surround him; and with a degree of severity according to the vindictiveness and brutality of the said mob. On the occasion of my witnessing a "welsher hunt," I was present at the races that in the autumn of 1868 were held in Alexandra-park at Muswell-hill. As the race for the Grand Prize was decided, looking down from the gallery of the stand, I observed a sudden commotion amongst the perspiring, bawling, leather-lunged gentry, who seek whom they may devour, in the betting-ring below, and presently there arose the magical cry of "Welsher!" I have heard the sudden cry of "Fire!" raised in the night, and watched its thrilling, rousing effect on the population; but that was as nothing compared with it. Instantly, and as though moved by one deadly hate and thirst for vengeance, a rush was made towards a man in a black wide-awake cap, and with the regular betting-man's pouch slung at his side, and who was hurrying towards the gate of the enclosure. "Welsher! welsher!" cried the furious mob of the ring, making at the poor wretch; and in an instant a dozen fists were directed at his head and face, and he was struck down; but he was a biggish man and strong, and he was quickly on his legs, to be again struck down and kicked and stamped on. He was up again, however, without his hat, and with his face a hideous patch of crimson, and hustled towards the gate, plunging like a madman to escape the fury of his pursuers; but the policeman blocked the way, and they caught him again, and some punched at his face, while others tore off his clothes. One ruffian —I cannot otherwise describe him—plucked at the poor devil's shirt at the breast, and tore away a tattered handful of it, which he flung over to the great yelling crowd now assembled without the rails; another tore away his coat-sleeves, and tossed them aloft; and in the same way he lost his waistcoat and one of his boots. It seemed as though, if they detained him another moment, the man must be murdered, and so the policeman made way for him to escape.

From the frying-pan into the fire. "Welsher! welsher!" The air rang with the hateful word, and, rushing from the gate, he was at once snatched at by the foremost men of the mouthing, yelling mob outside, who flung him down and punched and beat him. Fighting for his life, he struggled and broke away, and ran; but a betting-man flung his tall stool at him, and brought him to earth again for the twentieth time, and again the punching and kicking process was resumed. How he escaped from these was a miracle, but escape he did; and with the desperation of a rat pursued by dogs, dived into an empty hansom cab, and there lay crouched while fifty coward hands were stretched forward to drag him out, or, failing in that, to prog and poke at him with walking-sticks and umbrellas. At last, a mounted policeman spurred his horse forward and came to the rescue, keeping his steed before the place of refuge. Then the furious mob, that was not to be denied, turned on the policeman, and only his great courage and determination saved him from being unhorsed and ill-treated. Then other police came up, and the poor tattered wretch, ghastly, white, and streaming with blood, was hauled out and dragged away insensible, with his head hanging and his legs trailing in the dust, amid the howling and horrible execrations of five thousand Englishmen.

The next consideration was what to do with him. To convey him off the premises was impossible, since a space of nearly a quarter of a mile had to be traversed ere the outer gate could be reached. There was no "lock-up" at the new grand stand, as at Epsom and elsewhere. Nothing remained but to hustle him through a trap-door, and convey him by an underground route to a cellar, in which empty bottles were deposited. And grateful indeed must have been the stillness and the coolness of such a sanctuary after the fierce ordeal he had so recently undergone. Whether water was supplied him to wash his wounds, or if a doctor was sent for, is more than I can say. There he was allowed to remain till night, when he slunk home; and within a few days afterwards a local newspaper briefly announced that the "unfortunate man, who had so rashly roused the fury of the sporting fraternity at Alexandra races, was dead"!

To a close observer of the system that rules at all great horse-racing meetings, nothing is so remarkable as the child-like reliance with which the general public intrusts its bettings to the keeping of the "professionals," who there swarm in attendance. In the case of the bettors of the "ring" they may be tolerably safe, since it is to the interest of all that the atmosphere of that sacred enclosure, only to be gained at the cost of half-a-guinea or so, should be kept passably sweet. Besides, as was mentioned in the case of the unfortunate "welsher" at Alexandra races, the said enclosure is bounded by high railings; and the salutary effect of catching and killing a "welsher" is universally acknowledged. As regards the betting men themselves, it enables them to give vent to reckless ferocity that naturally waits on disappointed greed, while the public at large are impressed with the fact that strict principles of honour amongst gamblers really do prevail, whatever may have been said to the contrary. But at all the principal races the greatest number of bets, if not the largest amounts of money, are risked outside the magic circle. It is here that the huckster and small pedlar of the betting fraternity conjure with the holiday-making shoemaker or carpenter for his half-crown. For the thousandth time one cannot help expressing amazement that men who have to work so hard for their money—shrewd, hard-headed, sensible fellows as a rule—should part with it on so ludicrously flimsy a pretext. Here—all amongst the refreshment bustle, from which constantly streamed men hot from the beer and spirit counters—swarmed hundreds of these betting harpies; some in carts, but the majority of them perched on a stool, each with a bit of paper, on which some name was printed, stuck on his hat, and with a money-bag slung at his side, and a pencil and a handful of tickets. This was all. As often as not the name and address on the betting man's hat or money-bag was vaguely expressed as "S. Pipes, Notting-ham," or "John Brown, Oxford-street;" and who Pipes or Brown was not one man in a thousand had the least idea. Nor did they inquire, the silly gulls. It was enough for them they saw a man on a stool, ostensibly a "betting man," bawling out at the top of his great, vulgar, slangy voice what odds he was prepared to lay on this, that, or t'other; and they flocked round—enticed by terms too good to be by any possibility true, if they only were cool enough to consider for a moment—and eagerly tendered to the rogue on the stool their crowns and half-crowns, receiving from the strange Mr. Pipes or Mr. Brown nothing in exchange but a paltry little ticket with a number on it. This, for the present, con-cluded the transaction; and off went the acceptor of the betting man's odds to see the race on which the stake depended. In very many cases the exchange of the little ticket for the money con-cluded the transaction, not only for the present, but for all future; for, having plucked all the gulls that could be caught, nothing is easier than for Pipes to exchange hats with Brown and to shift their places; and the pretty pair may with impunity renounce all responsibility, and open a book on the next race on the pro-gramme. To be sure it is hard to find patience with silly people who *will* walk into a well; and when they follow the workings of their own free will, it is scarcely too much to say they are not to be pitied. But when a cheat or sharper is permitted standing room that he may pursue his common avocation, which is to cheat and plunder the unwary public, the matter assumes a slightly different complexion.

Of all manner of advertising betting gamblers, however, none are so pernicious, or work such lamentable evil against society, as those who, with devilish cunning, appeal to the young and in-experienced—the factory lad and the youth of the counting-house or the shop. Does anyone doubt if horseracing has attractions for those whose tender age renders it complimentary to style them "young men"? Let him on the day of any great race convince him-self. Let him make a journey on the afternoon of "Derby-day," for instance, to Fleet-street or the Strand, where the offices of the sporting newspapers are situated. It may not be generally known that the proprietors of the *Sunday Times, Bell's Life,* and other journals of a sporting tendency, in their zeal to outdo each other in presenting the earliest possible information to the public, are at the trouble and expense of securing the earliest possible telegram of the result of a horserace, and exhibiting it enlarged on a broad-sheet in their shop-windows. Let us take the *Sunday Times,* for instance. The office of this most respectable of sporting newspapers is situated near the corner of Fleet-street, at Ludgate-hill; and wonderful is the spectacle there to be seen on the afternoon of the great equine contest on Epsom downs. On a small scale, and making allowance for the absence of the living provocatives of excitement, the scene is a reproduction of what at that moment, or shortly since, has taken place on the racecourse itself. Three o'clock is about the time the great race is run at Epsom, and at that time the Fleet-street crowd begins to gather. It streams in from the north, from the east, from the south. At a glance it is evident that the members of it are not idly curious merely. It is not composed of ordinary pedestrians who happen to be coming that way. Butcher-lads, from the neighbouring great meat-market, come bareheaded and perspiring down Ludgate-hill, and at a pace that tells how exclusively their eager minds are set on racing: all in blue working-smocks, and with the grease and blood of their trade adhering to their naked arms, and to their hob-nailed boots, and to their hair. Hot and palpitating they reach the obelisk in the middle of the road, and there they take their stand, with their eyes steadfastly fixed on that at present blank and innocent window that shall presently tell them of their fate.

I mention the butcher-boys first, because, for some unknown reason, they undoubtedly are foremost in the rank of juvenile bettors. In the days when the Fleet-lane betting abomination as yet held out against the police authorities, and day after day a narrow alley behind the squalid houses there served as standing room for as many "professional" betting men, with their boards and money-pouches, as could crowd in a row, an observer standing at one end of the lane might count three blue frocks for one garment of any other colour. But though butcher-boys show conspicuously among the anxious Fleet-street rush on a Derby-day, they are not in a majority by a long way. To bet on the "Derby" is a mania that afflicts all trades; and streaming up Farringdon-street may be seen representatives of almost every craft that practises within the City's limits. There is the inky printer's-boy, hot from the "machine-room," with his grimy face and his cap made of a ream wrapper; there is the jeweller's apprentice, with his bibbed white apron, ruddy with the powder of rouge and borax; and the paper-stainer's lad, with the variegated splashes of the pattern of his last "length" yet wet on his ragged breeches; and a hundred others, all hurrying pell-mell to the one spot, and, in nine cases out of ten, with the guilt of having "slipped out" visible on their streaming faces. Take their ages as they congregate in a crowd of five hundred and more (they are expected in such numbers that special policemen are provided to keep the roadway clear), and it will be found that more than half are under the age of eighteen. Furthermore, it must be borne in mind that in the majority of cases a single lad represents a score or more employed in one "office" or factory. They cast lots who shall venture on the unlawful mission, and it has fallen on him. Again, and as before mentioned, the *Sunday Times* is but one of ten or a dozen sporting newspapers published between Ludgate-hill and St. Clement Danes; and in the vicinity of every office may be met a similar crowd. Let the reader bear these facts in mind, and he may arrive at some faint idea of the prevalence of the horse-gambling evil amongst the rising generation.

The significance of these various facts is plain to the advertising tipster, and he shapes his baits accordingly. He never fails to mention, in apprising his youthful admirers, that, in exchange for the last "good thing," postage-stamps will be taken. Well enough the cunning unscrupulous villain knows that in the commercial world postage-stamps are articles of very common use, and that at many establishments they are dealt out carelessly, and allowed to lie about in drawers and desks for the "common use." There is temptation ready to hand! "Send fourteen stamps to Dodger, and receive in return the *certain* tip as to who will win the Derby." There are the stamps, and the ink, and the pen, and the envelope, and nothing remains but to apply them to the use Dodger suggests. It is not stealing, at least it does not seem like stealing, this tearing fourteen stamps from a sheet at which everybody in the office has access, and which will be replaced without question as soon as it is exhausted. It is at most only "cribbing." What is the difference between writing a private note on the office paper and appropriating a few paltry stamps? It would be different if the fourteenpence was in hard money—a shilling and two penny-pieces. No young bookkeeper with any pretensions to honesty would be guilty of stealing *money* from his master's office—but a few stamps! Dodger knows this well enough, and every morning quite a bulky parcel of crummy-feeling letters are delivered at his residence in some back street in the Waterloo-road.

This is the way that Dodger angles for "flat-fish" of tender age:

"GREAT RESULTS FROM SMALL EFFORTS!—In order to meet the requirements of those of humble means, W. W—n, of Tavistock-street, is prepared to receive small sums for investment on the forthcoming great events. Sums as low as two-and-sixpence in stamps (uncut) may be sent to the above address, and they will be invested with due regard to our patron's interest. Recollect that at the present time there are Real Good things in the market at 100 to 1, and that even so small a sum put on such will return the speculator twelve pounds ten shillings, less ten per cent commission, which is Mr. W.'s charge."

"Faint heart never won a fortune! It is on record that the most renowned Leviathan of the betting world began his career as third-hand in a butcher's shop! He had a 'fancy' for a horse, and was so strongly impressed with the idea that it would win, that he begged and borrowed every farthing he could raise, and even pawned the coat off his back! His pluck and resolution was nobly rewarded. The horse he backed was at 70 to 1, and he found himself after the race the owner of nearly a thousand pounds! Bear this in mind. There are as good fish in the sea as ever came out of it. Lose no time in forwarding fourteen stamps to Alpha, John-street, Nottingham; and wait the happy result."

What is this but a plain and unmistakable intimation, on the part of the advertising blackguard, that his dupes should *stick at nothing* to raise money to bet on the "forthcoming great event"? Pawn, beg, borrow—*anything,* only don't let the chance slip. Butcher-boys, think of the luck of your Leviathan craftsman, and at once take the coat off your back, or if you have not a garment good enough, your master's coat out of the clothes-closet, and hasten to pawn it. Never fear for the happy result. Long before he can miss it, you will be able to redeem it, besides being in a position to snap your fingers at him, and, if you please, to start on your own "hook" as a bookmaker.

Another of these "youths' guide to the turf" delicately points out that, if bettors will only place themselves in his hands, he will "pull them through, and land them high and dry," certainly and surely, and with a handsome return for their investments. "No knowledge of racing matters is requisite on the part of the investor," writes this quack; "indeed, as in all other business affairs of life, 'a little knowledge is a dangerous thing.' Better trust *entirely* to one who has made it the one study of his existence, and can read off the pedigree and doings of every horse that for the past ten years has run for money. Large investments are not recommended. Indeed, the beginner should in no case 'put on' more than a half-sovereign, and as low as half-a-crown will often be sufficient, and in the hands of a practised person like the advertiser be made to go as far as an injudiciously invested pound or more."

It would be interesting to know in how many instances these vermin of the betting-field are successful, how many of them there are who live by bleeding the simple and the infatuated, and what sort of living it is. Not a very luxurious one, it would seem, judging from the shady quarters of the town from which the "tipster" usually hails; but then we have to bear in mind the venerable maxim, "Light come, light go," and its probable application to those harpies who hanker after "uncut" stamps and receive them in thousands. That very many of them find it a game worth pursuing, there can be no doubt, or they would not so constantly resort to the advertising columns of the newspapers. How much mischief they really do, one can never learn. The newspaper announcement is, of course, but a preliminary to further business: you send your stamps, and what you in most cases get in return is not the information for which you imagined you were bargaining, but a "card of terms" of the tipster's method of doing business. There is nothing new or novel in this. It is an adaptation of the ancient dodge of the medical quack who advertises a "certain cure" for "all the ills that flesh is heir to," on receipt of seven postage-stamps; but all that you receive for your sevenpence is a printed recipe for the concoction of certain stuffs, "to be had only" of the advertiser.

And well would it be for the gullible public if the mischief done by the advertising fraternity of horseracing quacks was confined to the "fourteen uncut stamps" they have such an insatiable hunger for. There can be no doubt, however, that this is but a mild and inoffensive branch of their nefarious profession. In almost every case they combine with the exercise of their supernatural gift of prophecy the matter-of-fact business of the "commission agent," and, if rumour whispers true, they make of it at times a business as infernal in its working as can well be imagined. They can, when occasion serves, be as "accommodating" as the loan-office swindler or the 60-per-cent bill-discounter, and a profit superior to that yielded by either of these avocations may be realised, and that with scarce any trouble at all. No capital is required, excepting a considerable stock of impudence and a fathomless fund of cold-blooded rascality.

Judging from the fact that the species of villany in question has never yet been exposed in a police-court, it is only fair to imagine that it is a modern invention; on that account I am the more anxious to record and make public an item of evidence bearing on the subject that, within the past year, came under my own observation.

It can be scarcely within the year, though, for it was at the time when an audacious betting gang "squatted" in the vicinity of Ludgate-hill, and, owing to some hitch in the law's machinery, they could not easily be removed. First they swarmed in Bride-lane, Fleet-street. Being compelled to "move on," they migrated to a most appropriate site, the waste land on which for centuries stood the infamous houses of Field-lane and West-street, and beneath which flowed the filthy Fleet-ditch. But even this was accounted ground too good to be desecrated by the foot of the gambling blackleg, and they were one fine morning bundled off it by a strong body of City police. After this they made a desperate stand on the prison side of the way in Farringdon-street, and for some months there remained.

It was at this time that I made the acquaintance of the subject of the present little story. I had noticed him repeatedly, with his pale haggard face and his dull eyes, out of which nothing but weariness of life looked. He was a tall slim young fellow, and wore his patched and seedy clothes as though he had been used to better attire; and, despite the tell-tale shabbiness of his boots and his wretched tall black hat, he still clung to the respectable habit of wearing black kid-gloves, though it was necessary to shut his fists to hide the dilapidations at their finger-tips.

He was not remarkable amongst the betting blackguards he mingled with on account of the active share he took in the questionable business in which they were engaged; on the contrary, he seemed quite out of place with them, and though occasionally one would patronise him with a nod, it was evident that he was "nothing to them," either as a comrade or a gull to be plucked. He appeared to be drawn towards them by a fascination he could not resist, but which he deplored and was ashamed of. It was customary in those times for the prosperous horse-betting gambler to affect the genteel person who could afford to keep a "man," and to press into his service some poor ragged wretch glad to earn a sixpence by wearing his master's "card of terms" round his neck for the inspection of any person inclined to do business. The tall shabby young fellow's chief occupation consisted in wandering restlessly from one of these betting-card bearers to another, evidently with a view to comparing "prices" and "odds" offered on this or that horse; but he never bet. I don't believe that his pecuniary affairs would have permitted him, even though a bet as low as twopence-halfpenny might be laid.

I was always on the look-out for my miserable-looking young friend whenever I passed that way, and seldom failed to find him. He seemed to possess for me a fascination something like that which horse-betting possessed for him. One afternoon, observing him alone and looking even more miserable than I had yet seen him, as he slouched along the miry pavement towards Holborn, I found means to start a conversation with him. My object was to learn who and what he was, and whether he was really as miserable as he looked, and whether there was any help for him. I was prepared to exercise all the ingenuity at my command to compass this delicate project, but he saved me the trouble. As though he was glad of the chance of doing so, before we were half-way up Holborn-hill he turned the conversation exactly into the desired groove, and by the time the Tottenham-court-road was reached (he turned down there), I knew even more of his sad history than is here subjoined.

"What is the business pursuit that takes me amongst the betting-men? O no, sir, I'm not at all astonished that you should ask the question; I've asked it of myself so often, that it doesn't come new to me. I pursue no business, sir. What business *could* a wretched scarecrow like I am pursue? Say that *I* am pursued, and you will be nearer the mark. Pursued by what I can never get away from or shake off; damn it!"

He uttered the concluding wicked word with such decisive and bitter emphasis, that I began to think that he had done with the subject; but he began again almost immediately.

"I wish to the Lord I had a business pursuit! If ever a fellow was tired of his life, I am. Well—yes, I *am* a young man; but it's precious small consolation that that fact brings me. Hang it, no! All the longer to endure it. How long have I endured it? Ah, now you come to the point. For years, you think, I dare-say. You look at me, and you think to yourself, 'There goes a poor wretch who has been on the down-hill road so long that it's time that he came to the end of it, or made an end to it.' There you are mistaken. Eighteen months ago I was well dressed and prosperous. I was second clerk to ——, the provision merchants, in St. Mary Axe, on a salary of a hundred and forty pounds—rising twenty each year. Now look at me!

"You need not ask me how it came about. You say that you have seen me often in Farringdon-street with the betting-men, so you can give a good guess as to how I came to ruin, I'll be bound. Yes, sir, it was horse-betting that did my business. No, I did not walk to ruin with my eyes open, and because I liked the road. I was trapped into it, sir, as I'll be bound scores and scores of young fellows have been. I never had a passion for betting. I declare that, till within the last two years, I never made a bet in my life. The beginning of it was, that, for the fun of the thing, I wagered ten shillings with a fellow-clerk about the Derby that was just about to come off. I never took an interest in horseracing before; but when I had made that bet I was curious to look over the sporting news, and to note the odds against the favourite. One unlucky day I was fool enough to answer the advertisement of a professional tipster. He keeps the game going still, curse him! You may read his name in the papers this morning. If I wasn't such an infernal coward, you know, I should kill that man. If I hadn't the money to buy a pistol, I ought to steal one, and shoot the thief. But, what do you think? I met him on Monday, and he chaffed me about my boots. It was raining at the time. 'I wish I had a pair of waterproofs like yours, Bobby. You'll never take cold while they let all the water out at the heel they take in at the toe!' Fancy me standing *that* after the way he had served me! Fancy this too—me borrowing a shilling of him, and saying 'Thank you, sir,' for it! Why, you know, I ought to be pumped on for doing it!

"Yes, I wrote to 'Robert B—y, Esq., of Leicester,' and sent the half-crown's worth of stamps asked for. It doesn't matter what I got in return. Anyhow, it was something that set my mind on betting, and I wrote again and again. At first his replies were of a distant and business sort; but in a month or so after I had written to him to complain of being misguided by him, he wrote back a friendly note to say that he wasn't at all surprised to hear of my little failures—novices always did fail. They absurdly attempt what they did not understand. 'Just to show you the difference,' said he, 'just give me a commission to invest a pound for you on the Ascot Cup. All that I charge is seven and a half per cent on winnings. Try it just for once; a pound won't break you, and it may open your eyes to the way that fortunes are made.' I ought to have known then, that either he, or somebody in London he had set on, had been making inquiries about me, for the other notes were sent to where mine were directed from—my private lodgings —but this one came to me at the warehouse.

"Well, I sent the pound, and within a week received a post-office order for four pounds eight as the result of its investment. The same week I bet again—two pounds this time—and won one pound fifteen. That was over six pounds between Monday and Saturday. 'This *is* the way that fortunes are made,' I laughed to myself, like a fool.

"Well, he kept me going, I don't exactly recollect how, between Ascot and Goodwood, which is about seven weeks, not more. Sometimes I won, sometimes I lost, but, on the whole, I was in pocket. I was such a fool at last, that I was always for betting more than he advised. I've got his letters at home now, in which he says, 'Pray don't be rash; take my advice, and bear in mind that great risks mean great losses, as well as great gains, at times.' Quite fatherly, you know! The infernal scoundrel!

"Well, one day there came a telegram to the office for me. I was just in from my dinner. It was from B—y. 'Now you may bag a hundred pounds at a shot,' said he. 'The odds are short, but the result *certain.* Never mind the money just now. You are a gentle-man, and I will trust you. You know that my motto has all along been 'Caution.' Now it is 'Go in and win.' It is *sure.* Send me a word immediately, or it may be too late; and, if you are wise, put a 'lump' on it.'

"That was the infernal document—the death-warrant of all my good prospects. It was the rascal's candour that deceived me. He had all along said, 'Be cautious, don't be impatient to launch out;' and now this patient careful villain saw his chance, and advised, 'Go in and win.' I was quite in a maze at the prospect of bagging a hundred pounds. To win that sum the odds were so short on the horse he mentioned, that fifty pounds had to be risked. But he said that there was *no* risk, and I believed him. I sent him back a telegram at once to execute the commission.

"The horse lost. I knew it next morning before I was up, for I had sent for the newspaper; and while I was in the midst of my fright, up comes my landlady to say that a gentleman of the name of B—y wished to see me.

"I had never seen him before, and he seemed an easy fellow enough. He was in a terrible way—chiefly on my account—though the Lord only knew how much *he* had lost over the 'sell.' He had come up by express purely to relieve my anxiety, knowing how 'funky' young gentlemen sometimes were over such trifles. Al-though he had really paid the fifty in hard gold out of his pocket, he was in no hurry for it. He would take my bill at two months. It would be all right, no doubt. He had conceived a liking for me, merely from my straightforward way of writing. Now that he had had the pleasure of seeing me, he shouldn't trouble himself a fig if the fifty that I owed him was five hundred.

"I declare to you that I knew so little about bills, that I didn't know how to draw one out; but I was mighty glad to be shown the way and to give it him, and thank him over and over again for his kindness. That was the beginning of my going to the devil. If I hadn't been a fool, I might have saved myself even then, for I had friends who would have lent or given me twice fifty pounds if I had asked them for it. But I *was* a fool. In the course of a day or two I got a note from B—y, reminding me that the way out of the difficulty was by the same path as I had got into one, and that a little judicious 'backing' would set me right before even my bill fell due. And I was fool enough to walk into the snare. I wouldn't borrow to pay the fifty pounds, but I borrowed left and right, of my mother, of my brothers, on all manner of lying pretences, to follow the 'advice' B—y was constantly sending me. When I came to the end of their forbearance, I did more than borrow; but that we won't speak of. In five months from the beginning, I was without a relative who would own me or speak to me, and without an employer—cracked up, ruined. And there's B—y, as I said before, with his white hat cocked on one side of his head, and his gold toothpick, chaffing me about my old boots. What do I do for a living? Well, I've told you such a precious lot, I may as well tell you that too. Where I lodge it's a 'leaving-shop,' and I keep her 'book' for her. That's how I get a bit of breakfast and supper and a bed to lie on."

[Since the above was written, the police, under the energetic guidance of their new chief, have been making vigorous and successful warfare against public gamblers and gambling agents. The "spec" dodge has been annihilated, "betting-shops" have been entered and routed, and there is even fair promise that the worst feature of the bad business, that which takes refuge behind the specious cloak of the "commission-agent," may be put down. That it may be so, should be the earnest wish of all right-thinking men, who would break down this barrier of modern and monstrous growth, that blocks the advancement of social purity, and causes perhaps more ruin and irreparable dismay than any other two of the Curses herein treated of.]

VII.

WASTE OF CHARITY.

Chapter XXIII.

Metropolitan Pauperism.

Parochial Statistics—The Public hold the Purse-strings—Cannot the Agencies actually at work be made to yield greater results?—The Need of fair Rating —The heart and core of the Poor-law Difficulty—My foremost thought when I was a "Casual"—Who are most liable to slip?—"Crank-work"—The Utility of Labour-yards—Scales of Relief—What comes of breaking-up a Home.

The following is a return of the number of paupers (exclusive of lunatics in asylums and vagrants) on the last day of the fifth week of April 1869, and total of corresponding week in 1868:

Unions and single Parishes (the latter marked*).	Paupers.				Corresponding Total in 1868.
	In-door. Adults and Children.	Out-door.		Total 5th week Apr. 1869.	
		Adults.	Children under 16.		
West District:					
*Kensington . .	809	1,379	1,545	3,733	2,874
Fulham . . .	364	988	696	2,048	1,537
*Paddington . .	460	1,004	660	2,124	1,846
*Chelsea . . .	702	896	744	2,342	2,272
*St. George, Han-over-square . .	753	852	642	2,247	2,127
*St. Margaret and St. John . .	1,131	1,791	1,313	4,235	5,742
Westminster . .	1,101	749	558	2,408	1,874
Total of West Dist.	5,320	7,659	6,158	19,137	18,272
North District:					
*St. Marylebone .	2,221	2,587	1,374	6,182	5,902
*Hampstead . .	143	126	57	326	347
*St. Pancras . .	2,141	3,915	2,847	8,903	8,356
*Islington . . .	909	1,996	1,590	4,495	4,792
Hackney . . .	695	2,909	2,952	6,556	5,385
Total of North Dist.	6,109	11,533	8,820	26,462	24,782

Unions and single Parishes (the latter marked*).	Paupers.				Corresponding Total in 1868.
	In-door. Adults and Children.	Out-door.		Total 5th week Apr. 1869.	
		Adults.	Children under 16.		
Central District:					
*St. Giles and St. George, Bloomsbury	869	587	538	1,994	2,246
Strand . . .	1,054	647	387	2,088	3,069
Holborn . . .	554	947	781	2,282	2,724
Clerkenwell . .	713	999	642	2,354	2,863
*St. Luke . . .	965	1,245	1,045	3,255	3,165
East London .	838	1,038	906	2,782	2,813
West London . .	598	701	542	1,841	1,965
City of London .	1,034	1,191	632	2,857	3,019
Total of Central D.	6,625	7,355	5,478	19,453	21,864
East District:					
*Shoreditch . .	1,440	1,966	1,770	5,176	5,457
*Bethnal Green .	1,510	1,265	1,389	4,164	5,057
Whitechapel . .	1,192	1,234	1,700	4,126	4,315
*St. George-in-the-E.	1,192	1,585	1,565	4,342	3,967
Stepney . . .	1,072	1,600	1,533	4,205	4,650
*Mile End Old Town . . .	547	1,228	1,055	2,830	2,705
Poplar	1,014	2,807	2,793	6,614	9,169
Total of East Dist.	7,967	11,685	11,805	31,457	35,320
South District:					
St. Saviour, Southwark . .	537	678	678	1,893	2,000
St. Olave, Southwark . .	478	393	464	1,335	1,349
*Bermondsey . .	712	554	752	2,018	1,860
*St. George, Southwark . .	660	1,260	1,646	3,566	4,120
*Newington . .	891	1,450	1,330	3,671	3,676
*Lambeth . . .	1,503	2,777	3,401	7,681	8,369
Wandsworth & Clapham . . .	887	1,678	1,439	4,004	3,876
*Camberwell . .	865	1,537	1,492	3,894	3,360
*Rotherhithe . .	288	638	518	1,444	1,338
Greenwich . . .	1,447	2,799	2,314	6,560	5,933
Woolwich . . .	—	2,506	2,173	4,679	3,110
Lewisham . . .	320	595	394	1,309	1,253
Total of South Dist.	8,588	16,865	16,601	42,054	40,244
Total of the Metropolis	34,609	55,097	48,857	138,563	140,482

TOTAL PAUPERISM OF THE METROPOLIS.

(Population in 1861, 2,802,000.)

Years.	Number of Paupers.		Total.
	In-door.	Out-door.	
Fifth week of April 1869 . .	34,609	103,954	138,563
" " " 1868 . .	34,455	106,027	140,482
" " " 1867 . .	32,728	96,765	129,493
" " " 1866 . .	30,192	71,372	101,564

This as regards parochial charity. It must not be imagined, how-ever, from this source alone flows all the relief that the nation's humanity and benevolence provides for the relief of its poor and helpless. Besides our parochial asylums there are many important charities of magnitude, providing a sum of at least 2,000,000*l.* a-year for the relief of want and suffering in London, independently of legal and local provision to an amount hardly calculable. We content ourselves with stating one simple fact—that all this charity, as now bestowed and applied, fails to accomplish the direct object in view. If the 2,000,000*l.* thus contributed did in some way or other suffice, in conjunction with other funds, to banish want and suffering from the precincts of the metropolis, we should have very little to say. But the fact is that, after all these incredible efforts to relieve distress, want and suffering are so prevalent that it might be fancied charity was dead amongst us. Now that, at any rate, cannot be a result in which anybody would willingly acquiesce. If the money was spent, and the poor were relieved, many people probably would never trouble themselves to inquire any further; but though the money is spent, the poor are not cured of their poverty. In reality this very fact is accountable in itself for much of that accumulation of agencies, institutions, and efforts which our statistics expose. As has been recently remarked: "A certain expenditure by the hands of a certain society fails to produce the effect anticipated, and so the result is a new society, with a new expenditure, warranted to be more successful. It would be a curious item in the account if the number and succession of fresh charities, year after year, could be stated. They would probably be found, like religious foundations, taking some new forms according to the discoveries or presumptions of the age; but all this while the old charities are still going on, and the new charity becomes old in its turn, to be followed, though not superseded, by a fresh creation in due time."

If it be asked what, under such circumstances, the public can be expected to do, we answer, that it may really do much by easy inquiry and natural conclusions. Whenever an institution is supported by voluntary contributions, the contributors, if they did but know it, have the entire control of the establishment in their hands; they can stop the supplies, they hold the purse, and they can stipulate for any kind of information, disclosure, or reform at their pleasure. They can exact the publication of accounts at stated intervals, and the production of the balance-sheet according to any given form. It is at their discretion to insist upon amalgamation, reorganisation, or any other promising measure. There is good reason for the exercise of these powers. We have said that all this charity fails to accomplish its one immediate object—the relief of the needy; but that is a very imperfect statement of the case. The fact is that pauperism, want, and suffering are rapidly growing upon us in this metropolis, and we are making little or no headway against the torrent. The administration of the Poor-law is as unsuccessful as that of private benevolence. Legal rates, like voluntary subscriptions, increase in amount, till the burden can hardly be endured; and still the cry for aid continues. Is nothing to be done, then, save to go on in the very course which has proved fruitless? Must we still continue giving, when giving to all appearances does so little good? It would be better to survey the extent and nature of agencies actually at work, and to see whether they cannot be made to yield greater results.

Confining ourselves, however, to what chiefly concerns the hardly-pressed ratepayers of the metropolis, its vagrancy and pauperism, there at once arises the question, How can this enormous army of helpless ones be provided for in the most satisfactory manner?—This problem has puzzled the social economist since that bygone happy age when poor-rates were unknown, and the "collector" appeared in a form no more formidable than that of the parish priest, who, from his pulpit, exhorted his congregation to give according to their means, and not to forget the poorbox as they passed out.

It is not a "poor-box" of ordinary dimensions that would contain the prodigious sums necessary to the maintenance of the hundred thousand ill-clad and hungry ones that, in modern times, plague the metropolis. Gradually the sum-total required has crept up, till, at the present time, it has attained dimensions that press on the neck of the striving people like the Old Man of the Sea who so tormented Sinbad, and threatened to strangle him.

In London alone the cost of relief has doubled since 1851. In that year the total relief amounted to 659,000*l.*; in 1858 it had increased to 870,000*l.*; in 1867 to 1,180,000*l.*; and in 1868 to 1,317,000*l.* The population within this time has increased from 2,360,000 to something like 3,100,000, the estimated population at the present time; so that while the population has increased by only 34 per cent, the cost of relief has exactly doubled. Thirteen per cent of the whole population of London were relieved as paupers in 1851, and in 1868 the percentage had increased to 16. In 1861 the Strand Union had a decreasing population of 8,305, and in 1868 it relieved one in every five, or 20 per cent, of that population. Besides this, the cost of relief per head within the workhouse had much increased within the last 15 years. The cost of food consumed had increased from 2*s.* 9*d.* per head, per week, in 1853, to 4*s.* 11*d.* in 1868; while we have the authority of Mr. Leone Levi for the statement that a farm-labourer expended only 3*s.* a-week on food for himself.

In 1853 the population of England and Wales was in round numbers 18,404,000, and in 1867 21,429,000, being an increase of 3,000,000. The number of paupers, exclusive of vagrants, in receipt of relief in England and Wales was, in 1854, 818,000, and in 1868 1,034,000, showing an increase of 216,000. The total amount expended in relief to the poor and for other purposes, county- and police-rates, &c., was, in 1853, 6,854,000*l.*, and in 1867 10,905,000*l.*, showing an increase of 4,000,000*l.* This total expenditure was distributable under two heads. The amount expended in actual relief to the poor was, in 1853, 4,939,000*l.*, as against 6,959,000*l.* in 1867, being an increase of 2,020,000*l.* The amount expended, on the other hand, for other purposes, county- and police-rates, &c., was, in 1853, 1,915,000*l.*, against 3,945,000*l.* in 1867.

And now comes the vexed question, Who are the people who, amongst them, in the metropolis alone, contribute this great sum of *thirteen hundred thousand pounds,* and in what proportion is the heavy responsibility divided? This is the most unsatisfactory part of the whole business. If, as it really appears, out of a population of two millions and three-quarters there must be reckoned a hundred and forty thousand who from various causes are helpless to maintain themselves, nothing remains but to maintain them; at the same time it is only natural that every man should expect to contribute his fair share, and no more. But this is by no means the prevailing system. Some pay twopence; others tenpence, as the saying is.

By an examination of the statistics as to the relative contributions of the different unions, we find the discrepancy so great as to call for early and urgent legislation; and despite the many and various arguments brought to bear against amalgamation and equalisation, there is no other mode of dealing with this great and important question that appears more just, or more likely to lead to the wished-for result. That the reader may judge for himself of the magnitude of the injustice that exists under the present system will not require much more evidence than the following facts will supply. The metropolis is divided into five districts, and these again into unions to the number of six-and-thirty, many of which in their principal characteristics differ greatly from each other. We find the West and Central Districts relieve each between 19,000 and 20,000 poor, the Eastern District about 32,000, and the North District some 27,000; but the Southern District by far exceeds the rest, as the report states that there are in receipt of relief no less than 43,000 paupers. These bare statistics, however, though they may appear at first sight to affect the question, do not influence it so much as might be imagined; the weight of the burden is determined by the proportion that the property on which the poor-rate is levied bears to the expenditure in the different unions. For example, St. George's, Hanover-square, contributes about the same amount (viz. 30,000*l.*) to the relief of paupers as St. George's-in-the-East; but take into consideration the fact that the western union contains a population of about 90,000, and property at the ratable value of nearly 1,000,000*l.*, and the eastern union has less than 50,000 inhabitants, and the estimated value of the property is only 180,000*l.*; the consequence is that the poor-rate in one union is upwards of five times heavier than the other, being 8*d.* in the pound in St. George's, Hanover-square, and no less than 3*s.* 5¾*d.* in St. George's-in-the-East. The reader may imagine that this great discrepancy may arise in some degree from the fact that the two unions mentioned are at the extreme ends of the metropolis; but even where unions are contiguous to one another the same contrasts are found. The City of London is situated between the unions of East London and West London: in the two latter the rates are not very unequal, being about 2*s.* 11*d.* in one and 3*s.* 1*d.* in the other; but in the City of London, one of the richest of the thirty-six unions in the metropolis, the poor-rate is only 7*d.* in the pound. The cause of this is that, if the estimates are correct, the City of London Union contains just ten times the amount of rateable property that the East London does, the amounts being 1,800,000*l.* and 180,000*l.* respectively. Again, Bethnal Green does not contribute so much as Islington, and yet its poor-rates are four times as high. In general, however, we find that in unions contiguous to one another, the rates do not vary in amount to any great extent. In the North, for instance, they range from 1s. to 1s. 7d., Hampstead being the exception, and below the shilling. In the South they are rather higher, being from 1s. 2d. to 2s. 11d., Lewisham alone being below the shilling. In the East, as might be expected, the figures are fearfully high, all, with one exception, being above 2s. 6d., and in the majority of cases exceeding 3s. Bethnal Green, that most afflicted of all unions, is the highest, reaching the enormous sum of 3s. 11d. in the pound, being nearly seven times the amount of the rate in the City of London. In the Central District, which is situated in an intermediate position, the rates range from 1s. 11d. to 3s., the City itself being excluded.

No one who reads the foregoing statistics can fail to be struck with the inequality and mismanagement that they exhibit. No one can deny that this state of affairs urgently needs some reorganisation or reform, for who could defend the present system that makes the poor pay most, and the rich least, towards the support and maintenance of our poor?

There appears to be a very general impression that the sum levied for the relief of the poor goes entirely to the relief of the poor; but there is a great distinction between the sum levied and the sum actually expended for that purpose. Taking the average amount of poor-rates levied throughout England and Wales for the same periods, it is found that for the ten years ending 1860 the average was 7,796,019l.; for the seven years ending 1967, 9,189,386l.; and for the latest year, 1868, when a number of other charges were levied nominally under the same head, 11,054,513l. To gain an idea of the amount of relief afforded, it was necessary to look to the amount which had actually been expended. For the ten years ending 1860 the average amount expended for the relief of the poor was 5,476,454l.; for the seven years ending 1867, 6,353,000l.; and in the latest year, 7,498,000l. Therefore the amount actually expended in the relief of the poor was, in the ten years ending 1860, at the average annual rate of 5s. 9½d. per head upon the population; for the seven years ending 1867, 6s. 1d.; and for the year 1868, 6s. 11½d. The average number of paupers for the year ending Lady-day 1849 was 1,088,659, while in 1868 they had decreased to 992,640. Thus, in 1849 there were 62 paupers for every 1,000 of the population, and in 1868 there were but 46 for every 1,000, being 16 per 1,000 less in the latter than in the former year. In 1834, the rate per head which was paid for the relief of the poor was 9s. 1d. If we continued in 1868 to pay the same rate which was paid in 1849, the amount, instead of being 6,960,000l. would be 9,700,000l., showing a balance of 2,740,000l. in favour of 1868.

The very heart and core of the poor-law difficulty is to discriminate between poverty deserving of help, and only requiring it just to tide over an ugly crisis, and those male and female pests of every civilised community whose natural complexion is dirt, whose brow would sweat at the bare idea of earning their bread, and whose stock-in-trade is rags and impudence. In his capacity of guardian of the casual ward, Mr. Bumble is a person who has no belief in decent poverty. To his way of thinking, poverty in a clean shirt is no more than a dodge intended to impose on the well-known tenderness of his disposition. Penury in a tidy cotton gown, to his keen discernment, is nothing better than "farden pride"—a weakness he feels it is his bounden duty to snub and correct whenever he meets with it. It is altogether a mistake to suppose that all the worthy strivers in the battle for bread, and who, through misfortune and sickness, sink in the rucks and furrows of that crowded field, find their way, by a sort of natural "drainage system," to the workhouse. There are poorer folks than paupers. To be a pauper is at least to have a coat to wear, none the less warm because it is made of gray cloth, and to have an undisputed claim on the butcher and the baker. It is the preservers of their "farden pride," as Bumble stigmatises it, but which is really bravery and noble patience, who are most familiar with the scratching at their door of the gaunt wolf FAMINE; the hopeful unfortunates who are content to struggle on, though with no more than the tips of their unlucky noses above the waters of tribulation—to struggle and still struggle, though they sink, rather than acknowledge themselves no better than the repulsive mob of cadgers by profession Mr. Bumble classes them with.

I have been asked many times since, when, on a memorable occasion, I volunteered into the ranks of pauperism and assumed its regimentals, what was the one foremost thought or anxiety that beset me as I lay in that den of horror. Nothing can be more simple or honest than my answer to that question. This was it— *What if it were true?* What if, instead of your every sense revolting from the unaccustomed dreadfulness you have brought it into contact with, it were your lot to grow used to, and endure it all, until merciful death delivered you? What if these squalid, unsightly rags, the story of your being some poor devil of an engraver, who really could not help being desperately hard-up and shabby, were all *real*? And why not? Since in all vast commercial communities there must always exist a proportion of beggars and paupers, what have I done that I should be exempt? Am I—are all of us here so comfortably circumstanced because we deserve nothing less? What man dare rise and say so? Why, there are a dozen slippery paths to the direst ways of Poverty that the smartest among us may stumble on any day. Again, let us consider who are they who are most liable to slip. Why, that very class that the nation is so mightily proud of, and apt at bragging about! The working man, with his honest horny hand and his broad shoulders, who earns his daily bread by the sweat of his brow! We never tire of expressing our admiration for the noble fellow. There is something so manly, so admirable in an individual standing up, single-handed and cheerful-hearted, and exclaiming, in the face of the whole world, "With these two hands, and by the aid of the strength it has pleased God to bless me with, my wife and my youngsters and myself eat, drink, and are clothed, and no man can call me his debtor!" He is a fellow to admire; we can afford to admire him, and we do—for just so long as he can maintain his independence and stand without help. But should misfortune in any of its hundred unexpected shapes assail him, should he fall sick or work fail him, and he be unable to keep out the wolf that presently eats up his few household goods, rendering him homeless, *then* we turn him and his little family over to the tender mercies of Mr. Bumble, who includes him in the last batch of impostors and skulkers that have been delivered to his keeping. I don't say that, as matters are managed at present, we can well avoid doing so; but that does not mitigate the poor fellow's hardship.

It is to be hoped that we are gradually emerging from our bemuddlement; but time was, and that at no very remote period, when to be poor and houseless and hungry were accounted worse sins against society than begging or stealing, even—that is to say, if we may judge from the method of treatment in each case pursued; for while the ruffian who lay wait for you in the dark, and well-nigh strangled you for the sake of as much money as you might chance to have in your pocket, or the brute who precipitated his wife from a third-floor window, claimed and was entitled to calm judicial investigation into the measure of his iniquity and its deserving, the poor fellow who became a casual pauper out of sheer misfortune and hard necessity was without a voice or a single friend. The pig-headed Jack-in-office, whom the ratepayers employed and had confidence in, had no mercy for him. They never considered that it was *because* he preferred to stave off the pangs of hunger by means of a crust off a parish loaf rather than dine on stolen roast beef, that he came knocking at the workhouse-gate, craving shelter and a mouthful of bread! But *one* idea pervaded the otherwise empty region that Bumble's cocked-hat covered, and that was, that the man who would beg a parish loaf was more mean and contemptible than the one who, with a proper and independent spirit, as well as a respect for the parochial purse, stole one; and he treated his victim accordingly.

Vagrancy has been pronounced by the law to be a crime. Even if regarded in its mildest and least mischievous aspect, it can be nothing less than obtaining money under false pretences. It is solely by false pretences and false representations that the roving tramp obtains sustenance from the charitable. We have it on the authority of the chief constable of Westmoreland, that ninety-nine out of every hundred professional mendicants are likewise professional thieves, and practise either trade as occasion serves. The same authority attributes to men of this character the greater number of burglaries, highway robberies, and petty larcenies, that take place; and gives it as his opinion, that if the present system of permitting professional tramps to wander about the country was done away with, a great deal of crime would be prevented, and an immense good conferred on the community.

There can be no question that it is, as a member of parliament recently expressed it, "the large charitable heart of the country" that is responsible in great part for the enormous amount of mis-applied alms. People, in giving, recognised the fact that many of those whom they relieved were impostors and utterly unworthy of their charity; but they felt that if they refused to give, some fellow-creature, in consequence of their refusal, might suffer seriously from the privations of hunger and want of shelter. As long as they felt that their refusal might possibly be attended with these results, so long would they open their hand with the same readiness that they now did. The only remedy for this is, that every destitute person in the country should find food and shelter forthcoming immediately on application. Vagrancy, says the authority here quoted, is partly the result of old habits and old times, when the only question the tramp was asked was, "Where do you belong to?" Instead of that being the first question, it should be the last. The first question should be, "Are you in want, and how do you prove it?"

In 1858 the number of vagrants was 2416; in 1859, 2153; in 1860, 1941; in 1861, 2830; in 1862, 4234; in 1863, 3158; in 1864, 3339; in 1865, 4450; in 1866, 5017; in 1867, 6129; and in 1868, 7946.

There can be no doubt, however, that a vast number of tramps circulate throughout the country, of whom we have no returns. "Various means," says the writer above alluded to, "have been tried to check them, but in vain. If I venture to recommend any remedy, it must be, that repression, if applied, must be systematic and general. It is not of the slightest use putting this repression in force in one part of the country while the remainder is under a different system. The whole country must be under the same general system, tending to the same general result. In the first place, let all the inmates of the casual wards be placed under the care of the police. Let them be visited by the police morning and night. Let lists be made out and circulated through the country; and in no case, except upon a ticket given by the police, let any relief be given more than once; and unless a man is able to satisfy the police that his errand was good, and that he was in search of work, let him be sent back summarily without relief. It is the habit of all this class to make a regular route, and they received relief at every casual ward, thus laying the whole country under contribution."

True as this argument may be in the main, we cannot take kindly to the idea, that every unfortunate homeless wretch who applies at night to the casual ward for a crust and shelter shall be treated as a professional tramp until he prove himself a worthy object for relief.

It is not a little remarkable, that, however legislators may disagree as to the general utility of the Poor-law under its present aspect, they are unanimous in approving of the "labour test;" whereas, according to the opportunities I have had of observing its working, it is, to my thinking, one of the faultiest wheels in the whole machine. The great error chiefly consists in the power it confers on each workhouse-master to impose on the tested such work, both as regards quantity and quality, as he may see fit. I have witnessed instances in which the "labour test," instead of proving a man's willingness to work for what he receives, rather takes the form of a barbarous tyranny, seemingly calculated as nothing else than as a test of a poor fellow's control of his temper. Where is the use of testing a man's willingness to work, if he is compelled in the process to exhaust his strength and waste his time to an extent that leaves him no other course but to seek for his hunger and weariness to-night the same remedy as he had recourse to last night? They manage these things better in certain parts of the country and in model metropolitan parishes, but in others the "test" system is a mere "farce." I found it so at Lambeth in 1866; and when again I made a tour of inspection, two years afterwards, precisely the same process was enforced. This was it. At night, when a man applied for admittance to the casual ward, he received the regulation dole of bread, and then went to bed as early as half-past eight or nine. He was called up at seven in the morning, and before eight received a bit more bread and a drop of gruel. This was the "breakfast" with which he was fortified previous to his displaying his prowess as a willing labourer.

The chief of the work done by the "casual" at the workhouse in question is "crank-work." The crank is a sort of gigantic hand-mill for grinding corn. A series of "cranks" or revolving bars extend across the labour-shed in a double or triple row, although by some means the result of the joint labour of the full number of operatives, forty or fifty in number, is concentrated at that point where the power is required. Let us see how "crank-work" of this sort is applicable as a test of a man's willingness and industry.

It may be safely taken that of the, say, forty-five "casuals" assembled, two-thirds, or thirty, will belong to that class that is, without doubt, the very worst in the world—the hulking villanous sort, too lazy to work and too cowardly to take openly to the trade of thieving, and who make an easy compromise between the two states, enacting the parts of savage bully or whining cadger, as opportunity serves. Thirty of these, and fifteen real unfortunates who are driven to seek this shabby shelter only by dire necessity. In the first place, we have to consider that the out-and-out vagrant is a well-nurtured man, and possesses the full average of physical strength; whereas the poor half-starved wretch, whose poverty is to be pitied, is weak through long fasting and privation. But no selection is made. Here is an extended crank-handle, at which six willing men may by diligent application perform so much work within a given time. It must be understood that the said work is calculated on the known physical ability of the able-bodied as well as the willing-minded man; and it is in this that the great injustice consists. Let us take a single crank. It is in charge of six men, and, by their joint efforts, a sack of corn, say, may be ground in an hour. But joint effort is quite out of the question. Even while the taskmaster is present the vagrants of the gang at the crank—four out of six, be it remembered—will make but the merest pretence of grasping the bar and turning it with energy; they will just close their hands about it, and increase the labour of the willing minority by compelling them to lift their lazy arms as well as the bar. But as soon as the taskmaster has departed, even a pretence of work ceases. The vagrants simply stroll away from the work and amuse themselves. Nevertheless, the work has to be done; the sack of corn must be ground before the overnight batch of casuals will be allowed to depart. But the vagrants are in no hurry; the casual ward serves them as a sort of handy club-room in which to while away the early hours of tiresome morning, and to discuss with each other the most interesting topics of the day. It is their desire, especially if it should happen to be a wet, cold, or otherwise miserable morning, to "spin-out" the time as long as possible; and this they well know may best be done by leaving the weak few to struggle through the work apportioned to the many; and they are not of the sort to be balked when they are bent in such a direction.

The result is, as may be frequently observed, that the labour-shed is not cleared until nearly eleven o'clock in the morning, by which time the honest and really industrious minority have proved their worthiness of relief to an extent that leaves them scarcely a leg to stand on. They have been working downright hard since eight o'clock. The slice of bread and the drop of gruel they received in the morning is exhausted within them; their shaky and enfeebled limbs are a-tremble with the unaccustomed labour; and, it being eleven o'clock in the day, it is altogether too late to hope to pick-up a job, and nothing remains for a poor fellow but to saunter idly the day through, bemoaning the desperate penalty he is compelled to pay for a mouthful of parish bread and the privilege of reposing in an uncomfortable hovel, till night comes again, and once more he is found waiting at the casual gate.

It may be said that no one desires this, that it is well understood by all concerned that a workhouse is a place intended for the relief of the really helpless and unable, and not for the sustenance of imposture and vagrancy; but that under the present system it is impossible to avoid such instances of injustice as that just quoted. This, however, is not the case. It has been shown in numerous cases that it is possible to economise pauper-labour so that it shall be fairly distributed, and at the same time return some sort of profit.

It appears that in Liverpool and Manchester corn-grinding by *hand-mills* is chiefly used as a task for vagrants or able-bodied in-door poor. In the absence of other more suitable employment, there is no reason why they should not be so employed. As, however, but one person can be employed at the same time on one mill, and the cost of each mill, including fixing, may be roughly stated at from 3*l.* to 4*l.*, it is clear that no very large number of persons is likely to be thus employed in any one yard. Despite this and other minor objections however, it appears that corn-grinding is as good a labour-test as you can have in workhouses. It is not remunerative; it is a work that is disliked; it is really hard; and being one by which there is no actual loss by accumulation of unsaleable stock, it has much to commend it. At the establishments in question a fairly strong able-bodied man is required to grind 120 lbs. of corn daily, and this is sufficient to occupy him the whole day. The male vagrants at Liverpool are required to grind 30 lbs. of corn each at night, and 30 lbs. the following morning. At Manchester the task for male vagrants is 45 lbs. each, of which one half is required to be ground at night, and the remainder the next morning. At the Liverpool workhouse they have 36 of these mills; at Manchester, 40 at the new or suburban workhouse for able-bodied inmates, and 35 at the house of industry adjoining the old workhouse. The mills at the latter are chiefly used for vagrants, but upon these able-bodied men in receipt of out-door relief are also occasionally employed. The ordinary task-work for these last is, however, either farm-labour at the new workhouse, or oakum-picking at the house of industry, according to the nature of their former pursuits. During the cotton famine there was also a large stone-yard, expressly hired and fitted-up for this class. Another large building was set apart during that period for the employment of adult females in receipt of relief in sewing and knitting, and in cutting-out and making-up clothing; a stock of materials being provided by the guardians, and an experienced female superintendent of labour placed in charge of the establishment.

The experiment of selecting a limited number of men from the stone-yard, and setting them to work in scavenging the streets, has now been tried for rather more than six months by the vestry of St. Luke's, City-road, with a fair amount of success; the men (fifteen from the stone-yard, and ten from the workhouse) were entirely withdrawn from the relief-lists, and employed by the vestry at the same rate of wages as the contractor who previously did the work was in the habit of paying. Of these men, according to the latest report, fourteen are still thus employed, and four have obtained other employment. The remaining seven were discharged—three as physically incapable, and four for insubordination. The conduct of the majority under strict supervision is said to have been fairly good, though not first-rate; and it is undoubtedly something gained to have obtained useful work from fourteen out of twenty-five, and to have afforded four more an opportunity of maintaining themselves by other independent labour.

At the same time it is clear that such a course is open to two objections: first, it must have a tendency to displace independent labour; and secondly, if these paupers are (as in St. Luke's) at once employed for wages, it would, unless guarded by making them pass through a long probationary period of task-work, tend to encourage poor persons out of employ to throw themselves on the rates, in order thus to obtain remunerative employment. The better course would seem to be, where arrangements can be made by the local authorities, for the local Board to provide only the requisite implements and superintendence, and for the guardians in the first instance to give the labour of the men to the parish, paying them the ordinary relief for such work as task-work. If this were done—and care taken to put them on as extra hands only, to sweep the pavements, or such other work as is not ordinarily undertaken by the contractors—there can be no doubt that an outlet might be thus afforded for some of the better-conducted paupers, after a period of real probationary task-work, to show themselves fit for independent employment, and so to extricate themselves from the pauper ranks.

"It would undoubtedly conduce much to the utility of these labour-yards if the guardians comprising the labour or out-door relief committee would, as they now do in some unions, frequently visit the yard, and thus by personal observation make themselves acquainted with the conduct and characters of the paupers, with the nature of the superintendence bestowed upon them, and with the manner in which the work is performed. A channel of communication may thus be formed between employers of labour when in want of hands and those unemployed workmen who may by sheer necessity have been driven to apply for and accept relief in this unpalatable form. The guardians themselves, frequently large employers of labour, are for the most part well acquainted with those who are compelled to apply for parish work; and when they see a steady and willing worker in the yard will naturally inquire into his antecedents. Where the result of these inquiries is satisfactory, they will, it may be expected, gladly avail themselves of the earliest opportunity of obtaining for such a one employment in his previous occupation, or in any other which may appear to be suited to his capacity. The personal influence and supervision of individual guardians can scarcely be overrated; and thus a bond of sympathy will gradually arise between the guardians and the deserving poor, which, coupled with the enforcement of real work, will, it may be hoped, prove not without an ultimate good effect upon even those hardened idlers who have been hitherto too often found in these yards the ringleaders in every species of disturbance."

The above-quoted is the suggestion of the Chairman of the Poor-law Board, and well indeed would it be, for humanity's sake, that it should be regarded. As matters are at present arranged, the labour-system is simply disgusting. Take Paddington stone-yard, for instance. Unless it is altered since last year, the peculiar method of doing business there adopted is this: a man gets an order for stone-breaking, the pay for which is, say, eighteenpence a "yard." At most workhouses, when a man is put to this kind of labour he is paid by the bushel; and that is quite fair, because a poor fellow unused to stone-breaking usually makes a sad mess of it. He takes hammer in hand, and sets a lump of granite before him with the idea of smashing it into fragments; but this requires "knack," that is to be acquired only by experience. The blows he deals the stone will not crack it, and all that he succeeds in doing for the first hour or two is to chip away the corners of one lump after another, accumulating perhaps a hatful of chips and dust. By the end of the day, however, he may have managed to break four bushels, and this at eighteenpence a "yard" would be valued at six-pence, and he would be paid accordingly.

But not at Paddington. I had some talk with the worthy yard-master of that establishment, and he enlightened me as to their way of doing business there. "Bushels! No; we don't deal in bushels here," was his contemptuous reply to a question I put to him. "I can't waste my time in measuring up haporths of stuff all day long. It's half a yard or none here, and no mistake."

"Do you mean, that unless a man engages to break at least half a yard, you will not employ him?"

"I mean to say, whether he engages or not, that he's got to do it."

"And suppose that he fails?"

"Then he don't get paid."

"He doesn't get paid for the half-yard, you mean?"

"He doesn't get paid at all. I don't never measure for less than a half-yard, and so he can't be paid."

"But what becomes of the few bushels of stone he has been able to break?"

"O, he sells 'em to the others for what they'll give for 'em, to put along with theirs. A halfpenny or a penny—anything. He's glad to take it; it's that or none."

"And do you have many come here who can't break half a yard of granite in a day?"

"Lots of 'em. But they don't come again; one taste of Pad-dington is enough for 'em."

What does the reader think of the "labour-test" in this case?

An institution has, it appears, been established by the Birmingham guardians since the autumn of 1867, for the employment of able-bodied women in oakum-picking for out-door relief, the result of which has been, that not only has the workhouse been relieved of a large number of troublesome inmates of this class, with whom it was previously crowded, but the applications for relief have diminished in a proportionate ratio. Every effort is made to induce the women thus employed to seek for more profitable employment, and the applications at the establishment for female labour are said to be numerous. The superintendent, who was formerly matron at the Birmingham workhouse, reports to Mr. Corbett, that "from the opening of the establishment about fifteen months ago, nineteen have been hired as domestic servants, ten have obtained engagements in other situations, and two have married." In addition to these, some forty have obtained temporary employment, of whom three only have returned to work for relief at the end of the year. The total estimated saving on orders issued for work, as compared with the maintenance of the women as inmates of the workhouse, during the year ending 29th September last, is calculated to have been 646l. 0s. 7d. Indeed, so satisfactory has been the working of the system during the first year of its existence, that the guardians have resolved to apply the same test to the male applicants for relief, and a neighbouring house has been engaged and fitted-up for putting a similar plan in operation with respect to men. The total number of orders issued during the first twelve months after this establishment for female labour was opened was 719; of which, however, only 456 were used, the other applicants either not being in want of the relief asked for, or having found work elsewhere. Each woman is required to pick 3 lbs. of oakum per diem, for which she receives 9d., or 4s. 6d. per week; and if she has one or more children, she is allowed at the rate of 3d. a-day additional relief for each child. The highest number paid for during any week has been 95 women and 25 children. Some days during the summer there has been but one at work, and in the last week of December last there were but eleven. The house is said to be "virtually cleared of a most troublesome class of inmates."

The guardians of St. Margaret and St. John, Westminster, have, it appears, adopted a system embracing that pursued both at Manchester and Birmingham, and have provided accommodation for employing able-bodied women out of the workhouse both in oakum-picking and needlework; and, say the committee, "a similar course will probably be found advantageous in other metropolitan parishes or unions, whenever the number of this class who are applicants for relief exceeds the accommodation or the means of employment which can be found for them within the workhouse. At the same time we would especially urge that provision should be made in every workhouse for a better classification of the able-bodied women, and for the steady and useful employment of this class of inmates. Those who are not employed in the laundry and washhouse, or in scrubbing, bed-making, or other domestic work, should be placed under the superintendence of a firm and judicious task-mistress, and engaged in mending, making, and cutting-out all the linen and clothing required for the workhouse and infirmary; and much work might be done in this way for the new asylums about to be built under the provisions of the Metropolitan Poor Act." This plan of a large needle-room presided over by an efficient officer has been found most successful in its results at the new workhouse of the Manchester guardians, as well in improving the character of the young women who remain any time in the house, and fitting them for home duties after they leave, as in deterring incorrigible profligates from resorting to the workhouse, as they were in the habit of doing. Many now come into our metropolitan workhouses who can neither knit nor sew nor darn a stocking. This they can at least be taught to do; and we gather from the experience of Manchester, that while at first to the idle and dissolute the enforced silence and order of the needle-room is far more irksome than the comparative license and desultory work of the ordinary oakum-room, those who of necessity remain in the house are found by degrees to acquire habits of order and neatness, and thus become better fitted for domestic duties.

The following scale of relief for able-bodied paupers, relieved out of the workhouse and set to work pursuant to the provisions of the Out-door Relief Regulation Order, is recommended for adoption by the various Boards of Guardians represented at a recent conference held under the presidency of Mr. Corbett:

For a man with wife and one child, 6d. and 4 lbs. of bread per day; for a man with wife and two children, 7d. and 4 lbs. of bread per day; for a man with wife and three children, 7d. and 6 lbs. of bread per day; for a man with wife and four children, 8d. and 6 lbs. of bread per day; for a man with wife and five children, 9d. and 6 lbs. of bread per day; single man, 4d. and 2 lbs. of bread per day; single women or widows, 4d. and 2 lbs. of bread per day, with an additional 3d. per day for each child; widowers with families to be relieved as if with wife living.

Where a widow with one or more young children dependent on her and incapable of contributing to his, her, or their livelihood, can be properly relieved out of the workhouse, that she be ordinarily allowed relief at the rate of 1s. and one loaf for each child; the relief that may be requisite for the mother beyond this to be determined according to the special exigency of the case. That widows without children should, as a rule, after a period not exceeding three months from the commencement of their widowhood, be relieved only in the workhouse. Where the husband of any woman is beyond the seas, or in custody of the law, or in confinement in an asylum or licensed house as a lunatic or idiot, such woman should be dealt with as a widow; but where a woman has been recently deserted by her husband, and there are grounds for supposing he has gone to seek for work, although out-door relief may be ordered for two or three weeks, to give him time to communicate with his family, yet, after such reasonable time has elapsed, the wife and family should, as a rule, be taken into the workhouse, and proceedings taken against the husband. That the weekly relief to an aged or infirm man or woman be from 2s. 6d. to 3s. 6d. weekly, partly in money and partly in kind, according to his or her necessity; that the weekly relief to aged and infirm couples be 4s. to 5s., in money or in kind, according to their necessities; that when thought advisable, relief in money only may be given to those of the out-door poor who are seventy years of age and upwards.

It appears from a recent statement that the guardians of Eversham union applied not long since for the sanction of the Poor-law Board to a scheme for boarding-out the orphan children of the workhouse with cottagers at 3s. a-week, and 10s. a-quarter for clothing; the children to be sent regularly to school, and to attend divine worship on Sundays; with the provision that after ten years of age the children may be employed in labour approved by the guardians, and the wages divided between the guardians and the person who lodges and clothes them, in addition to the above payments. In a letter dated the 3d April 1869, the Secretary of the Poor-law Board states that, provided they could be satisfied that a thorough system of efficient supervision and control would be established by the guardians, and the most rigid inquiry instituted at short intervals into the treatment and education of the children, the Board have come to the conclusion that they ought not to discourage the guardians from giving the plan a fair trial, though they cannot be insensible to the fact that a grave responsibility is thereby incurred. The Secretary mentions particulars regarding which especial care should be taken, such as the health of the children to be placed out, the condition of the persons to whom they are intrusted, and the necessary periodical inspection. The Board will watch the experiment with the greatest interest, but with some anxiety. They request the guardians to communicate to them very fully the detailed arrangements they are determined to make. The Board cannot approve the proposed arrangement as to wages. The guardians have no authority to place out children to serve in any capacity and continue them as paupers. If they are competent to render service, they come within the description of able-bodied persons, and out-door relief would not be lawful. Upon entering into service, they would cease to be paupers, and would have the protection of the provisions of the Act of 1851 relating to young persons hired from a workhouse as servants, or bound out as pauper apprentices. The hiring-out of adults by the guardians is expressly prohibited by 56 George III., c. 129."

The great principle of the Poor-law is to make people do anything rather than go into the workhouse, and the effect is to cause people to sell their furniture before they will submit to the degradation; for degradation it is to an honest hardworking man, and no distinction is made. The effect of the Poor-law has been to drive men away from the country to the large towns, and from one large town to another, till eventually they find their way up to London, and we are now face to face with the large army of vagabonds and vagrants thus created. A man, once compelled to break-up his house, once driven from the locality to which he was attached, and where his family had lived perhaps for centuries, became of necessity a vagrant, and but one short step was needed to make him a thief.

It would be a grand step in the right direction, if a means could be safely adopted that would save a man driven to pauperism from breaking-up his home. The experiment has, it appears, been successfully adopted in Manchester, and may prove generally practicable. The guardians in that city have provided rooms in which the furniture or other household goods of persons compelled to seek a temporary refuge in the house may be stored. It would not do, of course, to enable people to treat the workhouse as a kind of hotel, to which they might retire without inconvenience, and where they might live upon the ratepayers until a pressure was passed. Perhaps the confinement and the separation of family-ties which the workhouse involves would sufficiently prevent the privilege being abused; but even if such a convenience would need some limitation in ordinary times, it might be readily granted on an occasion of exceptional pressure, and it would then produce the greatest advantages both to the poor and to the rate-payers. The worst consequence of the workhouse test is, that if a poor man under momentary pressure is forced to accept it and break-up his home, it is almost impossible for him to recover himself. The household goods of a poor man may not be much, but they are a great deal to him; once gone, he can rarely replace them, and the sacrifice frequently breaks both his own and his wife's spirit. If the danger of thus making a man a chronic pauper were avoided, the guardians might offer the test with much less hesitation; relief might be far more stringently, and at the same time more effectually, administered.

CHAPTER XXIV

The Best Remedy.

Emigration—The various Fields—Distinguish the industrious Worker in need of temporary Relief—Last Words.

All other remedies considered, we come back to that which is cheapest, most lasting, and in every way the best—emigration. This, of course, as applying to unwilling and undeserved pauperism. These are the sufferers that our colonies are waiting to receive with open arms. They don't want tramps and vagrants. They won't have them, well knowing the plague such vermin would be in a land whose fatness runs to waste. But what they are willing to receive, gladly and hospitably, are men and women, healthy, and of a mind to work honestly for a liberal wage. New Zealand has room for ten thousand such; so has Australia and Canada.

It would be a happy alteration, if some milder term than "pauper" might be invented to distinguish the industrious worker, temporarily distressed, so as to be compelled to avail himself of a little parochial assistance, from the confirmed and habitual recipient of the workhouse dole. As was pertinently remarked by Colonel Maude, at a recent meeting held in the rooms of the Society of Arts, and at which the policy of assisting willing workers to emigrate to New Zealand was argued:

"There are people who are fond of putting forward the offensive doctrine, that a man who is a 'pauper,' as they call him, has thereby become unfit ever again to exercise the self-reliance and independence in any other country necessary to procure him a living, the want of which qualities has brought him to the abject condition he is now in. Like most sweeping generalities, this is both false and cruel. The condition of the wage-paid class is, in the nature of things, more dependent than that of any other; and without for a moment depreciating the wisdom of frugality and thrift, I would ask some of those who are in the enjoyment of independent incomes, whether their position would not be almost as desperate if their income were suddenly withdrawn? And this is constantly happening to large masses of our artisans, in many cases entirely without fault of their own; and then how does the State deal with them? It says, 'If you will wait until you have parted with your last penny and your last article of furniture, and then come to us, we will assist you, but only then, and only in the following manner; The allowance of food, clothing, and shelter which we will give you shall be the least which experience proves will keep body and soul together. We will break the law of God and of nature by separating you from your family. We will prevent you seeking for work elsewhere by confining you in a house where employers are not likely to search for you, and whence you cannot go to seek it yourself. The nature of the work you shall perform shall not be that in which you are proficient, but shall be of the most uninteresting and useless kind. Owing to the small quantity of food we give you, you will not be able to exert your powers to their best advantage. By resorting to us for assistance, you will be lowered in the estimation of your fellow-workmen; and in all probability, as experience tells us, you will return to us again and again, until you become a confirmed and helpless pauper.'

"We are fond of pointing to Paris, and of showing how dearly the French pay for their system of providing work for the people; but if it be true, as I have lately heard, that there are one million of paupers at this moment in England—and besides these, I am in a position to state that there cannot be less than one million persons who would be glad of permanent employment at reasonable wages —I do not think we have much to boast of. Besides, does anyone doubt that if the French Emperor were possessed of our illimitable colonies, with their endless varieties of climate, he would very soon transfer his surplus population to them, and be very glad of the chance? And we ought to consider the cost of our paupers. Let us take it at 10*l.* a head per annum. As a matter of economy, it would pay very well to capitalise this tax, and at two years' purchase we could deport large numbers in great comfort, and thus save a good deal of money to the ratepayers, even supposing none of the money were ever refunded; but I hope to show how that amount would be more than repaid. But I suppose that some people will say, 'Your system, then, is transportation?' My answer might be, 'If you are not ashamed to impose the humiliating and unpleasant condition which you at present force upon an applicant for relief, surely when you have satisfied yourselves that his lot will be much happier and brighter in the new home which you offer him, all your compunctions should vanish.' "

I have ventured to quote Colonel Maude at length, because he is a man thoroughly conversant with the subject he treats of, and all that he asserts may be implicitly relied on. And still once again I am tempted to let another speak for me what perhaps I should speak for myself—the concluding words of this my last chapter. My justification is, that all that the writer expresses is emphatically also my opinion; and I am quite conscious of my inability to convey it in terms at once so graphic and forcible. The gentleman to whom I am indebted is the writer of a leader in the *Times*:

"Here is a mass of unwilling pauperism, stranded, so to speak, by a receding tide of prosperity on the barren shores of this metropolis. Something must be done with it. The other object is more important, but not so pressing. It is, that people who cannot get on well at home, and who find all their difficulties amounting only to this—that they have not elbow-room, and that the ground is too thickly occupied—should be directed and even educated to follow the instructions of Providence, and go to where there is room for them. There is no reason why every child in this kingdom should not have the arguments for and against emigration put before it in good time, before it arrives at the age when choice is likely to be precipitated, and change of mind rendered difficult. Children in these days are taught many things, and there really seems no reason why they should not be taught something about the colonies, in which five millions of the British race are now prospering, increasing, and multiplying, not to speak of the United States. But we must return to the object more immediately pressing. It is surrounded by difficulties, as was confessed at the Mansion House, and as is evident on the facts of the case. But we believe it to be a case for combined operation. Everything seems to be ready—the good men who will take the trouble, the agency, the willing guardians, the public departments, or, at least, their functionaries—and the colonies will not complain if we send them men willing to work, even though they may have to learn new trades. The Boards of Guardians and the Government will contribute, as they have contributed. But they cannot, in sound principle, do more. The public must come forward. Sorry as we are to say the word, there is no help for it. This is not a local, it is a national affair. Chance has thrown these poor people where they are. It would be a good opportunity thrown away, if this work were not done out of hand, one may say. Here are some thousands attracted to the metropolis by its specious promises of a long and solid prosperity. They cannot go back. They must now be passed on. Where else to but to the colonies?

"It must be evident by this time to the poor people themselves that they may wait and wait for years and years without getting the employment that suits them best. The metropolitan ratepayers are losing temper, and making themselves heard. The colonies are all calling for more men and more women, and more children approaching the age of work. Several members of the Government attended the meeting, either in person or by letter, with promises of money, advice, and aid. There is the encouragement of successful millions, who within our own lifetime have established themselves all over the world. Every cause that operated forty years ago operates now with tenfold force. At that date the only notion of an emigrant was a rough, misanthropical sort of man, who had read *Robinson Crusoe,* and who fancied a struggle for existence in some remote corner, with a patch of land, some small cattle, constant hardships, occasional disasters and discoveries, welcome or otherwise. It was not doubted for a moment that arts and sciences and accomplishments must be left behind. There could be no Muses or Graces in that nether world. The lady, so devoted as to share her husband's fortune in that self-exile, would have to cook, bake, brew, wash, sew, mend, and darn, if indeed she could spare time from the still more necessary toil of getting something eatable out of the earth, the river, or the sea. That was the prevailing picture of emigrant life; and when missionary tracts and Mr. Burford's dioramas indicated houses, streets, and public buildings, it was still surmised that these were flattering anticipations of what there was to be, just as one may see rows of semi-detached villas, picturesque drives, shrubberies, miniature lakes, and gothic churches in the window of a land-agent's office, representing the golden futurity of a site now covered by cattle or corn. Forty years have passed, and where there might be then a few hard settlers, there are now cities, towns, and villages which England might be proud of; railways, and every possible application of art and science on a scale often exceeding our own. Large congregations meet in handsome churches, stocks and shares are brought and sold, machinery rattles and whizzes, ladies walk through showrooms full of the last Parisian fashions, dinners are given worthy of our clubs, and operas are performed in a style worthy of Covent Garden, in places where, forty years ago, men were eating each other."

THE END.